MANOMIN

MANOMIN
CARING FOR ECOSYSTEMS AND EACH OTHER

EDITED BY BRITTANY LUBY, MARGARET LEHMAN, JANE MARIOTTI, SAMANTHA MEHLTRETTER, AND ANDREA BRADFORD WITH NIISAACHEWAN ANISHINAABE NATION

ILLUSTRATED BY DANI KASTELEIN

UMP

UNIVERSITY OF MANITOBA PRESS

Manomin: Caring for Ecosystems and Each Other
© The Authors 2024

28   27   26   25   24   1   2   3   4   5

University of Manitoba Press
Winnipeg, Manitoba, Canada
Treaty 1 Territory
uofmpress.ca

Cataloguing data available from Library and Archives Canada
ISBN 978-177284-090-2 (PAPER)
ISBN 978-177284-092-6 (PDF)
ISBN 978-177284-093-3 (EPUB)
ISBN 978-177284-091-9 (BOUND)

Cover artwork by Arlea Ashcroft
Interior illustrations by Dani Kastelein
Cover and Interior design by Jess Koroscil

Printed in Canada

The University of Manitoba Press acknowledges the financial support for its publication program provided by the Government of Canada through the Canada Book Fund, the Canada Council for the Arts, the Manitoba Department of Sport, Culture, and Heritage, the Manitoba Arts Council, and the Manitoba Book Publishing Tax Credit.

This book has been published with the help of a grant from the Federation for the Humanities and Social Sciences, through the Awards to Scholarly Publications Program, using funds provided by the Social Sciences and Humanities Research Council of Canada.

Research by members of the Manomin Project was funded, in part, through the generosity of George Weston Limited and Loblaw Companies Limited as well as the Royal Bank of Canada's Ontario Resource Field Program, and occurred in partnership with Niisaachewan Anishinaabe Nation.

Funded by the Government of Canada | Canadä

This book, which has found you, is for you.

It has been written with the hope of deepening your understanding of Manomin and the sacred ecosystem that sustains life.

For our Indigenous readers whose ancestors nurtured the Manomin spirit, we hope this book reminds you that every seed is a sign of ancestral care. When you encounter Manomin in your home territory, may you recall these teachings and know that you have always been loved.

For those whose ancestors came from across the sea, we hope this book enriches your understanding of the plant-human relationships that fed Indigenous Nations and fuelled Indigenous diplomacy before European arrival. These lands and waters have never been vacant.

Whatever your origins, we'd like to share a teaching from Gizhigokwe, an Elder from Ojibways of Onigaming First Nation, at this point of your learning journey: "Anishinaabe Knowledge Keepers remind us to have manoomin present when we speak about this gift of the Creator, to honor our sacred and ongoing relationship."

CONTENTS

xi **A Note on Language**
by Brittany Luby and Margaret Lehman

1 **Introduction**
by Brittany Luby, Samantha Mehltretter, Margaret Lehman, and
Jane Mariotti with Niisaachewan Anishinaabe Nation

13 CHAPTER 1
Manito Gitigaan, the Great Spirit's Garden
by Kezhii'aanakwat Ron Kelly, Giizhiigokwe Sandra Indian,
Patees Dorothy Copenace, and Kathi Avery Kinew

21 CHAPTER 2
Migration
by Edward Benton-Banai

27 CHAPTER 3
Seeds and Soils
by Victoria Jackson

43 RECIPE 1
Manomin and Bergamot
by Sean Sherman

49 CHAPTER 4

Manomin as Teacher

by Brittany Luby with Niisaachewan Anishinaabe Nation

63 # Images from Anishinaabe-Aki: Harvest

by Brittany Luby with Niisaachewan Anishinaabe Nation

71 CHAPTER 5

Relational Vocabularies

by Joseph Pitawanakwat

83 RECIPE 2

Onush Lakchi/Manomin, Berries, and Love

by Michelle Johnson-Jennings, PhD, EdM

89 CHAPTER 6

Environmental Change, Environmental Care

by Samantha Mehltretter and Andrea Bradford with Niisaachewan Anishinaabe Nation

107 # Images from Anishinaabe-Aki: The Seasons

by Andrea Bradford

115 CHAPTER 7

Disconnection

by Hannah Neufeld

131 RECIPE 3
Manomin with Mushrooms
by Shane Chartrand

137 CHAPTER 8
Treaty and Mushkiki
by Jana-Rae Yerxa and Pikanagegaabo William Yerxa

155 CHAPTER 9
Promise
by Kristi Leora Gansworth

159 ## Epilogue
by Andrea Bradford and Brittany Luby

161 ## A Note on Copyright, Rights Reversion, and Indigenous Language Rights
by Brittany Luby and Jill McConkey

169 NOTES

197 GLOSSARY
by Jane Mariotti and Brittany Luby

199 SELECTED BIBLIOGRAPHY

208 CONTRIBUTORS

219 INDEX

FIGURE 1: A Diverse Wetland. Manomin has many relations, including other plant beings. Water lilies (shown in the open channel) are commonly found growing near Manomin. Perennial vegetation, sometimes in the form of floating mats (featured on the right side of the photograph), may include a diversity of species. Photograph by Jane Mariotti, 19 August 2023.

A Note on Language

by Brittany Luby and Margaret Lehman

Niisaachewan Anishinaabe Nation teaches that Manomin is a living being and deserves to be treated with the same respect with which we treat one another. In recognition of this, the editors have decided to capitalize "Manomin" in their writings as well as the front and back matter. This decision conflicts with Western botanical standards. Textbooks warn students not to anthropomorphize—or attribute human characteristics or behaviours—to plants.[1] For generations, scholars trained in the Western European tradition have been taught that plants are less than human. Aristotle assigned plants a "low-level soul," which "permitted only reproduction."[2] Christian writers subsequently framed plants as organisms who are acted on by human beings—but who are not considered "living thing[s] of all flesh."[3] Anishinaabe teachers have long held that plants are sentient beings. Only recently has the academy allowed for plant sentience, acknowledging that plants *may* "communicate, have a social life, and solve problems by using elegant strategies—that they are, in a word, intelligent."[4] We believe that scholars trained in the Western European tradition have conflated anthropomorphism with anthropocentrism, the tendency to centre human beings as the only rational ones. By capitalizing the "M" in "Manomin," we reject the anthropocentric practice of only capitalizing names for human peoples and places. We hold, instead, that within the past few decades, scientific study has struggled to prove that "plants and animals are dumber than we think."[5] Capitalizing Manomin is consistent with the editors' teachings and is not intended to impose a hierarchy among plants and animals who are capitalized and those who are not. Readers may note variations in capitalization (e.g., "Manomin" vs. "manomin") in this text, consistent with the authors' preferred approaches and teachings.

Readers will also see variations in the spelling of "Manomin"/ "Manoomin"/"Mnoomin." Given that Anishinaabemowin developed in relationship to the land, regional variations in pronunciation and spelling are both natural and expected. The Anishinaabe language reflects the lands and waters where it originated.

Along similar lines, in recognition of plant sentience, the editors invited contributors to use the relative and interrogative pronouns "who" and "whom" instead of "that" or "which" when referring to Manomin in their works. In her article, "Returning the Gift," Robin Wall Kimmerer explains that "in English grammar, a being is either a person or a thing."[6] When we refer to our fellow humans with relative pronouns like "who," we recognize and affirm their personhood. In English, "that" is reserved primarily for inanimate objects (which, in many English-speaking communities, are considered spiritless). We are grateful for Manomin's willingness to nourish our bodies in return for life-affirming harvesting and seeding practices. We have chosen to reflect this gratitude in our editorial work by acknowledging *who* feeds us.

We are not the first to consider alternative pronoun use as a strategy for indigenizing plant research. Before us, Kimmerer asked, "Are there ways to bring this notion of animacy into the English language"? She expressed discomfort with "calling the living world 'it.'"[7] Kimmerer found inspiration in Anishinaabemowin, particularly the word "bimaadiziaki" which translates roughly into English as "a living being of the earth." Kimmerer wondered, "Could we be inspired by that little sound at the end of the word, the 'ki,' and use 'ki' as a pronoun"?[8] While Kimmerer noted associations between "ki" and "qui," meaning "who" in French, we saw echoes of "gi," a personal prefix in Anishinaabemowin meaning "you [the one or ones spoken to; the second person]."[9] Both "ki" and "gi" were contemplated in earlier drafts of this manuscript; however, we found that more work is needed to develop a grammar of animacy in an English framework and reverted to "it" as the personal pronoun and "itself" as the reflexive pronoun in the interim. To paraphrase a question raised by contributor Jana-Rae Yerxa, "Should we be asking Anishinaabemowin to fit English grammar rules?" We encourage our readers to think about such questions as they engage with these pages and teachings.

Other editorial decisions about language came easier. We have used the term "Turtle Island" instead of "North America" to better recognize the Nations that predate colonial arrival. "North America" is not a neutral term. It is a Eurocentric term that celebrates the intellectual labour of Italian navigator Amerigo Vespucci, who posited that the lands Christopher Columbus sailed to were not, in fact, part of eastern Asia but rather an entirely separate and "new" continent.[10] The term "Turtle Island" prioritizes Anishinaabe origin stories over European ones, particularly the Anishinaabe flood story in which Turtle offered to carry the weight of Earth on its back.[11]

While reclaiming "Turtle Island," we also needed to find a language to refer to non-Indigenous persons who now inhabit the continent with Indigenous Nations. We have opted to use "settler-colonist" for individuals who followed Christopher Columbus across the Great Salt Water. We use the term "settler-colonist" to emphasize that Crown agents and Treaty beneficiaries after 1867 sought to permanently occupy Indigenous territories in what is now known as Canada. To achieve this goal, settler-colonists worked to limit Indigenous presence on the land and to extract Indigenous resources to grow the settler collective.[12] In his article, "Understanding

Colonialism and Settler Colonialism as Distinct Formations," Lorenzo Veracini identified three common forms of displacement in settler-colonial societies: assimilation, murder, and barriers to resource access and use.[13] Taking into consideration the ways in which Canada worked to displace Anishinaabeg by limiting their access to Manomin fields and incentivizing European-style agriculture, we argue that the term "settler-colonist" is both applicable and most appropriate.

We honour the unique linguistic expressions of plant-human histories by maintaining the spelling, capitalization, pronoun, and terminology preferences of the authors.

Introduction

by Brittany Luby, Samantha Mehltretter,
Margaret Lehman, and Jane Mariotti with
Niisaachewan Anishinaabe Nation

Within Anishinaabe-Aki, the Land of the Anishinaabeg, the name "Manomin" refers to a life-giving plant relative in the genus *Zizania*. There are three known species of *Zizania* on Turtle Island, the continent colonially known as North America. These aquatic grasses grow in the shallow, slow-moving waters of lakes and some rivers. *Zizania palustris*, about whom this book is written, is an aquatic plant who grows from seed each year. It is most common in the Great Lakes region. We remind our readers to enliven rather than objectify "it." Remember species of *Zizania* are living beings whose survival can shape ecosystems and, by extension, our well-being. *Zizania aquatica* is also an annual emergent macrophyte. It flourishes around what is currently known as the St. Lawrence River and in the southeastern United States. *Zizania texana*, a cousin of Manomin, is a perennial aquatic grass, meaning it can survive multiple seasons. This now-endangered species is found in what is currently known as Texas.[1]

Members of the *Zizania* genus have been called by many names, some more accurate than others. Often called "wild rice" in English, it is not, in fact, a member of the rice family. Species of the genus *Oryza*, most often thought of as "paddy rice," are morphologically different from *Zizania*

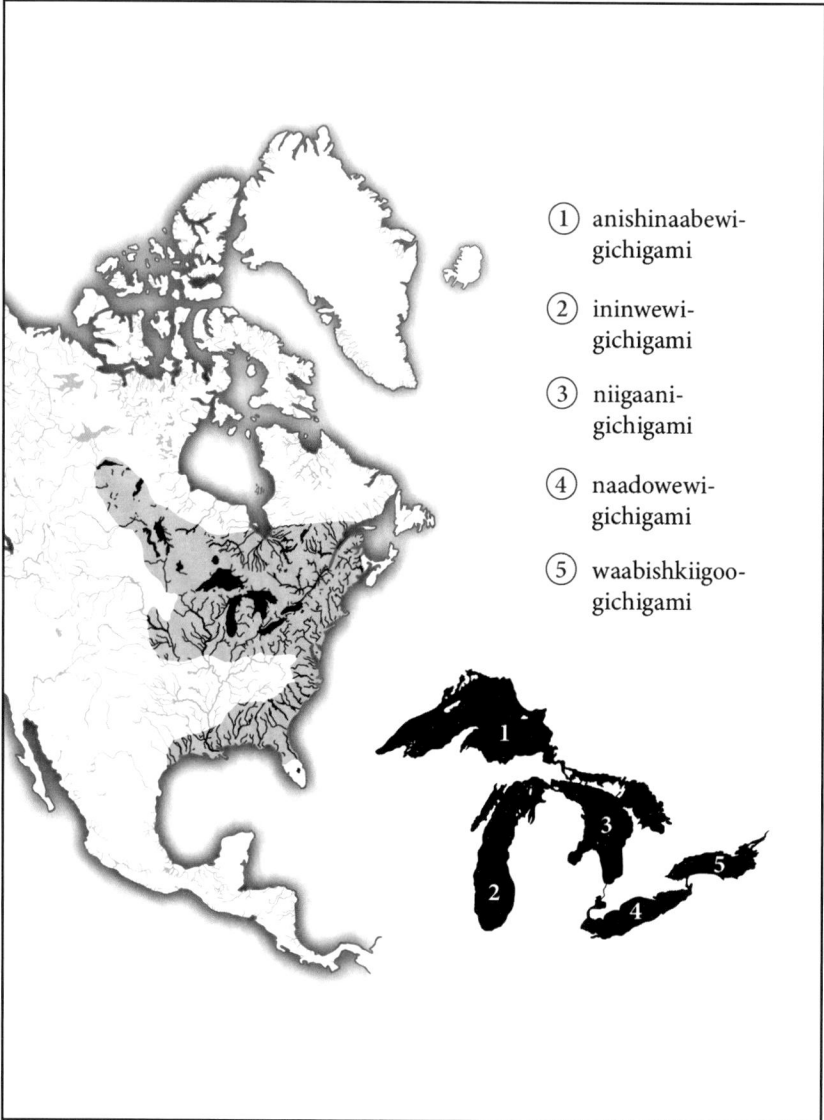

FIGURE 2: Geographic Range of *Zizania* spp. Map by Dani Kastelein, 2023.

Introduction

spp. and occupy different habitats. While the starchy, white-grained *Oryza* species exist as a staple at most grocery stores, the slender, brown-grained *Zizania* spp. are harder to come by in areas outside the Great Lakes. Like paddy rice, which has been traditionally farmed for centuries, *Zizania* spp. were (and continue to be) equally cared for by the humans they grow alongside. The difference lies not only in morphology, but in the fact that *Zizania* is traditionally cultivated without removing it from the natural ecosystem.

The information about *Zizania palustris*, henceforth Manomin, printed on these pages was gathered to fulfill a vision shared by Elder Clarence Henry Jr. at Niisaachewan Anishinaabe Nation in Anishinaabe-Aki. Clarence was raised along the Upper Winnipeg River in what is currently known as Canada. His guardians introduced him to the riches of his ancestral territory: riverbeds thick with Manomin, waters teaming with pickerel, and dense forests that could provide both shelter and fuel. At about six years of age, Clarence was removed from the land and forced to attend Indian Residential School.[2] Colonial law demanded Clarence's separation from his family and from his territory. Section 115 of the Indian Act, R.S.C. 1952 dictated that "every Indian child who has attained the age of seven years shall attend school."[3] Guardians who refused risked prosecution and were "liable on summary conviction to a fine of not more than five dollars or to imprisonment for a term not exceeding ten days or to both fine and imprisonment."[4] Section 115 formed part of Canada's aggressive assimilation program—from which Indian Residential Schools emerged—and complicated the transmission of Anishinaabe ecological knowledge. Anishinaabe guardians saw their children off—or found themselves traumatically separated by Indian Agents and police officers—before the harvest could be brought home.

When Clarence speaks about his childhood, harvesting season and Residential School are intertwined. His life story reminds us that the Canadian school year accommodates settler crops better than Indigenous ones. Federal agents forcibly removed children in late August or early September, a time that coincided with the completion of the wheat harvest.[5] Wheat has long been essential to Canada's economy. The first known exports were shipped from New France in 1654.[6] By the early 1800s, exporting wheat across the Atlantic supported a merchant and financial elite in what became Ontario.[7] After Confederation in 1867, the newly formed Canadian government envisioned the Prairie West as a vast agricultural expanse. Canada offered incentives to immigrants who were willing to build Canada's breadbasket—incentives like those encoded in the Dominion Lands Act, 1872. On paying a $10 administrative fee, homesteaders had "three years to build a habitable residence, clear the land for farming, and cultivate a certain area annually."[8] If homesteaders succeeded, colonial agents granted them ownership of the land.

Canada developed no comparable incentives for the expansion of Turtle Island's only native cereal crop: Manomin. The harvest of wheat and Manomin need not conflict. Rather, Manomin matures from late August to mid-September and, depending on climatic conditions, could be pulled in after the wheat. Colonial law, however, did not accommodate the harvest of both settler and native grains. Anishinaabe children like Elder Clarence Henry were torn from their ancestral territories before Manomin was harvested by their families. Indian Residential Schools thus interfered with the intergenerational transmission of knowledge about Anishinaabe aquaculture. This pain is not unique to Anishinaabe-Aki or the Land of the Anishinaabeg. It is shared by other Indigenous Nations who cared for *Zizania* spp. Dakota people, for example, who may know "Manomin" as "Psiŋ" would have been treated like "Indians" under Canadian federal law—their children, like Anishinaabe children, would be subject to Section 115.

Educational clauses within the Indian Act were not the first to interfere with Anishinaabe aquaculture. As Brittany Luby has argued, the Indian Act, 1876, could limit where Anishinaabeg harvested and potentially suppress migration between reserves (which sometimes enclosed Manomin fields). Section 11 read: "No person, or Indian other than an Indian of the band, shall settle, reside or hunt upon, occupy or use any land or marsh, or shall settle, reside upon or occupy any road, or allowance for roads running through any reserve belonging to or occupied by such band."[9]

"Marsh" was colonial shorthand for Manomin fields.[10] Carl Linnaeus, the father of binominal nomenclature, institutionalized the colonial association between Manomin and wetlands, naming the species who grows in Anishinaabe-Aki *Zizania aquatica,* translating roughly into English as "aquatic weeds."[11] By prohibiting Anishinaabeg from travelling freely between reserves, Canada jeopardized their ability to effectively harvest Manomin in fields that predated colonial boundaries. Botanist Taylor Steeves explains that "not all of the rice on a given head ripened at one time, and different plants matured at different times, it was necessary to repeat the harvest at intervals of a few days over the same areas."[12] Without colonial interference, Anishinaabe harvesters would therefore rotate between fields, providing "rest days" during which Manomin could continue to ripen. Penalties associated with migration could have restricted Anishinaabeg's ability to harvest, making it difficult to follow traditional practices and pass down knowledge about ensuring sustainable harvests.

Elder Clarence Henry Jr. recognizes that colonial law has long barred the intergenerational transfer of Anishinaabe aquaculture. Clarence also knows, in his bones, that exposure to cultural foodways is essential to the formation of a healthy Anishinaabe identity. His vision—which we attempt to enliven here—was to communicate Manomin teachings gathered from across Anishinaabe-Aki to empower Anishinaabeg to reclaim their culture and their fields. Ethnobotanists like Anne Garibaldi and Nancy Turner might refer to Manomin as a "cultural keystone species," meaning it is a "culturally salient species" who shapes Anishinaabe identity.[13] Unimpeded by colonial law, Manomin can unite families for harvesting season and nourish entire communities. Exposure to Anishinaabe plant ways can arm Anishinaabe youth against colonial stereotypes. Indeed, Manomin harvesting provides us with insight into complex Anishinaabe ecologies, which help to counter colonial stereotypes of the "Indian savage." Rooted in scientific racism, the emerging social evolutionary theories of the eighteenth and nineteenth centuries held that Indigenous Peoples were hunter-gatherers and, as such, lacked the necessary "skill, knowledge, and technology"[14] to subdue and master their physical environments.[15] To be "savage" was to be unlearned. Many settler-colonists believed that Indigenous Peoples could, however, evolve from their perceived state of savagery to civilization if they developed the land in accordance with settler standards of agriculture, which included single-crop cultivation (monoculture), domesticated livestock, and private land ownership.[16] The Indian Act, 1876, which restricted Anishinaabe movement and complicated intergenerational knowledge transmission, reflected and reinforced settler beliefs that First Nations needed "to be kept in a condition of tutelage and treated as wards or children of the State."[17] *Manomin: Caring for Ecosystems and Each Other* challenges these colonial narratives, which remain encoded in terms like "wild rice" and *Zizania palustris*, by celebrating Anishinaabe crop care over the centuries.

Anishinaabe ecological knowledge not only counters colonial stereotypes but also provides evidence that our generation has been loved into being. This is reflected in the Seven Generations Principle common in many Indigenous cultures.[18] Our parents, grandparents, and great-grandparents made choices that made our own lives possible. They considered how their actions would impact their environment and chose to behave in ways that would foster a world for us to thrive in. By planting Manomin seeds, the ancestors prepared for our arrival. Clarence wants each Anishinaabe child born into the world to know this: the ancestors have been waiting for you.

Now, as we make our own choices, we must also consider our children, grandchildren, and great-grandchildren. We must recognize how our actions influence one another, how they influence our environment, and how they will influence the generations that follow. We are all interconnected, and our actions reverberate through space and through time. Just as our ancestors prepared for our arrival, we must prepare for the arrival of the generations to come. This collection of essays has been prepared to help circulate Anishinaabe ecological knowledges throughout the Anishinaabe diaspora. It is an act of knowledge reclamation and transmission, which we hope will empower future harvesters.

We invite you to journey with us as we learn about and from Manomin. The text is organized in honour of the Seven Generations Principle. We start by learning from our ancestors through understanding how they and their other-than-human relations prepared for us. Next, we learn how to better know the relations that exist in our own generation, drawing on the language our ancestors left for us. Then, we must consider how our actions will impact our human and other-than-human kin and, consequently, the generations that follow. We conclude with a message to future generations.

Readers will find that Manomin teachings within this anthology appear in many forms—essay, poem, letter, and recipe—an editorial decision that reflects Anishinaabe teachings of self-expression. Many Anishinaabeg believe that the Creator bestowed each living being with unique gifts. Human beings may carry a vision for how best to exercise their gifts over the course of their lifetimes. Anishinaabe Elder Thomas Peacock explains that "because each of us has a different vision, it must be lived as we alone can understand it."[19] Some contributors are gifted Elders and academics. Others are gifted chefs and creatives. All were provided with knowledge of or experience with Manomin. By accepting a wider range of expression, we could invite more Indigenous teachers to participate as authors (rather than informants of academic essays). This helps to preserve the strength and quality of each teaching. Grand Chief of Treaty #3 Francis Kavanaugh explains that gifts have frequencies. To have the best reception, you want to be closest to the transmitter, the lands or the spirits from whom the teaching originated.[20] Each contributor provides readers with insight into Manomin that is rooted in their lived experiences.

Many Anishinaabeg also believe that all forms of creation form a circle. Manomin pushes "through the earth and reach[es] toward the sun. They seed, then wither with the seasons, and lay down on the earth to die. New plants grow from the seed."[21] Human beings also move in circles,

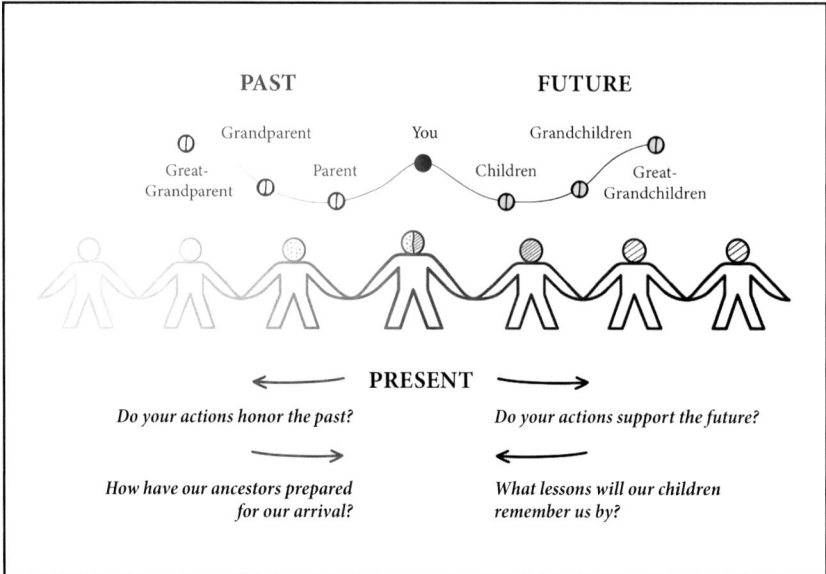

FIGURE 3: The Seven Generations Principle. Illustration by Dani Kastelein with annotations by Brittany Luby, 2023.

experiencing birth, enlivening their vision, and leaving behind their teachings for the next generation. Peacock explains that "the path forms a great circle, and within it are many circles within circles."[22] Each contributor's circle has overlapped with Manomin in some way. What we pass on to you, dearest reader, are seeds of plant knowledge.

This volume opens with a description of Manito Gitigaan or the "Great Spirit's Garden" by Kezhii'aanakwat Ron Kelly, Giizhiigokwe Sandra Indian, Patees Dorothy Copenace, and Kathi Avery Kinew. This chapter describes Anishinaabe relations with the environment, allowing readers to envision how life changes throughout the seasons. Readers are reminded that although this collection focuses on Manomin, the Manomin harvest is supported by an entire ecosystem, a complex network of relations. Kezhii'aanakwat Ron Kelly et al. remind us we are all related and all life is sacred.

We continue learning with Edward Benton-Banai's history of the Great Anishinaabe Migration. It is akin to an origin story as it roots Anishinaabeg around the Great Lakes. Origin stories provide an explanation of how the world came into being. They are also coded with information about how to live well in one's ancestral territories, one's place of becoming. Edward Benton-Banai's migration story does not teach us about the formation of Turtle Island. That is not its purpose. It provides us with his understanding of how the Anishinaabeg came to occupy lands and waters around the Great Lakes; however, regional variations of this teaching exist.[23] Benton-Banai also reminds us that Manomin, a plant being, is essential to Anishinaabe survival. In the oral history and teachings of the Anishinaabeg, the people and Manomin are so intertwined that Benton-Banai associates Manomin growth with feeling at home.

In "Seeds and Soil," settler scholar Victoria Jackson helps us to understand why this sacred crop has been desecrated by colonizing governments. It has been understudied in an archaeological and paleobotanical context. For generations, Manomin was considered a "wild" rather than cultivated foodstuff. In this chapter, we learn how past colonial designations shaped public knowledge of Anishinaabe aquaculture. Settler-colonists have yet to acknowledge Manomin has been cared for as a gift from the Creator for generations.

Working in partnership with Niisaachewan Anishinaabe Nation, Brittany Luby reveals how Anishinaabe guardians used Manomin to teach Anishinaabe philosophy, particularly relational and intergenerational thinking. Relational thinking encourages Anishinaabe children to recognize connections in the Great Web of Being. Intergenerational thinking prompts Anishinaabe children to think about the long-term consequences of their actions and to envision themselves as ancestors.

MANOMIN

Chef Sean Sherman's Manomin and bergamot recipe invites us to activate ancestral knowledges. Sherman empowers us to use generational knowledge and connect with Manomin as food, and as medicine.

With teachings from our ancestors, we can reflect on our own position in space (Mother Earth's Great Web of Being) and time (the Seven Generations). Joseph Pitawanakwat helps us achieve this by reminding readers that Anishinaabe ecological knowledges and plant relations can be reclaimed through language. When we learn the words of the ancestors, we can move toward deeper, more meaningful, anti-colonial connections with plant and animal beings. As contemporary learners, we can work to become teachers capable of carrying diverse plant knowledges into the future.

Dr. Michelle Johnson-Jennings's recipe encourages readers to connect with their plant relatives in the kitchen. She maintains that two essential ingredients in any meal are love and gratitude. These elements remind us that plant beings offered their lives to nourish human bodies, to support our growth today.

Understanding our own place in space and time allows us to examine how our current actions may impact future generations. Despite the best efforts of Anishinaabe ancestors to protect Manomin from encroachment, newcomers have jeopardized crop sustainability. Drawing on Manomin teachings, settler scholars Andrea Bradford and Samantha Mehltretter, working in partnership with Niisaachewan Anishinaabe Nation, reveal to readers the interconnectedness of our environment, its sensitivity to human actions, and its potential for resilience should we choose to help. Once we appreciate how our actions reverberate through space and time, we can not only adjust our own behaviour, but we can empower future generations to rebuild and deepen Anishinaabe foodways.

However, to really prepare for future generations, we must recognize that colonization has changed how Anishinaabeg live on the land and where on the land they live. Current and future urban Indigenous Peoples may face different harvesting challenges, including limited access to nourishing riverbeds. Hannah Neufeld reminds us of the unique challenges and creative adaptations of urban families to maintain connections to culture through food.

Introduction

Chef Shane Chartrand celebrates adaptation; he invites readers to adapt along with our environments and to reincorporate traditional food into our diet, however we are able.

Jana-Rae and Pikanagegaabo William Yerxa remind us that Manomin can be medicine—it provides us with an opportunity to reconnect with kin and culture and to counteract the colonial project.

We conclude with a reminder that other-than-human kin, if we allow them, can sustain us. Anishinaabeg have never forgotten that Manomin is essential to the survival of human, plant, and animal Nations. Anishinaabe poet and geographer Kristi Leora Gansworth makes clear that "after all that has been enacted to destroy all that is Anishinaabe, this existence is a miracle" (see Chapter 9). Through these pages, we seek to rekindle connections to place and feed an interest in reclaiming the fields.

FIGURE 4: An Interconnected Ecosystem. This image features an active beaver lodge within an ancestral Manomin field. The beaver cut through the Manomin field, moving from their lodge to the shore. Such movements may inadvertently knock ripe seeds into the riverbed, helping to reseed Manomin. Elder John Henry said, "Without them [the beavers] knowing it, I guess they were part of the whole system. Regenerating for the next season." Photograph by Jane Mariotti, 18 August 2023.

1

Manito Gitigaan, the Great Spirit's Garden

by Kezhii'aanakwat Ron Kelly, Giizhiigokwe Sandra Indian, Patees Dorothy Copenace, and Kathi Avery Kinew

We wish to share with you some traditional teachings of the Ojibways of Onigaming, who live along the waters of what is currently known as Lake of the Woods in Treaty #3 Territory and find common ground with traditional peoples across Turtle Island and beyond. Through the generations, our people have continued Anishinaabe teachings on the lands and waters through family camps, community gatherings, and, in recent years, through the Ojibways of Onigaming's fall harvests, where Elders share how to dance on and winnow manoomin, fillet and cook fish, gather and prepare plant medicines, and skin deer and singe partridge feathers with children and youth. We do our best to respond to the ever-changing needs of our people. Most recently, we have begun to share videos online. Now, we are honoured to open this volume.

MANOMIN

Manoomin, a cereal grain indigenous to Turtle Island, grows in Manito Gitigaan (the Great Spirit's Garden), and flourishes in the many inland and boundary waterways of Anishinaabe-Aki. For thousands of years, Anishinaabeg have been caring for and extending manoomin areas by seeding the crop during and after the fall harvest. We sow seeds where water levels and water movement are conducive to growth. Anishinaabeg support manoomin growth by eliminating both animal and vegetative predators. For example, Anishinaabeg trap muskrats who might eat manoomin roots, chase away birds who might want to feast in the fields, and remove or transplant water lilies and other plants which might emerge earlier than manoomin and stunt its growth. Anishinaabeg make efforts to protect the crop from wind, rain, or early frost, which might end the harvest. In earlier times, Anishinaabeg would tie stalks together to protect the unripened grain from the wind as the harvest neared.

Anishinaabeg also take care of manoomin through offerings and ceremonies. Traditionally, Elders are the first to pick some of the early crop to prepare and share in a feast. Before any pickers can turn their canoe to enter the manoomin fields and begin harvesting, they put asemaa (tobacco) into the water for the Creator, asking the winds and rain to stay away or be gentle, praying that the harvest does not end too early. Such care by the Anishinaabeg, the Elders teach, has been upheld in prayers to the Creator to help the manoomin harvest since time immemorial.

Anishinaabeg today remember and honour how Gete-Anishinaabeg, our Anishinaabe ancestors, incorporated manoomin and all the gifts of the Creator into the six seasons of care and thanksgiving. According to the late Elder Metekamiganang Doug Skead of Wauzhusk Onigum First Nation, there are six thanksgivings to respect the changes of the seasons.[1] Pagita'an (ice break up) is followed by iskaagamizigewin, usually a time of hot, sunny days when evaporation takes place quite rapidly. During the spring thaw, crows and geese return home to lay their eggs and raise their babies. The manoomin plant feels the sun's warmth and energy underwater.

FIGURE 5: Protecting Unripened Grains. Photograph by George Kemmerer, "Wild Rice Field," c. 1900–1909, University of Wisconsin Digital Collections Center, 80K album, p. 186.

Ziigwaan (spring) is when sap runs in the trees, enabling Anishinaabeg to prepare birch and maple syrup, and other essential items. Other vegetation begins to grow, which, like manoomin, can help to sustain the Anishinaabe Nation. Niibin (summer) offers its abundance of fruits and berries including miinan (blueberries), ode'iminan (strawberries), miskominag (raspberries), osasawiminan (chokecherries), and pawa'iminaanan (pin cherries), all of which Anishinaabeg can dry for future use or prepare as paashkiminisigan'an (sauces or jams). Niibin is also the time of mashkikiikewin (making medicines) and gitigewin (planting gardens). During this busy time, wiigwaas (birchbark) is collected and prepared for canoes and baskets of different sizes and purposes, all used in the harvest of manoomin, water medicines, and for other essential tasks. The manoomin plant now rises through the water to the floating-leaf stage, and within weeks, aerial shoots will appear.

Late summer leads into Manoominikewi-giizis (Harvest Moon)—a huge copper moon—and is accompanied by the preparation for migration by the ducks, geese, and other birds. An Elder chosen by the community who has been monitoring manoomin growth will advise harvesters when they can "pick" with the cedar sticks they carved weeks before. The appointed Elder will also determine when manoomin needs to rest, directing harvesters to pause to enable more ripening, and redirecting the harvest to an alternate field for a few days. Families traditionally sent pickers out into the fields, while those at camp processed (dried and winnowed) manoomin so that it would be available for months to come.

The first stage of fall, when the waters begin to freeze and trees lose their leaves, is called oshkitagwaagin, or dagwaagin. This is the harvesting time when Anishinaabeg practice andawenjigewin (hunting and trapping) and bagida'waawin (fishing with gill nets in open waters). Bagida'waawin will later be replaced by shaabozigaweba'igewin (pushing the gill nets under the ice).

Then kashkatin (freeze-up) heralds biboon (winter), the time when the Creator's gifts enter a stage of rest and renewal. In times of extreme cold, there is not much movement on the ground and families seek shelter together. Elder Kezhii'aanakwat Ron Kelly explains that the harshest times are reserved for storytelling as well as men's and women's teachings. Sagakinige is the time to make and put away leatherwork, beading, drums and drumsticks, and to complete numerous other activities that may not have been finished before the onset of winter. It is also an important time to discuss survival skills.

Caring for Mother Earth and all life through the seasons is a sacred and enduring responsibility. Every year, we must exert energy to care for, gather, and prepare foods and medicines. There is a need to maintain ceremonies of gratitude to the Creator for these gifts. Manoomin is with us in every ceremony as it is an esteemed gift that, once dried in processing, will not spoil. These responsibilities embody the Anishinaabe science of sacred ecology, respecting the relationships of all life that Anishinaabe teachings convey.

Understanding manoomin requires respect for the interrelationships of all the essential gifts of the Creator. Consider that cedar (or sometimes spruce) is needed for thrashing sticks to knock manoomin grains into the canoe during harvest. Cedar, spruce, and wiigwaas are needed to make the canoes and push poles to navigate manoomin fields. Reed mats are woven on which to dry manoomin. Anishinaabeg also depend on the animals who provide skins for wrap-around moccasins, which are used by those who dance on roasted manoomin to remove husks. Wiigwaas baskets of varying sizes are lovingly crafted to hold the manoomin and to winnow the grains from their husks. We hope that Anishinaabe teachings about manoomin (re)awaken within you an understanding of the relationship of spirit in all life—we Anishinaabeg are one with manoomin and all gifts of the Creator.

Anishinaabeg worked hard to protect all Creation during Treaty negotiations with Canada and the United States. Within Canada, Anishinaabe leaders, with hundreds of their supporters, negotiated with the Crown in the years 1869–73 to reach the Nation-with-Nation agreement called the Northwest Angle Treaty or Treaty #3. Treaty #3 covers an area of 55,000 square miles (about 142,449 square kilometres) from west of what is now known as Thunder Bay on the shores of Lake Superior into what is now known as the Whiteshell area of southeast Manitoba. Anishinaabeg negotiated for the continuation of their way of life, their traditional teachings, medicines, and governance, to be "free as by the past for their hunting and rice harvest."[2] Indeed, the final discussions that led to Treaty #3 were held while Anishinaabeg were harvesting manoomin. As self-governing First Nations citizens of Treaty #3, we have heard of the intentional impacts of the United States in undermining Anishinaabeg harvesting rights, as seen, for example, with the White Pine Treaty of 1837.[3]

Despite Nation-with-Nation negotiations, we understand that the Crown and other colonial governments deliberately misinterpreted treaties in their own favour—as "proof-of-purchase"—and encouraged settlers to claim the lands and use the waters.[4] Colonial governments tried to stop the interconnectedness in the Anishinaabe way of life and threatened the manoomin harvest by taking lands and children. The determined work of Indian Residential School survivors has ensured that Canadians and Americans are reckoning with their colonial history and their continuing colonization policies and practices. The awakening of Canadians to this country's true history of genocide,[5] including cultural genocide,[6] occurred with the release of the Final Report of the Truth and Reconciliation Commission of Canada (2015) and its 94 Calls to Action. The process of awakening has been strengthened by a Canadian law enacted on 21 June 2021, which was intended to bring Canadian laws in line with the United Nations Declaration on the Rights of Indigenous Peoples (UNDRIP).[7] Within the United States, there is an awakening to the intergenerational impact of Indian boarding schools on Native Americans and their lands and waters, although UNDRIP in the United States remains morally, but not yet legally, binding. There is hope that Canada and the United States will honour and implement Treaties specifically as they move to acknowledge international Indigenous Rights generally.

Although colonial governments have made efforts to diminish Anishinaabe harvesting rights in the English written record, we must remember, as Grand Council Treaty #3 states, that "there is no single document [that] completely covers all terms of the agreement known as Treaty #3."[8] Anishinaabe oral traditions are alive in Anishinaabemowin— the Anishinaabe language—as well as in the ceremonies and traditions that carry Treaty teachings. Anishinaabe teachings maintain that the Anishinaabeg never surrendered their right of self-governance nor the Inherent Rights they were born with. Anishinaabeg are finding innovative ways to share oral tradition through the written word and evolving social and other media. We share manoomin teachings through ceremony and practices of Anishinaabe ecological science to ensure the next generations will live our Treaty and Inherent Rights.[9]

FIGURE 6: Caretaking Responsibilities. While Manomin can grow without human intervention, it thrives in relationship. In this image, Elder Guy Henry surveys a Manomin field. Traditionally, an Elder was appointed to monitor fields to determine when the harvest could begin. Colour is one feature that was used to gauge readiness. Manomin's seeds turn from a milky green to a reddish-brown as they ripen. At this point, they are ready to leave their mother plant—destined either for the harvester's canoe or the riverbed where they may germinate the following spring. Photograph by Jane Mariotti, 17 August 2023.

❷

Migration[1]

by Edward Benton-Banai

When the seven prophets came to the Anishinabe, the nation was living somewhere on the shores of the Great Salt Water in the East. There are many opinions about where this settlement was. It is generally agreed that the Ojibways and other Algonquin [peoples] were settled up and down the eastern shores of North America. We have some idea of the size of the nation from these words that have been handed down: "The people were so many and powerful that if one was to climb the highest mountain and look in all directions, they would not be able to see the end of the nation." Bands and clans were scattered here and there.[2] There were berry pickers, wood carvers, fishermen, canoe makers, and stone carvers. There were those who were charged with raising food from Mother Earth. They were called the Gi-ti-gay'-wi-nini-wug' (planters or keepers of the Creator's garden). There was an active exchange and communication among all groups of people. They used the waterways of the land to travel by canoe. They had a system of overland trails. They used sleds and dog teams to travel in the winter. . . . There was ample food from the land and sea, and there were fish from many rivers. . . .

[The prophet of the First Fire had told the people: "If you do not move, you will be destroyed."][3] There was much discussion among all the Anishinabe about the migration. . . . Huge gatherings were held to discuss the plans of the nation. Many people did not want to move their families on the journey to the West. Others were ready to follow the believers in the migration and give their unselfish support to what they felt was the Creator's plan. . . .

The Mide people[4] remembered the words of the prophet of the First Fire [as they journeyed inland]. He had spoken of a turtle-shaped mi-ni-si' (island) that would be the first of seven stopping places during the migration.

Some people thought that this island of the beginning of their journey was surely a place of great power and that they were to go there and await further instructions from the Creator. Others thought that those who accepted the words of the prophets should seek out this island and go there for Sweat Lodge and purification ceremonies. Still others felt that the search for the island was a test of their strength by Gitchie Manito.[5] There was a great search throughout all the waters of the land for this island.

At last, a woman who was carrying a child in her womb had a ba-wa-zi-gay-win' (dream). In this dream she found herself standing on the back of a turtle in the water. The tail of the turtle pointed to the direction of the rising Sun and its head faced the West. The turtle was in a river that ran into the setting Sun.

The woman told her husband of her dream. Her husband took the dream to the old men of the Midewiwin Lodge. These elders accepted this dream in its totality and instructed the people to explore the rivers in search of such an island.

Such an island was finally found in the St. Lawrence River. . . . There were many Spirit Ceremonies and cleansing ceremonies held there as the people sought additional instructions.

After some time, the people resumed their journey to the West. . . . From [the second major stopping place at Niagara Falls], the people moved to a place identified by one of the earlier prophets as "a place where two great bodies of water are connected by a thin, narrow river." This river was described as a "deep and fast ribbon of water that slices through the land like a knife." Many lives were lost in crossing this river. This third stopping place was very likely the shores of the Detroit River that connects Lake St. Clair and Lake Huron in the North to Lake Erie in the South. . . .

The people picked up the Waterdrum[6] and continued their westward journey. They were attacked along the way by the nations later called the Sauks and the Foxes. The people pushed on until they came to a large body of fresh water. . . . It is possible that this camping place of the migration was on the eastern shore of Lake Michigan. At this point many people drifted off by groups to look for a place to cross the great water. They knew that their journey must take them to the West. . . . Many felt that the direction of the migration had become lost and that the people had missed their fourth stopping place. Time passed so that there were many births and deaths among the people. . . . [T]he prophecies said that "a boy would be born to show the Anishinaabe back to the sacred ways." It was prophesied that he would show the way to "the stepping stones to the future of the Anishinabe people." That boy did come among the people. He had a dream of stones that led across the water. The Mide people paid attention to this dream and led the people back to the river that cut the land like a knife. They followed the river to the North. The river turned into a lake, and at a place where the river was formed again, they rested a while on an island. This island is known today as Walpole Island. They continued following the river further and came to the northern sea of freshwater that they had heard about when they first came to this region. They followed its eastern shore until, at last, they discovered a series of islands that led across the water. By moving the people by canoe, a way was found to the West over these "stepping stones." They found "the path to their chosen ground, a land in the West to which they must move their families." . . .

MANOMIN

Manitoulin Island became the fourth major stopping place of the migration. . . . For some time the main body of the migration stayed on the island, but it was not until the people settled at Baw-wa-ting' that the Waterdrum was given a home in which to rest and sing. . . . There was a small island here where powerful ceremonies were held. People now call this place Sault Ste. Marie. The fishing was excellent in the fast water. Skilled fishermen could run the rapids with a canoe while standing backwards in the bow. They would be carrying an ah-sub-bi' (net) on the end of a long pole. By the time they got to the quiet water of the river, their canoe would be full of beautiful Mi-ti-goo-ka-maig' (whitefish). There was so much food in the village that this place came to support many families. Baw-wa-ting' became the fifth stopping place of the migration. . . .

From Baw-wa-ting', the migration split into two large groups. One group followed the shore of another great body of water to the West. The other group followed the northern shore. Both of these groups were attacked by people called the Ba-wahn'. . . . Their hunting territory was being invaded by the migrating newcomers and they fought fiercely. These conflicts illustrate the way that both of these nations were devoted to their purposes in life. The Ba-wahn' were later called Dakotas by the Light-skinned Race. . . .

[The two large groups of Anishinabe migrants came together on an island.] This island today is referred to as Spirit Island at the west end of Lake Superior. . . . It was near Spirit Island that the words of the prophets were fulfilled. Here the Anishinabe found "the food that grows on the water." . . . [Manomin] has always been regarded by the Ojibway as the sacred gift of their chosen ground. . . .

This island in the bay became the sixth major stopping place of the migration. The Elders of the Midewiwin Lodge sensed that the long journey of their people was near its end. But something was missing. One of the prophets long ago had spoken of a turtle-shaped island that awaited them at the end of their journey. . . . The people sought out this island and placed tobacco on its shore. . . . Here, the Waterdrum made its seventh and final stop on the migration. . . . This island was called Mo-ning-wun'-a-kawn-ing (the place that was dug) by the Ojibway. It was later called Madeline Island. This name has survived to this day. The main body of the Anishinaabe people gathered here and they became strong and powerful.

FIGURE 7: A Flowering Manomin Plant. Manomin is wind-pollinated, meaning that pollen, which is produced by male flowers featured in this image, is carried by the wind to nearby female flowers. The pollen must reach the female ovary for an edible Manomin seed to form. Photograph by Laura Legzdins, 25 August 2022.

3

Seeds and Soils

by Victoria Jackson

Approximately 11,000 years ago, a deep proglacial lake dubbed Lake O'Connor covered the basin where today's eleven-kilometre-wide Whitefish Lake rests in northwestern Ontario. White spruce, oak, elm, poplar, and various herbs and shrubs dominated the area. But as the climate became more arid around 10,500 years ago, the deep-watered proglacial lake gradually drained and shallowed. The surrounding landscape became populated with ragweed (*Ambrosia*) and chenopods (*Chenopodiineae*), willow trees (*Salix*), firs (*Abies*), alders (*Alnus*), and sedges (*Cyperaceae*). Fluctuations in climate and temperature caused these plant populations to increase or decrease over time, sometimes giving way to other species. Then, approximately 6,000 years before the present, as humidity increased and the lake deepened, the drought-hardy ragweed and chenopods and the shallow-water wetland plants like sedges and willows began to decline, giving way to coniferous forests. Manomin began to appear in Whitefish Lake, along with water lilies (e.g., *Nymphaea odorata*, *Nuphar variegatum*), broadleaf arrowheads (*Sagittaria latfolia*), and pondweed (*Potamogeton gramineus*). While it is unknown precisely when humans arrived at the lake, several archaeological sites (including Martin-Bird, McCluskey, and MacGillivray sites) indicate people were consuming Manomin in the area at least 2,000 years ago, and it would have been widely available to them at least 3,000 years before that.[1]

I begin with a long history of Whitefish Lake because any study of people's relationship with Manomin should consider the space in which it grows. Archaeological sites dot the landscape around this particular lake, and many of these sites contain evidence of Manomin use. The MacGillivray site, for example, has a number of features suggestive of rice husking pits (ricing jigs), and subsequent testing of pottery found Manomin residues in the ceramics.[2] Similarly, the pottery recovered at the Mound Island site (a habitation site) and the Martin-Bird site (which includes prominent burials) indicates Manomin consumption, and depressions at Martin-Bird likewise indicate Manomin processing in ricing jigs.[3] Each of these sites is roughly dated to the Middle Woodland period, approximately 600 to 900 AD, indicating people in the area over 1,000 years ago were aware of and making use of the bountiful food supply of the lake.

Whitefish Lake and its surrounding sites are not unique; Manomin grows across the Great Lakes region, predominantly in parts of Ontario, Minnesota, and Michigan. Likewise, there are dozens of known archaeological sites that feature Manomin, indicating humans have had a long history with the aquatic plant. However, Manomin is generally understudied in both an archaeological and paleobotanical context.

This chapter is intended as an introduction and overview of some of the methods and sources that archaeologists and paleoethnobotanists[4] use to learn about ancient Manomin and the plant-human relationship. I am *not* an expert on Manomin, and while I am familiar with archaeological processes and theoretical frameworks, I am not an archaeologist. I am an historian; while I do include archaeological research and material in my own work, my formal training in archaeology stopped after a Bachelor's with Honours in Archaeology and Biological Anthropology. As such, most of my experience with archaeology comes from my efforts to combine it with historical methods, theory, and practice, also known as ethnohistory. My intent with this chapter is not to break new ground in the research, but instead to clarify to other non-specialists some of the research already available. My purpose with this chapter is three-fold. First, it is my hope that this chapter can help make the study of ancient Manomin use accessible to non-archaeologists by discussing the kinds of evidence and research methods used in the field. Second, I seek to clarify some of the limitations of that research, including problems inherent in archaeology, to demystify the process of extracting knowledge from ancient landscapes. Finally, this chapter is intended to briefly introduce what the land can (and cannot) teach us about the ancient use of Manomin and how ancient Indigenous Peoples interacted with the environment in which it grows. This chapter is not an exhaustive analysis, only an introductory examination of some of the research of Manomin.

The Archaeology of Manomin

Manomin is an aquatic grass known to scientists as *Zizania* or wild rice.[5] On Turtle Island, there are three species of *Zizania*: *Z. palustris*, *Z. aquatica*, and *Z. texana*. Most of the best-studied archaeological sites for Manomin, primarily the *Z. palustris* and *Z. aquatica* species, are found in Ontario, Canada, and the northern parts of Wisconsin, Michigan, and Minnesota in the United States—essentially, the Great Lakes region.[6] This aquatic grass grows in a fairly specialized environment and is sensitive to weather and fluctuations in water level.[7] Manomin requires relatively shallow (ideally 0.3 to 1.5 metres deep) water with gentle but steady water movement.[8] Manomin tends to ripen in the late summer or early autumn over the course of approximately two weeks—unless plants are bundled together to encourage uniform ripening—and requires repeated visits for harvesting.[9] Manomin plants also serve as an important food source to a number of non-human species, including at least twenty-six species of birds, such as wood ducks, mallards, blackbirds, blue-winged teals, and Virginia rails.[10]

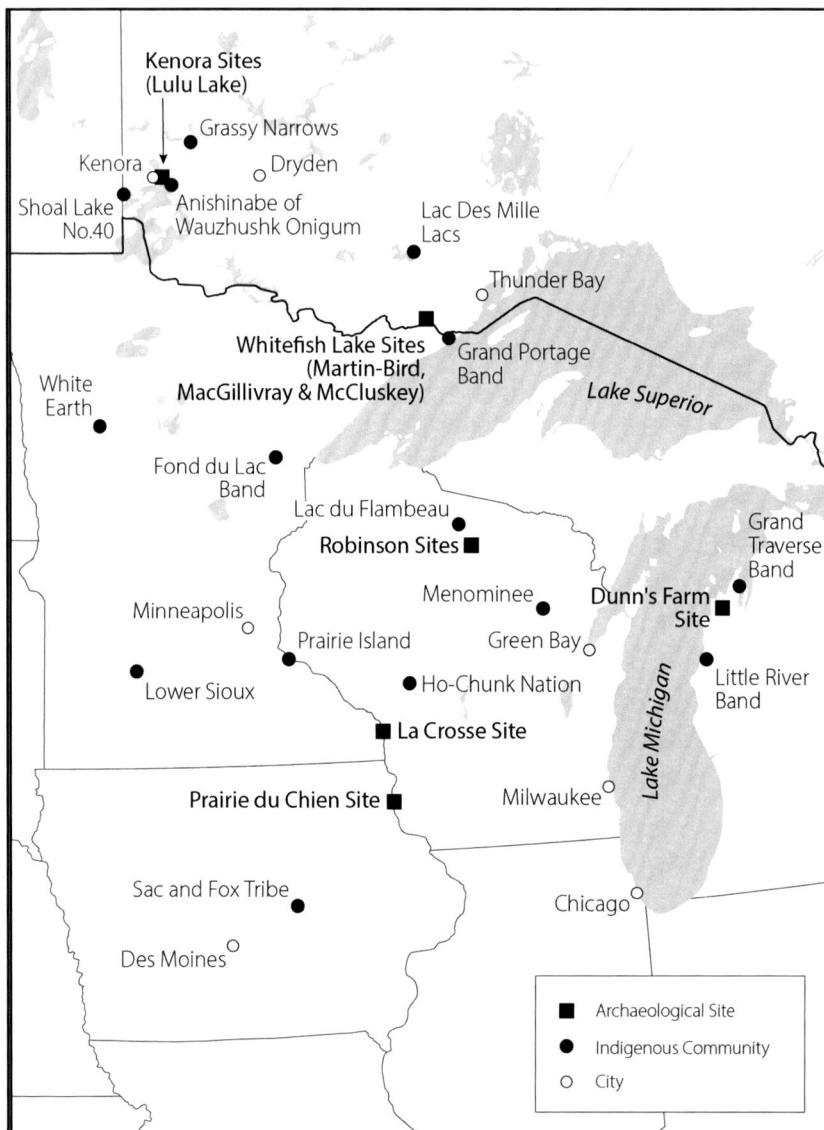

FIGURE 8: Archaeological Sites Proving Long-Term Plant-Human Relations. Map by Julie Witmer, 2024.

Seeds and Soils

Finding evidence of Manomin use at an archaeological site requires some specialized knowledge and tools. Paleoethnobotanists may look for macrobotanical (visible with the naked eye) or microbotanical (microscopic) remains.[11] Macrobotanical evidence for Manomin use mostly comes from preserved grains—usually charred from the parching process or from cooking. Indeed, charred Manomin grains have been recovered from pottery and threshing pits dating back hundreds of years.[12] Charred food remains have also been found inside of burials; Manomin is no different. At the Dunn's Farm site, a late Middle Woodland site located in Northwest Michigan, a burial (partially cremated) was uncovered, which contained some charred Manomin grains. While the Manomin may have been incorporated into the burial by accident, archaeologist David Brose suggested the Manomin could have been included deliberately as a spiritual offering.[13] Charred grains of Manomin, easily visible to the eye, are perhaps more familiar to archaeologists used to studying burials and village sites.

Microbotanical evidence, on the other hand, comes from pollen or phytoliths and tends to require some specialized knowledge and training for analysis. Pollen is often recovered from lake core sediments, but the remains are tiny and, in the case of Manomin, can be more difficult to interpret than other forms of evidence. Pollen from *Zizania* (Manomin) is "virtually indistinguishable from other native grasses" and requires scanning using specialized equipment and methods for diagnostic identification.[14] Pollen is also easily carried by the wind and other actors, and therefore Manomin pollen may not be found in the same place that Manomin grew. For example, one study of the Red Lake Peatland in northern Minnesota revealed *Zizania* pollen in the peat cores, but no macrofossils like phytoliths, which usually remain in place where the plant died; combined with the lack of evidence for modern Manomin stands in the area, it was concluded that the pollen likely came from the upland rather than from plants growing at the coring site.[15] However, palynological studies have also been used to successfully identify "wild rice lakes" and, especially in combination with other evidence, pollen can be a valuable source of information.[16]

Unlike pollen, phytoliths (microscopic silica structures that form naturally inside of some plant tissues) are usually found in situ, are often species-specific, and can be used to identify Manomin at a site. Because the silica deposits in the plant's tissues take on the shape and structure of the plant's cells, phytoliths provide a non-degradable record for scholars interested in determining the botanical history of an area. Phytoliths often have distinctive morphology and can be used to distinguish one type of plant from another; for example, several rondel phytoliths, which are produced in grasses, have distinctive characteristics only present in Manomin.[17] Phytoliths from Manomin chaff have been found in the charred food remains inside of nearly 3,000-year-old pottery in Minnesota,[18] as well as in sediment core studies, including in places like Lulu Lake near Kenora, Ontario.[19]

Much of the evidence of ancient Manomin is recovered through analysis of lake sediment cores from the lakes where these plants once grew. Sediment core studies may be conducted using a variety of core lengths depending on the timeline desired for analysis and the availability of equipment. Assuming the sediments in the lake were not disturbed by external forces, a lake's sediments will form natural layers, with the top layers logically having been deposited more recently, and the deeper layers representing progressively older periods of time.[20] A long core (for example, 4.5 metres) would, therefore, include sediments from a longer timeline than a short core of, for example, less than one metre. Sediment cores taken from lakes and marshes could include plant, animal, and inorganic matter, and they can be used both to provide a timeline for the appearance of new species in the area, as well as to give hints about what ancient environments would have looked like.[21] For example, palynological studies (plant pollen studies) of lake sediments have shown that Manomin became common in Minnesota and northern Ontario around 2,500 years BP.[22]

A study of pollen and phytolith evidence from lake sediments at the aforementioned Whitefish Lake was used to create a 10,000-year timeline of changing environments and flora in the area. The study revealed the appearance of Manomin in the lake at approximately 6,100 cal BP once the previously arid climate became more humid and the lake deepened enough to provide sufficient space for the Manomin to grow.[23] The researchers were able to determine the climatic changes by examining the pollen in the sediment cores; as the area became more humid and the waters deepened, there was a decline in drought-indicating plant species like *Ambrosia* and *Chenopodiineae*, and of shallow-water plants like sedge and *Salix*. Since Manomin pollen and phytoliths were dated to this climatic change, the evidence suggests that Manomin's appearance in Whitefish Lake was determined by climatic and associated changes rather than human intervention.[24]

Other scholars have used the food residues in pottery to determine the use and distribution of ancient Manomin. In one study, pottery pieces from three different sites kept at the New York State Museum were used to provide evidence of subsistence patterns in eastern New York. Although the study focused on dating the introduction of maize (corn) in the region, the researchers also found evidence of Manomin and other staples in the analysis, meaning that people were consuming Manomin in the seventh century AD and that they were using pottery for cooking and likely storing the Manomin.[25]

Finally, archaeologists may also look for evidence of Manomin harvest, process, or consumption. Manomin harvesting requires careful planning because of the limited window for its collection. To harvest Manomin, one paddles into the Manomin stand, pulls the stalk over the canoe, and carefully knocks the stalk to drop the ripened grains into the floor of the canoe.[26] This same harvest method may have been used in the ancient past, and therefore signs of ancient canoes in proximity to ancient Manomin may indicate a plant-human relationship.[27] For example, at the Misiano site near Gegoka Lake in northern Minnesota, archaeologist G.R. Peters found indirect evidence of dugout canoes in close proximity to ancient Manomin stands.[28] While still unconfirmed, the presence of canoes near a stable Manomin source may serve as indirect evidence of harvest and consumption.

Ricing jigs also provide evidence of Manomin processing. Ricing jigs are described as shallow pits dug into the earth and lined with skin or clay. People used ricing jigs to process Manomin in preparation for storage or consumption, which involved stepping on the rice in the pit so that the resulting friction would separate the grains from the chaff.[29] Finding ricing jigs near or at an archaeological site indicates the people were processing Manomin there, either for their own use or for trade. Ricing jigs, therefore, are particularly useful for being able to link specific groups of people or specific archaeological sites with the resources they used.

With these kinds of evidence and methods of data collection, the archaeological material tends to support a few common lines of inquiry. One of the most common questions archaeologists and paleoethnobot-anists try to answer revolves around the origins of food production: in other words, when did people on Turtle Island start plant husbandry and agriculture? While the origin(s) of maize agriculture dominates Canadian and American scholarly discussion of food production, there has been some limited research on the origins of Manomin in the Great Lakes area, and, more to the point for archaeologists, the origins of Manomin harvest, process, and consumption. For example, Constance Arzigian's study of a site at Prairie du Chien (southwestern Wisconsin) and Oneota sites at La Crosse dated Manomin use in the area to approximately 100–200 CE. Manomin was also associated with Prairie du Chien's earliest evidence for squash, sunflower, and sumpweed cultigens, as well as wild resources such as nuts, seeds, fish, and mussels. Arzigian's analysis indicates that Manomin was used whenever it was available, but that the people living at Prairie du Chien and La Crosse also used alternative food sources to supplement their diet and were able to shift to other resources when the Manomin stands grew poorly.[30] From other sites, it would seem that Manomin may have become widely available in a region long before it was used by humans. For example, Matthew Boyd et al.'s study of the Whitefish Lake area indicated that although Manomin had appeared in the area by 6,100 BCE, the oldest evidence of its process and consumption dates to approximately 300 BCE.[31] Manomin also appears in harvestable quantities in parts of Minnesota by approximately 10,000 BCE, and had become a major food source by approximately 2,500 BCE.[32] As such, it is clear from the archaeological record that Manomin appears in the landscape long before humans can be definitively said to be consuming it.

Many archaeologists are also concerned with the changes in food production over time. Some early studies were particularly interested in determining whether Manomin use continued after the introduction of maize to an area, but now it seems more widely held that Manomin was used when it was available because the people preferred its use, rather than because they had no other choice.[33] In some studies, maize and Manomin have been found together in cooking vessels, indicating that people may have either planted corn as well as gathered Manomin, or they were receiving one or both of those foodstuffs in trade and consumed them together out of preference; this also suggests people were unlikely to simply abandon Manomin when maize became available.[34] Indeed, it would seem that maize and Manomin were "closely intertwined components of diet in many northern Woodland societies," and the traditional emphasis on Manomin harvest may have even influenced the ways in which domesticated plants were adopted into or excluded from peoples' diets over time.[35]

The Limits to the Archaeological/Paleoethnobotanical Study of Manomin

Archaeology and paleoethnobotany can be very useful in tracing the ancient history of Manomin. However, there are a number of difficulties inherent in these studies. Some of the issues are rooted in the evidence and its collection; others are methodological or conceptual.

Manomin is not a common research subject in archaeology or paleobotany, nor is evidence easy to find. Direct and verifiable evidence of Manomin in subarctic archaeological sites is particularly rare, even though Manomin was both prevalent in the environment and culturally important to the peoples living in the region.[36] Part of the problem is the inaccessibility of sites in the North, but all sites of Manomin growth would be complicated to access. As an aquatic grass, most of the evidence of Manomin's ancient history is underwater in lakes and buried under centuries of silt. Most archaeology is conducted on land; archaeologists tend to look for signs of villages, burial grounds, and other permanent or semi-permanent features to determine where to dig. Archaeologists looking for evidence of food production, collection, trade, and consumption would tend to look for where the Manomin is stored (e.g., pottery, storage pits), processed (e.g., ricing jigs, hearths), or lost or deliberately discarded (e.g., middens, inside buildings or other structures, in burials). Finding evidence in lakes and streams requires specialized equipment and expertise, which also adds expense and time to the work. Likewise, in the northern Great Lakes region, Manomin may be plentiful, but the soil is often acidic and makes for poor preservation at sites where Manomin might be processed or consumed.[37] As such, evidence at archaeological sites may be scant and poorly preserved.

The environment presents other challenges. Waterways tend to change over time; sometimes this is because of climate shifts, but human and other-than-human (e.g., beaver) activity, such as damming, can also change the landscape, complicating the finding of ancient sites as well as their processing. Manomin is sensitive to environmental changes, and even small changes in water depths or currents can mean the difference between whether Manomin grows in a waterway or does not. In the ancient past, Manomin stands may have gone through cycles in which they were fruitful and plentiful for decades or even centuries and then disappeared because there was a change in its environment, sometimes permanently.[38] Over thousands of years, the environment can change substantially, complicating scholars' ability to find and examine useful sites.

When a site is located, finding and collecting evidence also presents certain challenges. On land, trace Manomin evidence is often found in places like burials and village sites, but the evidence is very small. Flotation, which involves mixing soil samples with water and then removing the plant materials that float to the surface so that they can be examined further, is a standard evidence recovery technique used to collect and sift through material from fire, storage, and midden pits, among other notable features.[39] However, although a valuable source of information, flotation is not always utilized. Archaeologist Clarence Surette points out that "flotation techniques have not been attempted at many sites" where Manomin might otherwise be found,[40] and in their survey of paleoethnobotany in Canada's Northeast, archaeologists Gary Crawford and David Smith point to the lack of comprehensive flotation use as standard procedure at Early and Middle Woodland sites.[41] When samples for flotation *are* collected for a site, sampling strategies vary, sometimes from season to season at the same dig site, as do flotation methods.[42] For other sites and studies, although flotation samples may have been collected, complete processing may not happen right away, or at all. For example, in Christine Branstner's report on the archaeological work at the Cloudman Site, flotation samples were collected and examined but not fully processed, limiting what the evidence can tell us.[43]

Sampling biases could also be inadvertently introduced to the study. As archaeologists Heidi A. Lennstrom and Christine A. Hastorf point out, efforts to maximize information while minimizing cost and labour means that archaeologists may inadvertently contribute to sampling bias. For example, archaeologists may collect materials for flotation by focusing their efforts on recognizable features, without realizing that those features may not be the best places to find plant material. For example, in their paleobotanical study of the Pancán site in Peru, Lennstrom and Hastorf found that hearths, pits, animal offerings, and human burials all had different ethnobotanical characteristics and patterns. Lennstrom and Hastorf suggested that analysis of these kinds of features at future sites would not only benefit from differential treatment, but also that these particular features might not be the best places to find botanical evidence.[44] Closer collaboration with experts in paleoethnobotany and further training in the nuances of paleoethnobotany for archaeologists would seem to be one way to avoid accidental sampling bias.

Similarly, evidence from lake cores has its own sampling bias. In their study of phytoliths recovered from lake sediment cores, Chad L. Yost et al. raised concerns about the practice of collecting cores from lake centres (as they did in their study). Their analysis indicated that Manomin phytoliths tended to be present in greater numbers in places where the largest Manomin stands were located.[45] If sample cores are collected from areas where Manomin may not grow—and since Manomin requires shallow waters, it is less likely to be found in the centre of a lake—this will affect what kind of evidence is recovered. This is an especially important consideration when subsequent studies are being conducted on archaeological material that had been gathered from previous studies.

Then there are dating issues. When evidence of Manomin is found, it is most useful to archaeologists if it can be accurately dated. Unfortunately, not all materials are found in datable contexts. While lake cores reflect the sedimentary stratigraphy and can provide at least a fairly reliable relational timeline, carbonized Manomin grains, on the other hand—which are easier to locate on land than pollen or phytoliths—are rarely recovered in datable contexts. In order to properly date Manomin use, "directly dated carbonized rice grains in association with diagnostic artifacts" would be ideal; however, this is not always possible, and in many sites the contexts are mixed, with ricing features, for example, being used periodically over the course of several centuries, making it impossible to reliably date the evidence.[46]

There is also a simple lack of knowledgeable paleoethnobotanists and archaeologists working on Manomin research, which means new research is published and distributed slowly. Most of the archaeological reports of "wild rice" in the Northeast (of Canada and the U.S.) were produced in the 1980s and 1990s, with a few notable examples in the 1970s; as of 2003, at least thirty-seven sites had been identified across the Northeast with evidence of Manomin.[47] However, most of the paleoethnobotanical data for that same region pertains not to Manomin but to the plants falling under "the Northern Mixed Economy pattern," which is dominated by maize, beans, squash, tobacco, and "wild" plants like chenopods, knotweed, and little barley.[48] The difficulty in finding academic experts to examine archaeological evidence of Manomin is unlikely to improve, as "the demand for [botanical] research is outstripping our ability to train paleoethnobotanists."[49]

Even when care is taken to mitigate potential bias, expertise is available, and evidence is collected with the utmost care, archaeology can only tell us about the evidence that survives to the present. While carbonized rice grains, pollen, phytoliths, and indirect evidence like ricing jigs and pottery provide information about Manomin, its harvest, and its consumption, there are also a number of ways Manomin can be collected, processed, and consumed without leaving any archaeological traces. Canoes and ricing jigs are commonly associated with the harvesting and processing of Manomin, but it is also possible to harvest and process without those tools. In the shallow waters, it is possible to simply walk through the Manomin stands to collect the grains,[50] and while ricing jigs are useful for separating the grains from the chaff, the same can be done by rubbing the grains in between one's hands. Likewise, although Manomin consumption has long been associated with pottery[51] and charred remains can be found inside many samples of ancient ceramics—even hundreds of years after they were used for that purpose—it is also possible to cook Manomin without using pottery. As such, humans may work with Manomin without leaving much or any archaeological record, suggesting the possibility that people have been harvesting, processing, and consuming Manomin for a lot longer than the roughly 2,500-year timeline presented in the archaeology.[52]

The Future of Research into Ancient Harvests

With all of this, what do we know, definitively, about the ancient history of Manomin? We know that the archaeological (and paleoethnobotanical) record places Manomin's appearance in the Great Lakes region at around 10,000 years ago. We know that people were definitely processing and cooking Manomin at least 2,500 years ago. We know that the people harvesting, processing, and cooking Manomin 2,500 years ago were using some of the same techniques that are used today. Unfortunately, the archaeological record does not show if people always used canoes to gather the Manomin, or if they used other techniques. The archaeological record does not tell us if ancient peoples always cooked Manomin in pots, or how frequently they gathered Manomin for ritual use rather than consumption. And the archaeological record does not tell us, conclusively, when people started harvesting Manomin (only that it was *at least* 2,500 years ago), or why some groups preferred Manomin over other food sources.

Archaeology of Manomin is still an underdeveloped field of study in Canada, although in the United States, there has been quite a bit of work coming from Michigan and Minnesota. Most of this research, however, attempts to trace the origins of Manomin use rather than analyze the actual relationship between humans and Manomin. Indeed, many scholars still refer to Manomin as "wild rice" and write about its appearance and continued growth as if there was never any human involvement, even though ethnographic, historical, and archaeological evidence suggests that at least some Manomin stands were actively and intensively cultivated, with people even reseeding to ensure new growth.[53]

More research is needed in this field. However, the research needs to be collaborative. Archaeology is not perfect and cannot tell us everything we would like to know about the plant-human relationship. In Canada, there is an increasing shift toward collaboration with Indigenous communities to create ethical research projects; unsurprisingly, the collaborative approach would greatly benefit research into Manomin's ancient history. Many Indigenous communities in the northern Great Lakes region still harvest Manomin today, and they know their own history with the plant, passed down through families and through generations in stories and by working the land and waters. Moreover, oral histories and traditions and archaeology can be used effectively together.[54] Archaeological digs already tend to bring in different kinds of experts to conduct their analyses of the evidence; a dig site at an ancient village might uncover pottery and ceramics, stone tools, human burials, animal burials, and charred food remains in a hearth pit, all of which might require specialized analysis for a complete understanding of the site. Talking to Indigenous Elders about the histories of sites on their territories should be understood as seeking another form of expertise. Fortunately, it does seem as though the research is moving more and more in this direction. In Ontario, archaeological organizations increasingly consult with Indigenous partners, and scholarly research projects are increasingly carried out with Indigenous collaboration.

Indigenous leadership is also important. There is increasing interest in reclaiming and repatriating traditional foods and foodways, and this has some significant implications for scholars interested in Manomin. For example, James Whetung of Curve Lake First Nation plants, harvests, processes, and sells Manomin from the lake, citing its nutrition as one of the benefits of bringing back the plant. In a *CBC Life* video available on

YouTube, Whetung explained that he went to local Elders to ask where Manomin used to grow, and he replanted in those areas.[55]

With Manomin, scholarly research can only benefit from partnerships with Indigenous knowledge-carriers. Elders and other knowledgeable persons in communities that traditionally harvested Manomin may know where the grass grew in the past and how people gathered and processed it. With more interest in reclaiming and repatriating traditional foods, there is also more lived experience and contemporary expertise to enhance understanding of long ago practices. Collaboration may well be the future of Manomin research.

MANOMIN AND BERGAMOT

by Sean Sherman

————

As we define Indigenous foods for a new generation, it is important to think about the methods and traditions of our ancestors. Our Indigenous ancestors were so privileged to have the thousands of generations of knowledge passed down to them, teachings that empowered them to use all of the flora around us for food and medicine. Keeping the simplicity of the food and flavours is important to remember. It allows the food to truly speak for itself with its clean, subtle flavours—flavours that offer so much wisdom and nutrition and are a direct connection to our communities of the past. This recipe uses some modern equipment but could be done with the year-end harvest of Manomin and seasonal farm produce.

Serves: 4 | *Prep time:* 30 mins | *Cook time:* 60 mins

Dried
Bergamot Leaves

Sunflower Oil

Salt

Maple Syrup

Dried & Seeded
Rosehip

Water

Manomin

Leek
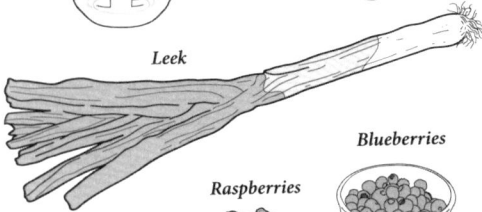

Blueberries

Raspberries

Turnip

Blackberries

Watercress

Sunflower Seeds

Butternut Squash

INGREDIENTS

Dumplings:

3 cups Manomin, cooked

1/2 cup Manomin, puffed
and ground into powder

1/4 cup turnip,
large dice and roasted

1/4 cup butternut squash,
large dice and roasted

1/4 cup leek, minced

1/4 cup pure maple syrup

3 tbsp sunflower oil

1/2 cup sunflower seeds,
toasted and unsalted

2 tbsp salt

Broth:

1 cup blackberry

1 cup blueberry

1 cup raspberry

2 tbsp rosehips,
dried and seeded

1/4 cup pure maple syrup

2 cups water

2 tbsp
bergamot leaves, dried

Garnish:

Watercress, fresh

Manomin and Bergamot

PREP

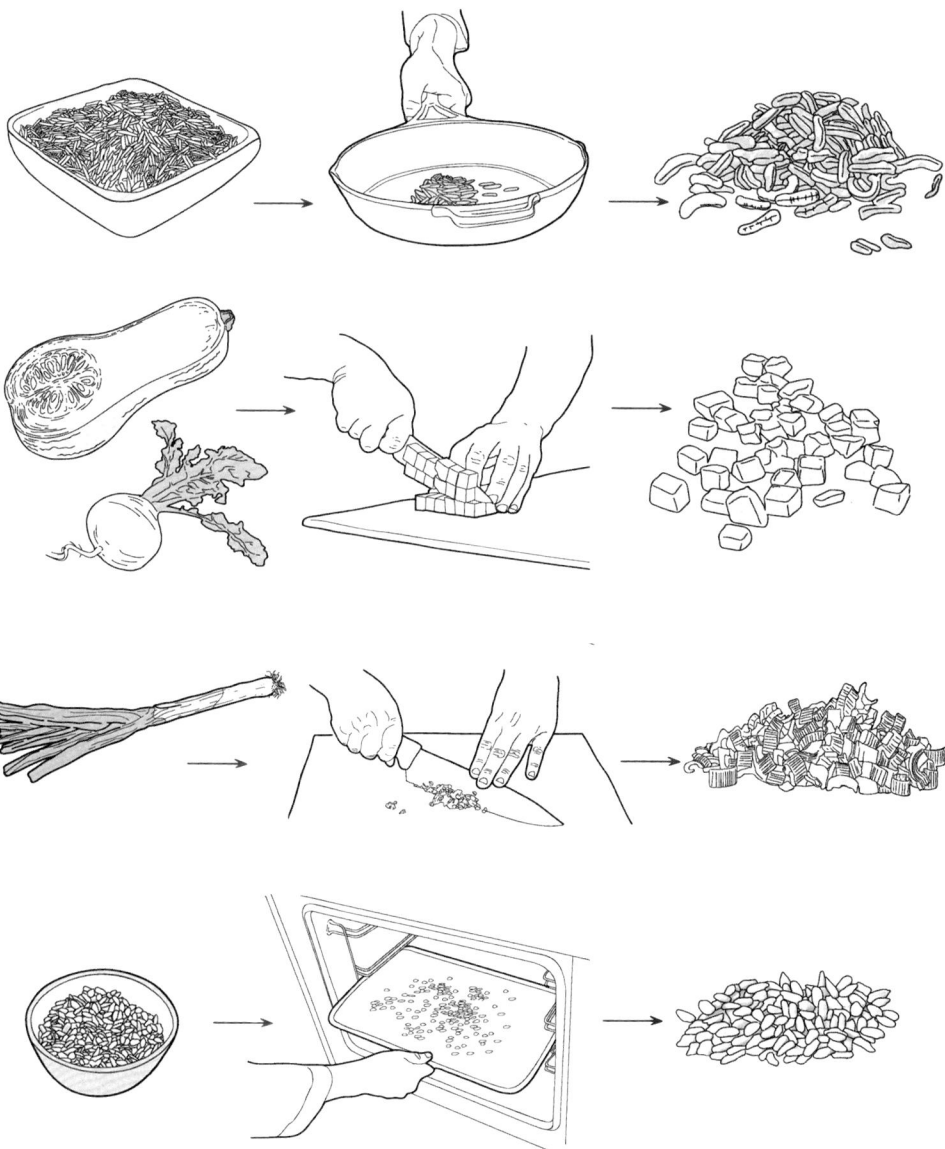

INSTRUCTIONS

Dumplings:

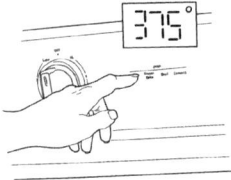

1 Preheat oven to 375 degrees Fahrenheit.

2 Toss squash and turnips in a little sunflower oil.

3 Lay a single layer on a sheet pan. Sprinkle with salt and bake for 14 minutes.

4 In a food processor, add all dumpling ingredients and purée until paste is thickened.

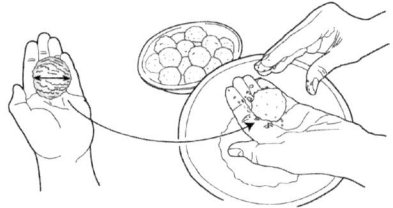

5 Scoop the dough into small balls the size of wild black walnuts.

6 Roll into popped Manomin powder. (To puff Manomin, heat a skillet on medium heat and add a small amount of raw Manomin directly to a hot pan with no oil and gently shake the pan as the Manomin puffs out, being careful not to burn. Remove puffed Manomin and repeat). Place dumplings back onto a sheet pan and bake for 12 minutes.

Broth:

7 Add all broth ingredients to
a pot and bring to a simmer.
Simmer for 15 minutes.

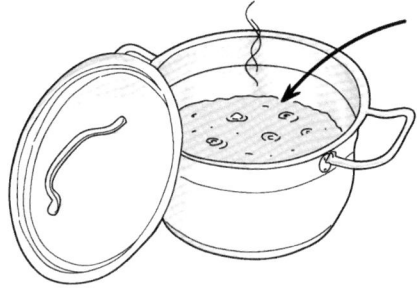

8 Then using a whisk, break
all the berries down into
the liquid. Continue to
simmer and whisk for the
next 10 minutes. Add more
water if too thick.

Assembly:

9 Place three dumplings
in a bowl, pour hot
berry broth over the
dumplings, garnish
with watercress on
top, and serve.

Reminder:

Make sure to purchase as many
products from Indigenous producers
as possible and continue to
decolonize your diet.

FIGURE 9: Barbed Husks. In this image, Elder Guy Henry holds unripe Manomin seeds in his hand, showing us their barbed husks. These barbs help Manomin seeds lodge in the soft soil of river- and lakebeds. They also pose a risk to harvesters. To care for Manomin, we must also take care of ourselves. Forms of self-care might include wearing protective gear, such as personal flotation devices (PFDs), safety glasses, and UV-resistant clothing, and pacing the work so that you can stay focused on the movements needed to bring Manomin safely home. Photograph by Jane Mariotti, 15 August 2023.

4

Manomin as Teacher

by Brittany Luby with Niisaachewan Anishinaabe Nation

The contemporary occupation of Anishinaabe-Aki is explained through a migration story. As we learned from Edward Benton-Banai in Chapter 2, the Anishinaabeg once lived "somewhere on the shores of the Great Salt Water in the East," suggesting an ancestral root that extends to the Atlantic Ocean.[1] The Anishinaabeg harvested animals from the land and fish from the waters. Their bellies were full, and their families thrived— but prophets proclaimed that the Creator had another plan for them. If Anishinaabeg were to survive, they had to leave the Great Salt Water and travel inland. The first of seven prophets stated that Anishinaabeg could settle when "they found the 'food that grows on the water,'" a symbol of their "chosen ground."[2] The third prophet agreed. And so, Anishinaabeg pushed west until Manomin welcomed them home.

My paternal ancestors settled along the north shore of Lake of the Woods, a region bemoaned by federal administrators for difficult treaty negotiations in 1871, 1872, and 1873. Treaty Commissioners wrote, "They [Anishinaabeg] seem fully alive to their own interests." Commissioners recognized that Anishinaabeg were attuned to the value of natural resources, including Manomin, in the region.[3]

My earliest memory of Manomin is associated with the dock at my grandfather's house. In this memory, I'm sitting in a boat watching my father adjust the tiller motor. Dad doesn't pull into the slip but edges toward shore. We idle alongside a tall grass with tassels. Dad reaches a hand over the side of the boat to gently greet the plant. "This is Manomin," he says. "When it's ripe, you can eat it." I scan the shoreline. I want to be able to identify plant relatives like my father. I long to know the plant that symbolizes "home." But all I see is an indecipherable mass of greens.

When my father introduced Manomin to me, he created a pathway for learning about Anishinaabe culture. Anishinaabeg have transmitted cultural teachings to children through Manomin for generations. Manomin has been and can be used to reinforce knowledge that we each have a sacred purpose; it can contribute positively to our communities, regardless of a person's age. Manomin reinforces lessons about interspecies dependencies; it reveals how all organisms on Earth are intertwined. Manomin can also be used to transmit the Seven Generations Principle, helping children understand how the present reflects past activities and predicts future opportunities. In this way, Manomin reminds youth of their duty to honour past generations and their responsibility to provide for future ones. As this chapter reveals, each of these cultural teachings provides children with a sense of belonging in Anishinaabe-Aki.

Although scholars have long referred to Manomin harvesting as a family affair, their research to date has focused on the labour-intensive activities of able-bodied women and men. In the late 1920s, ethnographer Frances Densmore observed women who "stirred two parching kettles" and "tossed a winnowing tray" while men rested on rush mats.[4] She described children "running about" purposelessly.[5] About twenty years later, biologist John B. Moyle asserted that both genders worked in the fields: "The man usually stands in the rear to shove the push-pole [to steer the canoe] and the woman . . . remove[s] the grain."[6] Youth are absent in Moyle's account.

Manomin as Teacher

In the 1980s, ethnographer Thomas Vennum linked gender discrepancies in adult labour to economic demand. He claimed that "more men began to take an active role" in the harvest in the twentieth century as "wild rice became increasingly central to the economy."[7] But boys receive scant attention for hulling Manomin in Vennum's account.[8] Girls go unmentioned. Most recently, Amanda Raster and Christina Gish Hill noted that "old and young alike" contributed to the harvest.[9] But the unique experiences of children are outside the purview of their article, which focuses on treaty and food security. Despite these limitations, each of these authors reminds us that families were active in Manomin fields.

What is missing is a sense of how children lived and learned in these spaces. My understanding of childrearing in the Manomin fields has been shaped by personal experience and oral testimony from Niisaachewan Anishinaabe Nation, a community on the Upper Winnipeg River in what is currently known as northwestern Ontario. Nine Elders—Archie Wagamese, Clarence Henry, Danny Strong, John Henry, Josephine Kylne, Larry Kabestra, Nancy McLeod, Terry Greene, and Theresa Jourdain (née Kabestra)—agreed to share harvesting experiences as part of the Manomin Project, a community-driven, multidisciplinary initiative to restore Manomin at ancestral sites. Oral testimony was communicated through recorded interviews in the band office. It was also shared on boat tours of ancestral fields and during community feasts. Interviews and related events were co-organized with Elder liaison and translator Barry Henry following a series of community workshops during which band members established the project's parameters.[10] The oldest Elder to share their experiences was born in 1943. The youngest started their life journey in 1963. While Elders experienced Manomin harvesting in the mid- to late twentieth century, they emphasized traditional practices and cultural continuity. Elders saw their harvesting experiences as an activation and affirmation of ancestral knowledge and lifeways that had originated generations beforehand. As such, their testimonies provide insight into traditional Anishinaabe childrearing.

Interconnected Families

Manomin fields were never occupied year-round. Instead, families established ricing camps as part of their seasonal rounds. Information about these family migrations can be gleaned from the names of Anishinaabe moons, which overlap roughly with months in the Gregorian calendar. For example, the Anishinaabemowin word for June (Ode'miin giizis) translates roughly into "Strawberry Moon," July (Mskomini giizis) means "Raspberry Moon," and August (Manoominike giizis) means "Ricing Moon."[11]

In these rounds, toward the time of ripening, experienced ricers began to monitor the crop. When the milky seed hardened, transitioning from a pale green to a sun-kissed brown, the plant would be deemed ready to yield. Anishinaabe scholar Linda LeGarde Grover explains that "the elders and other experienced ricers" opened the harvest.[12]

The camps that formed varied in size. Smaller fields might accommodate two to five extended families whereas larger lakes (with high yields) could attract fifteen to twenty families.[13] Each camp included cooking and sleeping quarters, and areas to process Manomin were laid out. Individuals needed to be able to parch, hull, winnow, and pack the Manomin brought off the river. At Niisaachewan Anishinaabe Nation (NAN), families also established a "rough area" where they trained adolescents to harvest Manomin without injuring the plant.[14]

Once the shelters and working spaces were set up, able-bodied adults began the laborious process of harvesting Manomin. Elders at NAN suggested that husbands and wives often worked together. The husband navigated while the wife knocked grains into the canoe. However, alternative pairings also existed: siblings partnered up, grandparents trained grandchildren, and Elders worked collaboratively with able-bodied youth who might have been unrelated. Elder Clarence Henry indicated that "the elderly woman . . . would get a young guy pushing the pole. They would split-split, half, [then] proceed."[15] Even within spousal partnerships, one's position in

FIGURE 10: A Mixed Gender Harvesting Team. Photograph by Monroe P. Killy, "Wild Rice Harvest," 1939, Minnesota Historical Society (MHS), Reserve album 243, p. 47, no. AV1981.193.600.

the boat depended on capability more than gender. Elder Terry Greene noted that a "big woman—more powerful" could manage the push pole.[16]

Back at the camp, children were monitored by adolescents, who were monitored by Elders, who also parched, winnowed, and cleaned Manomin.

Children were kept out of working canoes until they developed sufficient strength to navigate the fields. Manomin grows best in water of 0.3 to 0.9 metres.[17] Pushing a canoe through such shallow water using a pole required muscle. Elder Danny Strong indicated that "the good stuff was around the edges [shore] [where] it was still like mud. . . . You'd have to be pretty strong to pull your partner to get through that mud."[18] Gathering, holding, and knocking the Manomin over and over again likewise required strength and coordination. Manomin seeds ripen at different times, and the same plant can be knocked two to three times per season. Youth needed to demonstrate bodily awareness to avoid damaging the plants. A rough hand might break the stalk, thus limiting the family's ability to increase their food stores that season.[19]

Anishinaabe guardians also watched for signs of cognitive development. Very young children, from birth to about three years, explore the world through touch. Child development specialist Christine Todd and safety specialist Robert Aherin state that children "learn about the properties of things by putting them in their mouths at this age."[20] Children seeking to explore Manomin before it was processed were at risk of choking because the barbed husk could lodge in their throats.[21] Guardians needed to ensure that children understood and knew how to avoid risks before harvesting by canoe.

From ages four to six, children continue to explore the world through feel, but they rely less on touch sensors in their mouths.[22] Anishinaabe guardians needed to see evidence a child would not explore the world primarily by touch. A child of this age might reach for an object outside of the canoe, tip harvested food into the river, and drown. Between the ages of ten and fifteen, children can articulate risks and describe how they would manage danger. Anishinaabe guardians required proof that a child understood the dangers of harvesting before inviting them to do so. Awareness, not age, was the determining factor.

When I was in my mid-thirties, Elders repeatedly told me that barbed husks could cause eye damage and lead to blindness.[23] Only upon suggesting that I could wear safety glasses (at best) or sunglasses (at worst) did they invite me to work with unprocessed Manomin. I also assured them that I had access to medical care in town should my eye protection fail. These safety precautions allowed me to participate in a workshop on parching and winnowing Manomin in the summer of 2018. The cereal itself was harvested by Elder John Henry. At the end of the following summer, Elder

Danny Strong handcrafted a set of knocking sticks for me, indicating that I would soon be ready to harvest by canoe.

Although children were not allowed to help loosen seeds from stalks in the canoe, Anishinaabe guardians emphasized that children had a vital role in the harvest. They scaled jobs according to ability, allowing, as Métis scholar Kim Anderson found, "even the youngest children [to] make a contribution."[24] Elders from Niisaachewan Anishinaabe Nation suggest that what ethnographer Frances Densmore classifies as unstructured play was understood by Anishinaabe guardians as productive labour. Anishinaabe children who were too young to harvest were informed that their play deterred bears.[25] Children were also encouraged to alert harvesters to other dangers such as human poachers. Elder Clarence Henry described a poacher as "a lazy person who wants to steal a bit of rice here and there" and noted that "the kids are supposed to keep an eye on the wild rice that the parents pick."[26] Elder Theresa Jourdain associated positive emotions with the job she was provided as a child: "It was really good. . . . We're there to watch the rice for poachers."[27]

Watching Manomin reinforced the Anishinaabe teaching that every living creature—no matter how large or how small—is part of an inter-connected whole. Anishinaabe children who may have lacked the bodily strength and coordination to work in the fields had the gift of sight and voice to protect food brought in by older family members. Given that Manomin was "intended to last until the next year's harvest,"[28] children were taught that their job had a direct impact on family well-being: it would ensure their family could eat throughout the lean winter months.

Anishinaabe guardians coded children's play as a contribution, but they understood how children's responsibilities changed as they aged. Youth who outgrew child's play—but did not yet have adult bodies—helped Elders supervise younger individuals. Once their bodies matured, they trained in the "rough area." They practised navigating the canoe by using a push pole (generally identified as a "man's job") and knocking Manomin into the

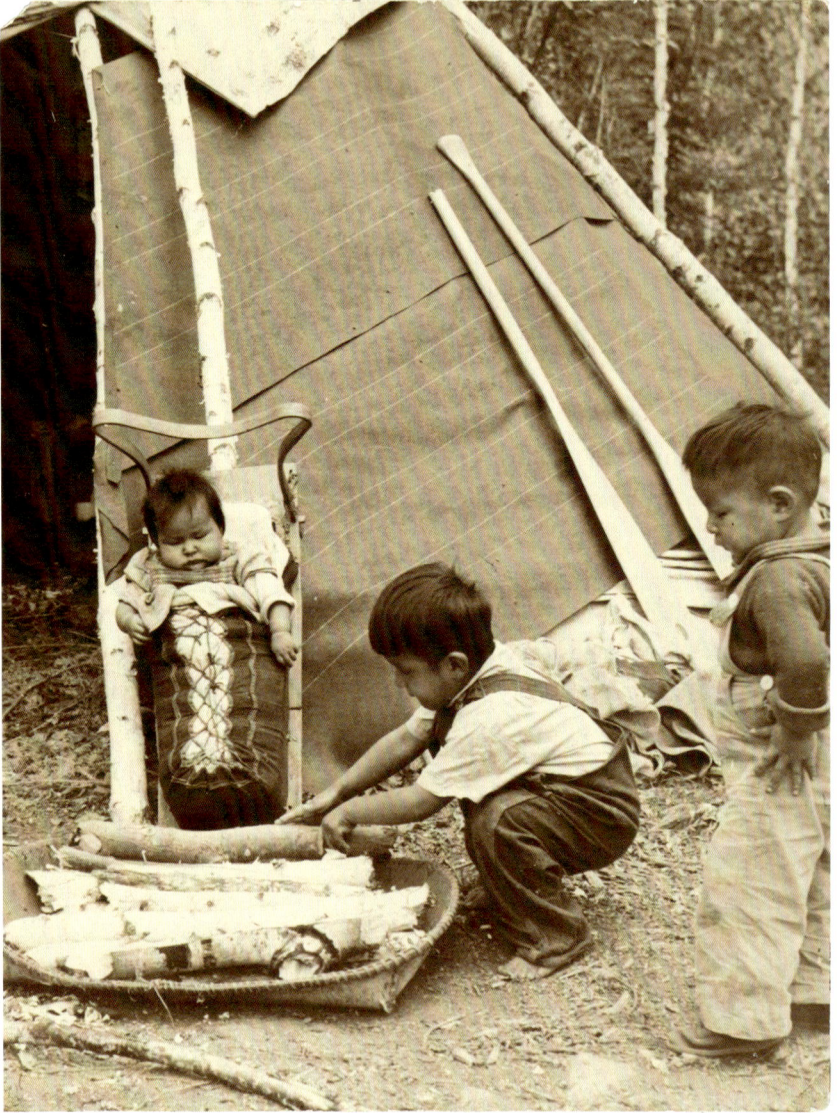

FIGURE 11: Children Organizing Firewood at Camp. Photographer unknown, "Chippewa Children in Rice Camp," 1940, MHS, E97.33, p. 2, no. 3934.

canoe (frequently coded as a "woman's job"). Children, regardless of sex, were versed in both tasks. Elder John Henry explained, "When you are beginning, they put you in a rough area and you learn from there." The training zone ensured that youth "don't destroy [the crop] when they are out there."[29] Elders indicated that the transition from childminding to harvesting often occurred between fifteen and nineteen years of age.[30] Younger children could see the "rough area," so they had a clear understanding of how their contributions would change. Because Anishinaabe children could visualize how their responsibilities would evolve as they aged, they knew they would remain contributing members of their community.

Anishinaabe guardians taught children that their contributions impacted community well-being. But, more than that, children were taught that their contributions were uniquely important. Although able-bodied adults were responsible for gathering, parching, and winnowing Manomin, children were encouraged to hull (or "dance on") it. Anishinaabe children were taught that their stature made them suited to this job. Elder Danny Strong explained, "If we get somebody like an adult, they'd just be breaking [the rice]. If you dance on it too hard, you won't have that rice."[31] Strong remembers receiving a special pair of deer hide moccasins for this task.

No life stage was without purpose. From cradle to grave, children were taught that functioning members of Anishinaabe society worked to ensure the well-being of others. Belonging was made possible by sharing gifts and entering a web of human relationships that assured—in this case—food security.

Interconnected Species

Anishinaabe guardians also worked with Manomin to teach children about their relationship with other-than-human beings. Manomin was (and is) perceived as a gift from the Creator. Indeed, the word translates roughly into English as "spirit berry."[32] To maintain the Creator's gift, Anishinaabeg must respect it. There is no sense that humans control the harvest; rather, Manomin offers itself to the Anishinaabeg when reciprocal relationships are established and maintained.

At Niisaachewan Anishinaabe Nation, youth are encouraged to lay tobacco in fields where Manomin might be harvested. A failure to acknowledge Manomin through such offerings could result in crop failure. Anishinaabe Elder Dorothy Dora Whipple from Leech Lake explained that "the reason why the Indians got the rice, because they put out tobacco for the thunder not to come to destroy the rice."[33]

In Anishinaabe oral stories, plants and animals have agency. They have options. Manomin offers itself to Nanabush, a half-human trickster, during a vision. Nanabush relays this message to the Anishinaabeg. Manomin thus gifted itself to the people.[34] A failure to offer tobacco, to honour the gift, can lead to its revocation. The emphasis on honouring other-than-human contributions to human well-being is not unique to the Upper Winnipeg River. In many Indigenous stories, as Robin Kimmerer notes, "legions of offended plants and animals and rivers rise up against the ones who neglected gratitude."[35]

Anishinaabe youth were taught that it is impossible to have an exclusive relationship with Manomin. Instead, Manomin and humankind are part of the Great Web of Being. Reciprocal and respectful relationships must be maintained with diverse species to ensure a successful harvest. Different species (referred to as "relatives") play a vital role in protecting Manomin at different stages of its life cycle. Moose, for example, feasts on aquatic plants. Moose's hooves help to churn the soil, uprooting other plants which may compete with Manomin for nutrients and space. Moose may also play a role in oxygenating the soil. In this way, Moose creates healthy growing conditions for Manomin in return for a meal.[36] The Anishinaabeg, who plant Manomin seed, help to feed Moose, who help Manomin. And so, by feeding Moose, the Anishinaabeg could also feed themselves.

Hawk was another helper species provided for in the fields. Cultural educator Kathi Avery Kinew notes that Hawk stands were erected by the

Anishinaabeg.[37] In return for a perch, Hawk helped human beings manage Red-Winged Blackbird (who, much like the Anishinaabeg, enjoyed eating Manomin). A failure to provide for one's other-than-human relations could negatively impact Manomin yields. For example, a failure to provide for Hawk could increase competition for food in the field. Anishinaabe guardians taught that family collaboration ensured Manomin processing in the winter months, whereas collaboration with plant and animal relatives ensured a crop would be harvested. As Anishinaabe poet Kristi Leora Gansworth writes, "From . . . scale to feather and branch, intertwined powers work together each day, constantly renewing this life that you belong to. As you exist, so do they; there is no separation" (see Chapter 9).[38] By teaching children about interspecies dependencies, Anishinaabe youth developed a sense of belonging: in Anishinaabe-Aki, you are never alone.

Interconnected Generations

Anishinaabe children were raised with an awareness of their interconnections with human and other-than-human relatives. But Manomin could also be used to teach children about their relationship with the ancestors and children yet to be born. The Seven Generations Principle is a decision-making framework through which Anishinaabeg learn that time is interconnected. The present is not isolated from the past or the future. Cultural educator Ron Deganadus McLester explains: "Each one of us has parents. . . . We also, therefore, had grandparents. . . . And though many of us may not remember it, and perhaps neither do they, we have had time with our great-grandparents. . . . If we're lucky, we'll each have a child. If we're really lucky, we'll also spend time with our grandchildren . . . and our great-grandchildren. The point is we spend time in each one of those areas. . . . Our choices, our behaviours, our mistakes reverberate that far throughout history."[39]

Actions carried out must, therefore, be evaluated intergenerationally. Individuals are taught to ask, "Am I honouring my ancestors? Would those who walked this Earth before me support my decisions?" They are also prompted to consider, "Am I protecting my descendants? Will those who come after me be served by my actions?" If you can answer "yes" to each of these questions, you can forge ahead having minimized the risk of harm. As a decision-making framework, the Seven Generations Principle prompts individuals to consider the long-term consequences of seemingly immediate decisions. According to McLester, "We challenge ourselves, we challenge each other, to make our decisions and our impacts within Creation within that timeline." By doing so, the Seven Generations Principle strengthens connections to Anishinaabeg past, present, and future.

During ricing moon, seed selection and planting allowed Anishinaabe guardians to transmit the Seven Generations Principle. After a successful harvest, Anishinaabe guardians divvied up food for home consumption, barter or sale, and reseeding. Seed that would be returned to the river could not be parched. In the words of American agriculturalist Joseph Bowron: "Germinating power is killed in the drying."[40] Elder Danny Strong revealed that a portion of his family's harvest, approximately 135 to 180 kilograms, was returned to the river.[41]

Children were not involved in identifying Manomin for storage. They were, however, actively involved in reseeding the river. Former Chief Allan Luby explained that Anishinaabe youth contributed to reseeding by forming mud balls and inserting seed into the balls.[42] Children likely threw the mud balls into the river from the shore, as parents were advised "not to take their kids out on the canoe" during the harvest to help prevent "tipping over."[43] Able-bodied adults reseeded the farthest reaches of the field by canoe. Strong observed that "some of them would go back around . . . throwing rice back into where we picked it."[44] But mud balls were not required for reseeding. Indeed, Strong explained that Manomin could be returned to the river loose: "You could just grab a handful and [*mimics throwing seed over the side of the boat*]" so long as "the skin" or husk was on.[45] The barbed husk helps the seed latch into the soil below. Mud balls were not essential to reseeding locally, but they were critical to teaching children how their actions influenced future Manomin growth.[46]

Packing mud balls helped children consider and understand how their actions reverberated across time. A failure to reseed could have dire consequences the next season. In the short term, their family might suffer from hunger; in the long term, they could (and can) starve future generations. As traditional harvester Fred Ackley Junior from northern Wisconsin warned, "We believe if we stop that tradition the world will stop."[47] Children who failed to reseed would not only cause Manomin shortages; they would limit access to other essential foodstuffs dependent on Manomin.

In this way, using the Seven Generations Principle to think through the long-term effects of seeding reinforced teachings about interspecies dependencies. Consider that Moose may no longer visit harvesting sites without aerial shoots to consume. Hunters, in turn, must reconsider their harvesting strategies. If Goose no longer descends on the fields during long-distance migrations, proteins will be less available during the fall. By seeding the field, Anishinaabe children learned that their actions would have a direct impact on the well-being of future generations.

Similarly, camping in established fields offered children evidence of ancestral love. Children were taught to plant as their ancestors had planted. More than that, children were taught that their ancestors had planted in anticipation of their arrival. Fields became evidence of past ceremonies and the prayers intended to provide for them. In this way, Manomin fields provided a sense of belonging in Anishinaabe-Aki. Children knew that food had been put aside to nourish them years before they were born.

Anishinaabe youth also learned that the ancestors were (and are) ever present. Healthy yields are not the only marker of intergenerational connections. During a feast in 2012, Elder Alice Kelly taught me that the ancestors can communicate with us non-verbally. While I was eating, a morsel fell from my fork onto the table. I felt embarrassed and sought to relocate this bit to the side of my plate. Alice gently touched my hand and stated, "I am going to teach you something." She encouraged me to wrap the fallen morsel into a paper napkin and set it aside. When I scrapped my plate at the end of the feast, she told me to save the napkin.

Once the band office emptied, Alice led me outdoors. "Your ancestors are hungry," she said. "They are asking you to feed them." Alice taught me how to offer a portion of my meal to the ancestors. They had made efforts to nourish me that day. They did not harvest Deer before her fawns could care for themselves. They seeded Manomin fields and took other precautions. I had a responsibility to nourish them in return. Alice taught me to be attuned to messages from the spirit world and to care for those who cared for me.

Conclusion

For centuries, Anishinaabe guardians collaborated with Manomin to teach children that they belonged to the Great Web of Being. By sharing the gifts of youth—such as the sound of child's play—with adult harvesters, Anishinaabe children helped to build food stores and thus contributed to the survival of their human families. They belonged to a network in which each member influenced the well-being of the others. Children were taught that their actions influenced not only the well-being of human relatives but also of the crawlers, swimmers, fliers, and four-leggeds. By entering a reciprocal relationship with plant and animal relations, Anishinaabe youth could ensure the survival of future generations. Each action (or inaction) in the field reinforced connections to all Creation. More than that, the field reminded Anishinaabe youth that they had been dreamed of by the ancestors, that all Creation had collaborated to prepare for their arrival.

IMAGES FROM
ANISHINAABE-AKI:
HARVEST

by Brittany Luby with Niisaachewan Anishinaabe Nation

———

Before travelling along the water or entering Manomin
fields, tobacco is offered to request permission to do so.

FIGURE 12A: Tying Manomin. In some parts of Anishinaabe-Aki, Anishinaabe women tie Manomin with basswood fibre to help allot food for their families. This practice occurs before the harvest and is not universally adhered to. Photograph by Frances Densmore, "Wild Rice Harvest. Woman in Boat Tying Wild Rice Stalks with Basswood Fiber," n.d., MHS, Reserve Album 96, p. 27, no. 55295.

MANOMIN

FIGURE 12B: Gathering Manomin. Teams of two collaborate to gather seed. The "push-poler" is responsible for navigating the field. The "knocker" is responsible for separating seeds from the panicle. Photographer unknown, "Gathering Wild Rice," c. 1938, MHS, E97.33 W, p. 9, no. 3935.

FIGURE 12C: Sorting Manomin. Parched Manomin cannot be used as seed. For this reason, a portion of Manomin is set aside for planting. Parched Manomin may also be sorted for home use or commercial sale. Photographer unknown, "Parching and Sorting Wild Rice, White Earth Reservation," c. 1935, MHS, E97.32 W, p. 48, no. 10663.

FIGURE 12D: Protecting Seed. To help ensure the survival of Manomin, Anishinaabeg return a portion of each year's harvest to the field. It is important to prevent Manomin from drying out before it can be replanted. For this reason, portions of Manomin are set aside for planting. To help Manomin retain its moisture, it can be inserted into clay balls or wrapped in damp moss. Photograph by Kenneth Melvin Wright, "Wrapping Rice in Wet Moss for Planting," c. 1930, MHS, E97.32 W, p. 21, no. 2091 B.

FIGURE 12E: Parching Manomin. In this stage of the process, Manomin is dried, preparing it for long-term storage. Dried Manomin will keep for up to one year if properly cared for. Traditionally, women were most likely to be responsible for parching Manomin. Photograph by Frances Densmore, "Wild Rice Harvest. Woman Parching Rice," c. 1910–1918, MHS, Reserve Album 96, p. 30, no. 13135.

FIGURE 12F: Threshing Manomin. In this stage of the process, Manomin is "danced" or "treaded" on to help loosen the seed coat (which is inedible) from the tasty kernel. Men, boys, and prepubescent girls were traditionally responsible for threshing Manomin. Photographer unknown, "Treading Wild Rice," c. 1938, MHS, E97.32 W, p. 5, no. 10662.

FIGURE 12G: Winnowing Manomin. This process helps remove loosened husks and other organic matter from the edible seed. Photograph by Monroe P. Killy, "Winnowing Threshed Wild Rice," 1939, MHS, E97.32 W, p. 40, no. 28153.

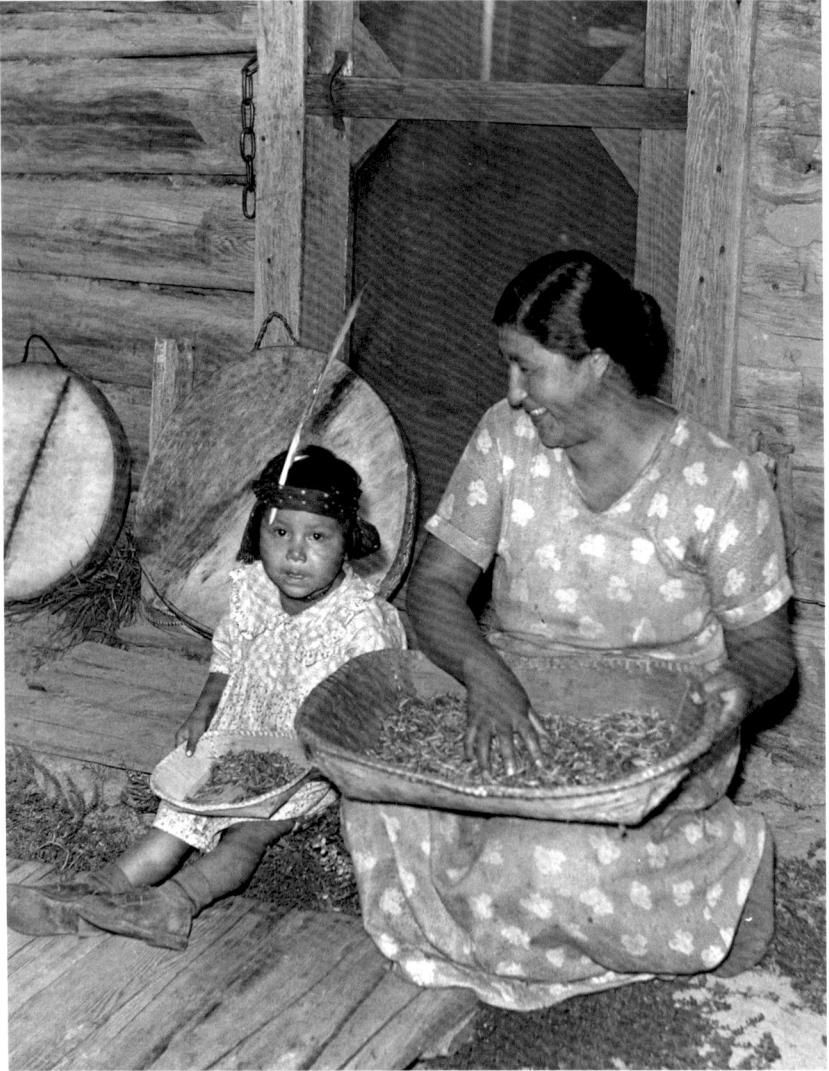

FIGURE 12H: Cleaning Manomin. Parched and threshed Manomin is placed into large baskets. Individuals of all ages remove leftover unwanted organic matter from the finished Manomin before storing it. Photographer unknown, "Indian Woman and Child Holding Baskets of Wild Rice," c. 1938, MHS, E97.32 W, p. 2, no. 13970.

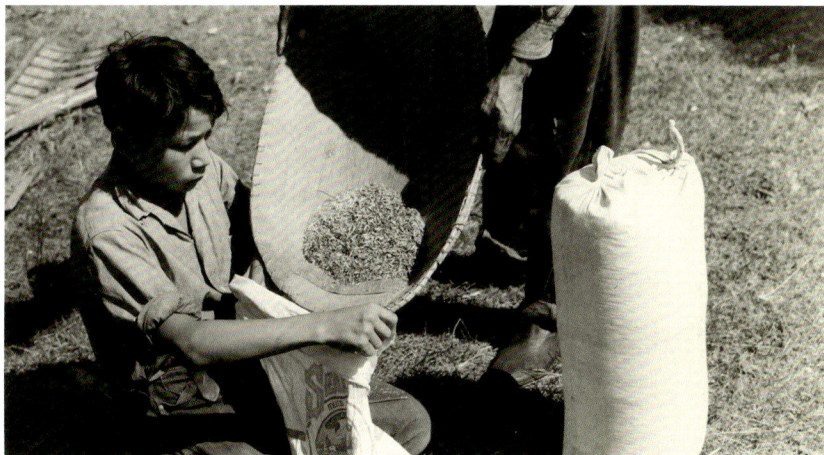

FIGURE 12I: Bagging Manomin. Parched and cleaned Manomin is bagged for future use. Bags can be sold or cached for ceremonial use or household consumption. Photographer unknown, "Bagging Wild Rice," c. 1938, MHS, E97.32 W, p. 4, no. 40144.

FIGURE 12J: Seeding Manomin. Families often work together to seed the fields. Manomin can be replanted by throwing loose seed from the shore or from the canoe. Seed can also be packed into clay balls. These clay balls can be transported to extend the area under cultivation. Photographer unknown, "Ojibwe Family by Their Canoe," c. 1900, MHS, E97.35, p. 2, no. 31679.

FIGURE 13: A Resting Canoe. This image features a canoe that has been pulled onto shore, and stored beside Manomin in flower. Manomin is considered a "monoecious plant," meaning it has both male and female flowers on the same plant. To avoid self-pollination, Manomin evolved so that the tassel-like male flowers—visible here—become active after the feather-like female flowers. To support Manomin growth, human beings must avoid damaging immature plants like these. Damage can be limited by paddling gently rather than motoring through Manomin fields as stalks may be broken or plants may become tangled in the motor. Photograph by Laura Legzdins, 25 August 2022.

⑤

Relational Vocabularies

by Joseph Pitawanakwat

We, as human beings, are surrounded and supported by plant beings. The air that we breathe is enriched with oxygen that our plant relations produce during the day through the process of photosynthesis. Plants can be significant for humanity as food, as medicines, and as tools.[1] By establishing relationships with plant beings, we can begin to understand how they shape our day-to-day lives. More than that, we can begin to understand how plant beings interact with other organisms and form complex ecologies.

Experience has taught me that healthy relationships (and ecological systems) begin with an introduction, with learning preferred names. Imagine that you are waiting to catch the subway. A stranger approaches you. Time passes as you wait side-by-side. Perhaps you try to open a conversation to help pass the time: "Do you know what time the train is expected?" If the conversation progresses, you are likely to share your name and receive theirs in return. People often forget to extend the same courtesy to plants. Shortly after meeting, people might ask, "Is that plant edible? Can I make it into tea? What can it be used for?" Imagine asking a stranger, "Can I nibble your elbow?" You would never do that to another human being. Plant-human relations should mirror human-with-human relations.[2] Healthy relationships begin with the commitment of time. We commit to learning *who* the being is before asking *what* the being does (or *what* the being can do for us).

In this chapter, I will introduce some plant beings found growing in wetlands. We will explore their names and the Anishinaabe ecological knowledge encoded within wetland vocabularies. A wetland is broadly defined as "an ecosystem that arises when inundation by water produces soil dominated by anaerobic processes, which, in turn, forces the biota, particularly rooted plants, to adapt to flooding."[3] Here, anaerobic processes refer to microorganisms breaking down small pieces of organic matter in oxygen-limited habitats, such as underwater.[4] For our relationships with wetlands to deepen, however, we must exchange more than names. Once we are introduced to a plant being, we must observe its environment and identify its needs. As human beings, we are responsible for returning the gift of life by supporting our plant relations in turn. In this chapter, I will also discuss acts of return, empowering you, the reader, to meet and connect with all your relations.

One of my favourite examples to show the power of Anishinaabemowin to communicate plant knowledge is Gziibinashk. The Latin name for this ancient genus is *Equisetum*, of which the most common species to occur in Ontario is *Equisetum hyemale*.[5] In English, this species is commonly known as "Scouring Rush" or "Horsetail." It is called Scouring Rush because "up to 25% of this plant's dry weight can be made up of silica, depending on the species."[6] Scouring Rush pulls silica from the soil and deposits it in the outer layer of the plant. And so, the outside of the plant is full of silica.[7] Silica is what you glue onto a piece of paper to make sandpaper. It is like a hard abrasive crystal. You can use it to scour things down. Before the industrialization of steel wool after World War I, Scouring Rush was the scouring pad that everyone used. The common English name, "Scouring Rush," teaches us how English-speaking settlers worked with this plant for generations.

FIGURE 14: Gziibinashk, also known as "Scouring Rush" in English and *Equisetum hyemale* in Latin. Photograph by Michael John Oldham, "Western Scouringrush (*Equisetum hyemale* ssp. *affine*)," 31 May 2023, iNaturalist, https://www.inaturalist.org/observations/165206903.

We learn that everyday people invited Scouring Rush into their homes and forged relationships around household maintenance. Ethnobotanist and educator Sandra Walker writes that "Indigenous People [first] used the properties of the plant for polishing and cleaning," adding that "you can file your nails or scrub pots with it," as well as use it for "cleansing minor wounds, reducing bleeding and mitigating infections."[8]

Gziibinashk, the Anishinaabe name, is multi-layered and teaches us about Anishinaabe household use, harvesting locations, as well as sensory cues that would help harvesters determine whether they successfully iden-tified their plant relative. Much like the name Scouring Rush, Gziibinashk reminds us that this plant relative can support our cleaning activities. This connection was made for me during a community meeting. I had delivered a presentation to the language committee. During my talk, one woman had her arms crossed. I thought my presentation upset her. So, I asked, "Hey, what's up?" This question prompted an important teaching:

> *Elder: How does your dad tell you to have a shower?*
>
> Pitawanakwat: "What kind of question is that?" He says gziibiigdiiye, to clean my butt.
>
> *Elder: What does that mean?*
>
> Pitawanakwat: I don't know—clean my butt? Use soap? I don't know what you mean.
>
> *Elder: How does your dad tell you to do the dishes?*
>
> Pitawanakwat: Gziibiignaagnen.
>
> *Elder: Gzii—what does that mean?*
>
> Pitawanakwat: I don't know. Clean?
>
> *Elder: Gzii means you scrub something. Gziibinashk—this name is telling you how it can be used. This relationship allows you to scrub things down.*

It was in this way that I learned that the name Gziibinashk teaches us about the plant-human relationship. This relationship allows you to scrub things down and to care for your body and your home.

Gziibinashk also teaches us about where to locate this plant relation. In general, the location where a plant may be found is constrained by its specific tolerance range to environmental factors such as soil water content, and thus, and thus, it will only grow in places where all its needs are met. Gziibinashk grows along the edges of rivers and creeks. In Anishinaabemowin, the word for *river* is *ziibi*. The water origins of Gziibinashk are coded into our language.

The Anishinaabe word for Scouring Rush, Gziibinashk, contains additional plant identifiers. Our ancestors coded teachings about sound into the language. Gziibinashk is hollow on the inside. But, the ridges on the perimeter are full of silica—a crystal-like substance. When you squeeze a bundle of Gziibinashk together, these crystals emit a scream-like sound. My great-grandmother once approached my grandmother from behind with a big bundle of dried Gziibinashk. My grandmother was frightened by the sound. She jumped up and ran away. When she reached a safe distance, my grandmother turned around. My great-grandmother was standing on the dock laughing with her bundle. My great-grandmother explained that Gziibinashk can scream—it can make us, human beings, scream. The Anishinaabe word for *scream* is *aazhikwe*. And so, when you say "Gziibinashk," you get two teachings in one word. If we focus on "ziibi'" in Gziibiinashk, we learn the plant grows near water. If we focus on Gziib'nashk, we learn how to identify the plant by sound.

When I shared this teaching with a plant and language expert in my community, he continued to deepen my understanding of the name Gziibinashk. He is a tea drinker. Sometimes, he makes tea with Scouring Rush. This tea tastes sweet when it is inside your mouth. But, when you swallow it, it turns sour. "Zhiiwizi" is how we say "s/he is sour" and "s/he is sweet." This sound is coded into many Anishinaabe plant names to teach us of their taste. Zhiiwibag is the Anishinaabe name for Rhubarb. The Anishinaabe name for *vinegar* is *zhiiwaaboo*. If we focus on Gziibinashk, we learn how Scouring Rush will taste. In this way, the names our ancestors gifted to our plant relatives can teach us the sound and taste to know them by, where to go to build a relationship, and how to work collaboratively once that relationship is forged.

For the Anishinaabeg, Manomin is an important carbohydrate. The only other large source of carbohydrates that the Anishinaabeg could access in a wetland is from Apakweaashk or Cattail. Cattail is a large reed-like plant that can grow up to three metres above the water within which its lower stalk and roots sit.[9] Once harvested, cattail roots can be dried and sifted free of fibres to create a starch-rich powder usable in the same way as flour. To create cattail flour, Anishinaabeg would collect, wash, and peel the roots. As you break up the roots under water, starch will begin to separate from the fibres. Once all the fibres have been separated, you can remove them and drain the excess liquid. The remaining materials can be dried near a fire or with the sun. What remains will become your flour.[10]

In Anishinaabemowin, the word for *roof* is *paakwan*. We see this word echoed in the Anishinaabe word for cattail: Apakweaashk. Now, Apakweaashk does not make the best thatching material. It shrinks in size as it dries. While there is a process that can be undertaken to make Apakweaashk waterproof, certain barks make better roofing material. However, this plant relative can be used to make a blind when hunting for waterfowl. In a wetland system, Apakweaashk can outcompete Manomin for sunlight, and thus reduce Manomin yields through competitive exclusion. Apakweaashk spreads by extending rhizomes through the mud at the bottom of the marsh. As the rhizomes spread outwards, they branch off from axillary buds to form an expansive network. These axillary buds on the rhizomes also send off new Apakweaashk shoots that rise from the rhizome mat, through the water and into the sunlight to start photosynthesizing.[11] If that mat of rhizomes extends over the substrate (i.e., underwater sediment) where Manomin grains lie awaiting germination, forming a "roof" over the seed bed, then Manomin seedlings cannot access sunlight. Following germination, young Manomin plants survive off stores of starch contained within the seed until they can create their own food through photosynthesis. However, the seed provides finite resources to the young plant, and if Manomin cannot make its way into the sunlight before its reserves run out, then the seedling will die.[12] In this way, a cattail roof or paakwan can cause low Manomin yields. For this reason, the Anishinaabeg used to nurture a wetland to grow either Manomin or Apakweaashk.

The Anishinaabeg were professional manipulators of both Manomin and Apakweaashk. Manipulation in this context refers to the basic responsibilities Anishinaabeg have to diversify the territory. Anishinaabeg nurtured both Manomin and Apakweaashk in what appears as monocrop systems; however, Anishinaabe horticultural activities supported an entire ecosystem. If these plants could grow thick and healthy, they supported villages. Access to healthy fields also reduced the labour required to gather food. But, we are not alone in the Great Web of Being. When we engage with a plant relative, we can encourage it to live to its fullest potential. When Manomin fields are cultivated, Manomin can grow in a thick mat. These thick mats attract Yellow Rails, a type of wading bird. By manipulating the environment to grow more Manomin, Anishinaabeg enabled a diversity of species, including Yellow Rail, to thrive in the fields. Yellow Rails are identifiable by their small size and dark banding, which is segmented by white bars. They can also be recognized by their unique call, which sounds like two stones being struck together.[13] As they move through the fields, you can see seeds flying into the river. The interdependency of these two species, Manomin and Yellow Rails, is captured in the Anishinaabemowin name for the bird: Minominkeshiihn.

Everywhere you go, even isolated Anishinaabe communities, there is Minominkeshiihn. This name translates more directly into English as "wild rice bird": Minominkebineshii. These birds remind me of fat chickens that run around the wetlands, knocking seed into the water. When the Anishinaabeg harvest Manomin, it is protocol to knock the seed into your canoe. Whatever falls into the river is left to reseed the field for future generations. Anishinaabe harvesters are taught never to take all of the seed. Minominkeshiihn has an important job and helps to ensure that other-than-human predators cannot over-consume the seed.

Minominkeshiihn flies in and out of the fields. It is the Yellow Rail's job to ensure that not all of the seed gets eaten and that some is planted for future generations. In Anishinaabemowin, Manominike means "s/he goes ricing." The Anishinaabeg and Yellow Rail play an important role in the harvest—both go ricing: Minominkeshiihn. Their activities in the field help to ensure that seed is replanted for the future.

Minominkeshiihn reminds us that when we interact with a plant, we are influencing the Great Web of Being. Minominkeshiihn plants Manomin with the Anishinaabeg and, by so doing, provides food for human beings, Muskrat, Red-Winged Blackbird, and even Rice Worm. As we learn Anishinaabe names, we must also commit to learning the plant's relationship with everything else. Lily Pads, called Kandamo in Anishinaabemowin, teach interconnection well. Water Lilies are an ancient group of plants that survive by keeping their stems and root systems submerged in water. The flower rises above the surface to be pollinated by animals.[14] Kandamo (which commonly refers to Lily Pad) has more than one meaning. It is also a hunting term. When you spot a bunch of moose tracks, you can state confidently "Oh! Moose are coming by all the time!" and "kando," or "sit and wait." You sit and wait because you know Moose will walk by sooner or later—their path is clear. Frogs also kando. They see Lily Pads and say, "I'm just going to sit there and all the food's going to come right to me." Frogs use Lily Pads to hunt for food. In recognition of shared hunting techniques, the ancestors named Lily Pads "Kandamo."

Kandamo and Manomin grow in partnership. Kandamo will attract Moose to Manomin fields during the fall. Moose will dedicate hours to eating as many Kandamo roots as possible. Kandamo is muscle medicine. Moose uses it to prepare for mating season. This plant will nourish Moose, allowing them to run, fight, and mate without fatigue. By watching Moose, the Anishinaabeg learned that they, too, could use Kandamo medicinally for muscles. It is best given to someone who is aging, who is becoming frail. Kandamo supports glucose uptake, your muscles' ability to metabolize sugar, or to use sugar for energy. It is also an important plant for diabetes management.[15] By observing Moose, the Anishinaabeg learned they could use Kandamo as they kando. This plant is also used in smoke medicine during winter hunts. Once there is snow and ice, Moose loses access to this favourite food and medicine. This can make Moose sad in winter. And so, we burn Kandamo. When Moose smell this smoke, it overrides part of their instinct. Even if they could smell you downwind, Moose would walk toward you and the smoke. Moose will edge closer and closer. I tell everyone that the use of smoke medicine makes hunting a more ethical experience. One of the worst things you could do is wound an animal by misfiring. A hunter's margin of error increases the further they are from the animal. When you wound a plant or an animal, when you cause unnecessary harm, you are no longer in a healthy relationship with them. But, when you understand plant-animal relationships, you can use plants' unique gifts as necessary. Kandamo allows the Anishinaabeg to make the hunt, their kando, as ethical as possible by increasing the chance of a clean shot.

Let us return to the Manomin fields. The roots of Kandamo can grow up to a metre deep. Moose will dive down and work to dig up these roots. They will come up to finish eating—Moose cannot swallow underwater. When you observe Moose foraging for Kandamo, you will see them dive and return to the surface to chew. There are teachings to suggest that Moose prepares the soil by digging up these roots. William G. Dore, who wrote *Wild-rice* for the Canada Department of Agriculture, claimed that "anything that might disturb or 'cultivate' the bottom sediments should increase the amount of oxygen, particularly if that disturbance also destroys the living roots of established perennial plants."[16] Captain Bill Holden, a bush pilot, informed Dore that "a strip of wild-rice" was "cultivated" by a Moose he watched "churning and splashing, across the muddy waters of a lake."[17] Anishinaabe and settler observations reveal Moose can increase productivity in Manomin fields.[18] We learn that Kandamo supports Moose, and Moose supports Manomin. They are connected by the life they give each other.

The first step toward understanding how you, as a human being, might connect with a plant being is by learning their name. Once you learn a name, you can begin to understand what makes that plant special, the gifts they can give you. The gift may be food (e.g., Manomin), medicine (e.g., Kandamo), or utilitarian (e.g., Gziibinashk). As human beings, to access gifts from plant beings, we must be willing to engage in a reciprocal relationship. We might determine, "We need to save these seeds for the future." We might decide, "We need to help this plant spread by seeding it." When we do not exercise the gift of reciprocity, there is suffering to be had in human health. For this reason, we must seek understanding from each plant about what it needs from us. It is through observation and appropriate action that we, the Anishinaabeg, can preserve the well-being of our Nation.

The Pitcher Plant can teach us about plant-human reciprocity.[19] They are called "Pitcher Plant" in English because their leaf is shaped like a pitcher of water. In Anishinaabemowin, we call it Mak'akiimdaas, which translates more accurately into English as "frog long johns," because the leaf looks like a sock a frog could wear. Botanists trained on Turtle Island may refer to this plant as *Sarracenia purpurea*. The genus *Sarracenia* contains many carnivorous plants, of which only *S. purpurea* grows in what is currently known as Canada. The Pitcher Plant can be found in nutrient-poor soils (for which it compensates by obtaining nutrients from its animal prey) on the edges of bogs or on floating mats of organic matter.[20] Mak'akiimdaas can give you the gift of medicine for back pain. They can draw out the calcium from sensory neurons in your lumbar.[21] They inhibit the toxic effects of glucose on the sciatic nerve, allowing it to heal. Mak'akiimdaas is a powerful medicine for injury, childbirth, or even degenerative conditions like diabetes.[22] When you look at this plant, this plant with an amazing gift to share, you must ask, "How can I help them?" As you ask yourself this question, you might notice that the plant has a long stem—up to forty-five centimetres—with a cluster of hundreds of seeds at the tip. Although Mak'akiimdaas produces many seeds, they compete for space. If these seeds

FIGURE 15: Mak'akiimdaas, also known as the "Pitcher Plant" in English and *Sarracenia purpurea* in Latin. Photograph by Alex Manders, "*Sarracenia purpurea*," n.d., Shutterstock, 2332552759.

fall within thirty centimetres of the parent plant, the parent will hormonally sterilize all their seeds. Seeds must fall beyond a foot away to germinate. However, the stem of Mak'akiimdaas is so rigid that the seeds will not naturally fall at a distance. Mak'akiimdaas is waiting for another being—like Moose or you or I—to knock it.

There can be joy in the act of reciprocity. My friend, my wife, and I were once out harvesting Mak'akiimdaas in the bog. My friend asked, "How can I help this one?" I took a seed pod and teasingly threw it at my wife. The seeds splattered everywhere. She laughed and threw a seed pod back at me. We played with the seed pods and, through our play, made it possible for thousands of Mak'akiimdaas to grow. Plant-human relationships are like any other relationship. They can bring us joy. But they can also disintegrate if we do not nourish our bond. We, as human beings, distance ourselves from people who take without reciprocating. We make ourselves scarce when our needs are consistently unmet. Plants do, too. If you take without reciprocating, the plants will leave. They do not grow legs and run away. They go extinct.

I will repeat my key message. I encourage you to repeat it with me: "Plant-human relationships are like any other relationship." By learning plant names, you can begin to learn about their unique bond with human beings. By spending time with plants, you can begin to decode Anishinaabe ecological knowledge built into the names of relatives by our ancestors. By understanding local ecologies, you can learn how to reciprocate. By reciprocating, you learn how to seed the future. As human beings, we have the unique gift or ability to observe and plan for the future. It is our responsibility to reciprocate and seed a future that supports all our relations.

ONUSH LAKCHI/
MANOMIN, BERRIES, AND LOVE

by Michelle Johnson-Jennings, PhD, EdM

———

Each time I smell "wild rice," my spirit rises to attention. I feel the gentle movement of the canoe. I recall the ways in which my hands move with the knockers to gently tap the seeds into the canoe. I smile, remembering how I cover my face and body as I am enveloped in both seeds and our insect relatives. Most of all, I recall feeling a sense of love and peace upon the waters. Being Choctaw, my body knows Onush Lakchi, a variation of *Zizania* (and relative of Manomin) that nourished my ancestors and other southeastern tribes. I married Dr. Derek Jennings (Sac, Fox/Miami–Anishinaabe, and Quapaw–Dhegiha Sioux), who knows a variation of *Zizania* as Manomin. We have joyfully launched our canoes, harvested, and provided this food to our loved ones together. At times, we have filled the canoe; but often we have worked for days and leave with just a small

---

Serves: 4 | *Prep time:* 10 mins | *Cook time:* 30 mins

gift of sacred foods. As in our lives, we have explored several bodies of water to harvest our sacred foods, and one of our greatest honours has been to share our Manomin with others. Together, we have provided our children with the sacred foods of their ancestors.

From Manomin, I have forged deep connections with my ancestral stories of love and kinship and realized the overlaps and connections that Indigenous Peoples share. One particular Manomin teaching stands out to me. At dawn, Derek and I placed our offerings and entered the dark still waters, excited to gather the Manomin that called. We paddled alone on this placid lake. Once I began to tap and Derek to pull, the overcast sky began to clear. Amafo Hashi, Grandfather Sun, caressed our faces with warmth. The water danced and sparkled, lighting our path. We both marvelled and quietly moved forward. Then, as we gazed out across the waters, I saw them. They initially appeared as rainbows flowing across the sky. They ebbed and flowed closer to our canoe. I glanced at Derek, who also stood transfixed. As they glided closer, I yelled, "chunkash," or spider in Choctaw. They were gracefully flying across the sky and momentarily lighting on the heads of grain. I immediately recalled my ancestral tale of loving and humble Spokni Chunkash, Grandmother Spider, who brought the Choctaw people fire when all others had failed. Woven within this teaching, Spokni Chunkash flew across the skies upon her webs to locate Thunderbird and to carry and nurture a small ember of fire back for the people. I had always wondered if a spider could actually travel great distances using only their webs.

Among the Manomin, I witnessed this incredible feat of flight, love, and connection. The chunkash illuminated and rested upon me, the boat, and Derek—as though to briefly greet and welcome us. I was honoured, grateful, and ecstatic. Outside of my tribal territory, I had witnessed and recalled our ancestral teaching of self-sacrifice and love for our people. To bring back a small grain seemed a similar act of love. In that moment, I realized that our ancestors shared their love across time, land, and kin. As I returned home and began to share and feed my children their ancestors' stories, food, and kinship, I realized that the process of gathering Manomin, or Onush Lakchi, is an act of love, cultural continuity, and revitalization. Hence, I decided that our berries that represent love not only pair well with Manomin but further feed our spirits with love and ancestral perseverance. The following is one recipe that is a favourite among our four children.

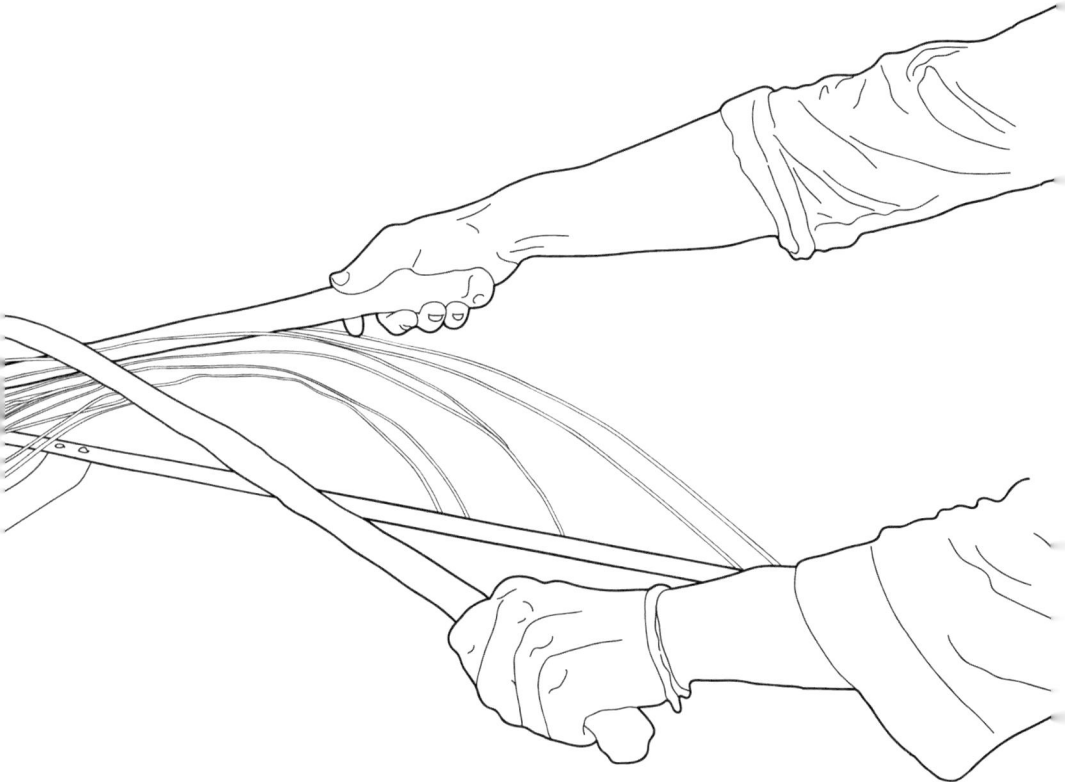

Water

Nuts

Berries

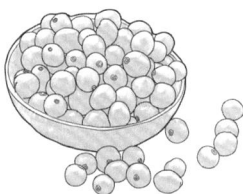

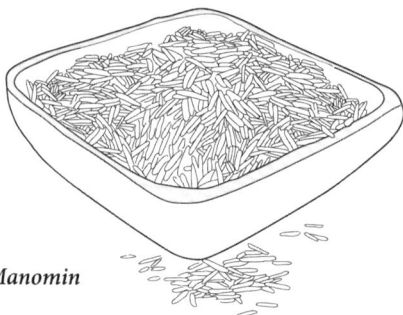
Manomin

INGREDIENTS

1 cup
Onush Lakchi/Manomin

2 1/2 cups water

1/2 cup berries and
1/2 cup of nuts of your
choosing

___

Gather the Onush
Lakchi/Manomin
that has been lovingly
tapped from the stems
of stalks, sitting quietly
in the still waters. The
Manomin that has been
danced upon by the
women and their ances-
tors, who still whisper
the ways to their
hearts and well-being.
Manomin, which after
being caressed by the
winds, is shared by
those who still care and
hold it dear.

INSTRUCTIONS

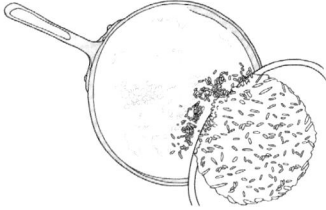

1 Take one cup of Onush Lakchi/Manomin and combine it with 2 1/2 cups of sacred oka/ waters, which have touched the lips of ancestors past and future, in a pot that contains sacred minerals.

2 Reflect upon the labour and love going into each grain while you bring it to a boil, and reduce it to a simmer as you give thanks to all beings who have contributed to this meal (approximately 20–30 minutes).

3 As the seeds begin to swell, remove them from the heat and gently place them in a large bowl. Optional: add salt and butter to taste.

4 Add a half cup of berries, which remind us of our delicate relationship with Mother Earth. Our family chooses dried cranberries with both sweetness and sourness, similar to our life experiences. Next, add nuts, which demonstrate the power that can reside in small ones. We select rich roasted hazelnuts for this task.

5 Serve to your loved ones and yourself, who all hold ancestors past and future. Ingest with gratefulness and gentle prayer as your body becomes one with medicines that have nourished generations.

FIGURE 16: Manomin's Riverine Habitat. This image depicts a stretch of the Winnipeg River known to sustain Manomin growth. At this moment in time, water levels were too high to support healthy Manomin stands. Manomin seeds remain dormant in the soil, ready to grow once conditions improve. Photograph by Samantha Mehltretter, 15 July 2022.

6

Environmental Change, Environmental Care

by Samantha Mehltretter and Andrea Bradford
with Niisaachewan Anishinaabe Nation

From the boat, there are no cities, factories, or highways in sight. To a couple of academics[1] from the big city in the south, the Upper Winnipeg River appears untouched by settler development.

But Elder Theresa Jourdain (née Kabestra) from Niisaachewan Anishinaabe Nation points to a bay with sparse growth of Manomin in a few places. In a hushed voice, she tells us that when she was a child, the area was filled with Manomin.

Elder Terry Greene agrees: "There used to be thousands of ducks here. Here and at the Dalles. Thousands of mallards. You can see them in the evenings. You can see flocks of them. Flying back and forth from rice field to rice field."[2]

MANOMIN

As we looked more closely, listened more attentively, and learned more astutely, the settler activities that upset relationships with Manomin and other-than-humans on the Upper Winnipeg River came into focus.

Since the late 1800s, the Upper Winnipeg River has been regulated by control structures (e.g., dams) that have affected patterns of water levels and flows. Upstream discharges of wastewater from an urban area and a pulp and paper mill have also impacted water and sediment quality. The cumulative effects of settler-imposed environmental changes led to a decline in Manomin.

Manomin translates into English as "spirit berry" or "gift from the Creator."[3] Manomin is a nutritious food that was historically part of a healthy diet for the Anishinaabeg and other-than-humans. Niisaachewan Elders taught us that Manomin is also an animate spirit being with agency.[4] Manomin is capable of expressing its desire to support human life and activities, capable of choosing not to regenerate, and capable of teaching humans.[5] Manomin is considered kin. Manomin both supports us and requires our support. It should not come as a surprise, then, that Elders express a deep sense of loss when they talk about Manomin decline.

Caretaking responsibilities are necessary to heal the reciprocal relationship between Manomin and humans. The story of Pine Portage, a bay that historically supported prolific Manomin growth on the Upper Winnipeg River, offers hope for Manomin recovery and guidance on caretaking.

As in many ancestral Manomin stands near Niisaachewan Anishinaabe Nation, a mat of other wetland vegetation (locally referred to as the "bog") was displacing Manomin, leaving little suitable habitat for its growth. Elders expressed concern about the loss of balance associated with the vegetation's encroachment. At Pine Portage, however, Elders explained, a large storm tore the mat of floating vegetation from the shore, ripped it into smaller mats, and carried them downstream. Although not as thick as it historically grew, Manomin has returned to Pine Portage.

As far as we are aware, there have been no efforts to reseed the bay, suggesting that Manomin is lying in wait for an opportunity to grow again.

This seems to be a clear teaching from Manomin; it remains resilient, but it needs a little help.

Here, we share what Manomin and its relations have taught us about ecosystem interconnectedness, disruptions at different scales, and resilience and restoration. We draw on Elder testimony, the documentary record, and our own experiences to interpret Manomin's teachings about human impacts on the river and what actions can be taken to build resilience in this socio-ecological system.

We came to this work with formal training and life experiences that fostered a deep understanding of the interconnectedness of living and non-living things and a deep appreciation of the need for humanity to look after our environment so that it can continue to sustain us. Our personal values also align with the belief that Manomin and other living things have intrinsic value. But, as settler scholars, we also come from a society that places humans at the top of a hierarchy, above other-than-humans, a worldview that does not mesh with Anishinaabe relational philosophies. Dabasendiziwin (commonly translated into English as "humility")—one of the Seven Grandfather Teachings—encourages each of us "to think lower of oneself in relation to all that sustains us."[6]

Interconnectedness

"Everything is connected" has become a familiar refrain in the teachings of Niisaachewan Anishinaabe Nation Elders. But from a distance, the richness of species in Manomin's community was not evident to us. It was not until we visited the Manomin stands with Elders and spent hours paddling through them on our own that we came to appreciate the biodiversity and complexity of this ecosystem. The relationships between organisms in this place were revealed to us gradually, story by story, and over the course of the seasons.

An ecosystem's complexity increases with species diversity.[7] When there are many different species, of relatively similar abundance (meaning there is not a single species that dominates), an ecosystem becomes more complex because numerous relationships occur simultaneously. Whether through pollination, providing nutrients, or being part of the food web, the animals and plants living in one place influence one another. Biota with similar ecological niches may also compete for resources with one another.[8] Manomin is important to many human and other-than-human beings, and many of these beings are important to Manomin.

Earlier chapters in this volume examine how moose oxygenate the soil and open up space for Manomin while feeding on aquatic plants. Other fauna support Manomin by assisting with pollination and reseeding. While Manomin is mostly wind pollinated, waterfowl and insects will spread pollen and help to maintain diversity among Manomin plants.[9] Elder John Henry explained that birds fly around the Manomin stands on the Winnipeg River and assist with reseeding: "The geese and the ducks, different ducks, and the blackbirds . . . [they] fly like a hundred at a time. They will swoop down, and that's when they knock the rice over. . . . [They'll] knock two down, and they'll eat two. . . . And whatever they leave behind is next year's crop. That's how these animals helped out."[10]

Another Elder, Terry Greene, shared how waterfowl, as "carriers of wild rice," helped establish new stands. The ducks, he said, would eat the rice, "and, well, of course they would poop. Some of their poop would, they would digest a lot of it, but some would be left, so wherever they went there would be more rice growing in different areas. . . . Planting wild rice naturally."[11]

Ducks and geese also feed on the rice worms that grow within the Manomin panicle, a loose, branching cluster of flowers. In the process, they disturb the pollen, and the wind carries it to another plant for pollination.[12] Once pollinated, the Manomin seeds form. At first, the seeds are white and fluid-like beneath the pericarp or seed coat, but eventually, over approximately ten days, the seeds ripen into firm black grains: Manomin.[13] The streamlined shape of Manomin seeds facilitates reseeding next year's crop. Rather than falling into the water and being carried by the current, Manomin seeds plunge into the water and lodge into the soft sediment adjacent to their parent plant.

In addition to ducks, Manomin is an important food source for many other-than-humans in wetland habitats. Elders spoke about "all sorts of bugs, spiders, and insects that feed off the wild rice."[14] The rice worm that feeds the duck (*Apamea apamiformis*), for example, lays larvae in the pistillate florets (the female flowers containing ovaries), where the Manomin seeds form.[15] The larvae are protected from predators and have a source of food in the grain that is forming simultaneously with them.[16] At this time in Manomin's life cycle, the grains are milky and soft, an excellent source of nutrients for growing rice worms.[17] Too many rice worms can be detrimental to a Manomin stand, so waterfowl feeding on them creates another essential link in the food web.[18]

During their migrations south in the fall, waterfowl rely on Manomin for food and shelter.[19] In *Wild-rice,* William Dore describes how small birds such as red-winged blackbirds and sparrows come through ripening Manomin fields in late August and early September. These smaller birds perch on the stalks and often knock grains into the water while they eat.[20] The ducks arrive later when Manomin is fully ripened, and most of it has already fallen in the water. Given their ability to dive for their food, ducks retrieve seeds that have already lodged into the wetland's sediments rather than eating directly from the plant.[21]

Muskrats, beavers, and sometimes larger mammals like moose also graze on Manomin. These animals tend to prefer vegetative portions of the plant, such as stems and leaves, rather than tiny seeds.[22] The Manomin stands also provide safe, sheltered areas for muskrat and beavers to build their homes. We saw many of these small dome-shaped mounds of woody debris and mud (see Figures 17 and 18). With the guidance of the Elders, we learned to identify the inhabitants.

FIGURE 17: A Muskrat Home amongst Manomin on the Upper Winnipeg River. Photograph by Samantha Mehltretter, 2020.

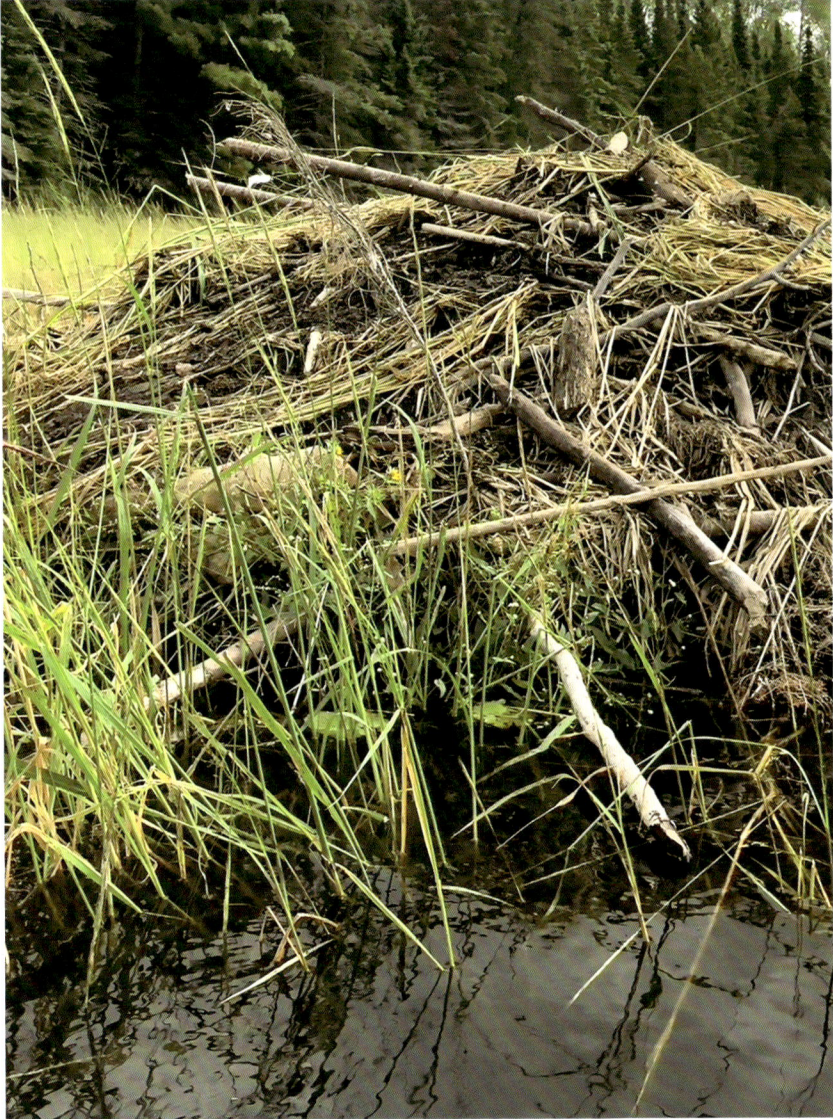

FIGURE 18: A Beaver Lodge amongst Manomin on the Upper Winnipeg River. Photograph by Samantha Mehltretter, 2020.

There are also relationships between Manomin and other flora. Robbins's pondweed (*Potamogeton robbinsii*), for example, support healthy Manomin crops by increasing tillering.[23] Tillering is when multiple shoots form from the same Manomin plant, resulting in more panicles, and more seeds. Biologists Robert W. Pillsbury and Melissa A. McGuire found several aquatic plants, or macrophytes, that were associated with healthy Manomin stands, including multiple species of pondweed (*Potamogeton natans, P. foliosus,* and *P. richardsonii),* white water lily (*Nymphaea odorata),* and star duckweed (*Lemna trisulca).*[24] Pillsbury and McGuire suggest that these plants can tolerate the shaded conditions created by the tall Manomin plants. Manomin also protects the smaller plants from being injured or uprooted by wind and waves.[25] The reduced wave action helps reduce turbidity—the murkiness of the water. Clear water increases the amount of sunlight that can penetrate the water column to support submerged vegetation. Manomin also takes up nutrients from the sediment during the growing season and reduces the amount remaining in the water, helping to prevent algal blooms, especially in areas adjacent to agricultural fields.[26] Manomin supports healthy biota as well as healthy abiotic conditions.

Within the Great Web of Being, some plants compete with Manomin for the same ecological niche. Although the presence of a competitor may elicit concern, competitors are, in reality, important members of healthy ecosystems. Competition among native species supports biodiversity and resilient communities, ensuring that no single being dominates over all others, helping keep the Great Web of Being in balance.

Settlers, however, have introduced beings from different parts of the world into Anishinaabe-Aki. If these beings outcompete native species and have no predators or competitors to keep themselves in balance, the ecosystem's biodiversity will decline, along with its resiliency.

Anishinaabeg have different views on introduced species. In their research, Nicholas Reo and Laura Ogden found that, according to Anishinaabe teachings, humans are obligated to learn why the newcomers arrived and what responsibilities we have toward them. Introduced species are not unwelcome or inherently bad.[27] Elders suggested making an offering to the newcomers and asking them why they came.[28]

At Pine Portage, Elders are concerned when competitors result in imbalance and the displacement of cultural species like Manomin. When newcomers take over quickly, there is little time to learn what gifts they offer and how to fulfill caretaking responsibilities to maintain balance. Balance makes an ecosystem more resilient when faced with environmental change.

Environmental Change

Elders at Niisaachewan Anishinaabe Nation associate the drastic decline of Manomin with the installation of hydroelectric dams on the Winnipeg River. Elder Clarence Henry explained: "Yeah, it's the water level, water level that's being released from Lake of the Woods. And you got a backlog from the other dam behind us. So, if they open Lake of the Woods, and they close Whitedog Falls, that ends up killing the—it would be flooding the rice fields."[29]

Manomin has taught us that, near Niisaachewan Anishinaabe Nation, it can grow in almost 1.5 metres of water. But, Manomin is no longer as healthy or productive as it was when it grew in shallower conditions. In deep water, more energy goes into elongating the plant's main stalk than into producing tillers (additional stems on the same plant) and seeds.[30] This results in lower yields and fewer seeds for next season's crop. Manomin showed us this in 2022, when the water level was very high. When Manomin managed to reach the surface, it was very thin and delicate, with only one tiller. A few seeds in the shallowest locations developed into stout Manomin plants with many hearty tillers. Unfortunately, the total number of Manomin plants we saw on the Upper Winnipeg River in 2022 was similar to the number we saw in a single, 0.5–square metre sampling plot in 2021.

Although Manomin has somewhat adapted to high water levels, it cannot thrive when stressors are persistent. Elder Archie Wagamese commented: "Ever since they built up those dams, they just ruin everything for the Native people."[31] While hydroelectric operations may not be the only determinant of Manomin decline, they are responsible for numerous ecological and social impacts globally.[32]

The root cause of many of these impacts is the alteration of the river's natural flow patterns. Streamflow is sometimes referred to as the "master variable."[33] Plants and animals that live on and around a river adapt to natural flow patterns.[34] And their habitats are formed and sustained through a river's natural dynamic character.[35] This character includes the magnitude, frequency, timing, duration, and rate of change of flows.[36] The variability of water conditions through the year and between years is part of a river's unique flow pattern. When dams are installed and operated based on human needs, fluvial processes are altered, channels may erode, fish may miss flow signals for migration, and emergent plants may drown.

Manomin's sensitivity to water level is reasonable, given it must grow from seed each year. If the water is too deep in the spring, there may be insufficient energy stored in the seed for the plant to grow large enough to access the sunlight needed for further growth. If Manomin does reach the water's surface, it remains vulnerable to changes in the water level. Throughout its life cycle, its roots tend to be short and loosely secured to a soft substrate, which means they can be easily uprooted if the water level rises too quickly.[37] This is a greater concern during the floating-leaf stage because the large ribbon-like leaves make Manomin very buoyant. If the water level rises more than 0.25 metres rapidly, Manomin yields will decline significantly that season.[38] Falling water levels are also a concern because the emergent macrophyte, once mature, can grow a couple metres above the water's surface, and without the support of the water, the tall stalks can break.[39] Whether the water level is too high, rising too quickly, or falling too fast, Manomin's success is at the mercy of water levels.

Climate change and land development also affect hydrology. The literature suggests that the mean annual streamflow in Canada has declined

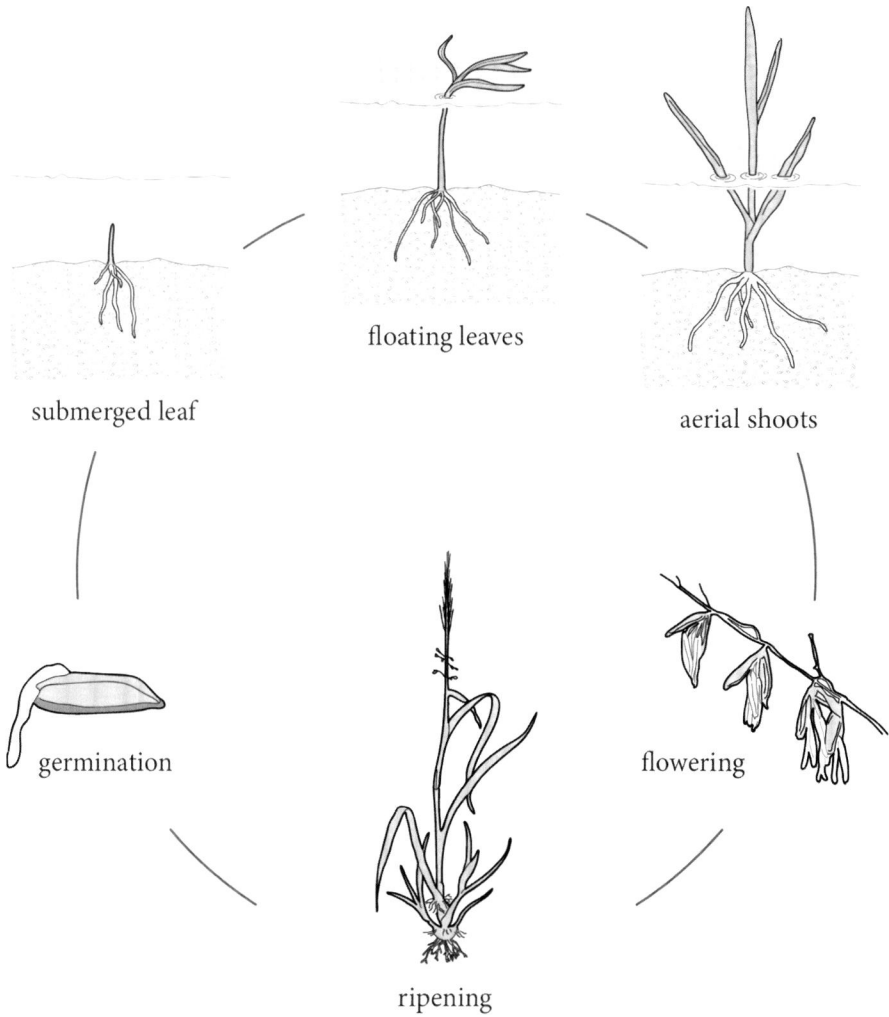

FIGURE 19: Life Stages of Manomin. Illustration by Dani Kastelein, 2023.

significantly over the twentieth century.[40] Findings from the Winnipeg River Drainage Basin suggest the opposite.[41] Scott St. George's trend analysis of hydrometric gauges on the Winnipeg River reveals that mean annual stream-flow has increased significantly since 1924.[42] In particular, mean flows in the winter months (November to April) experienced a significant increase.[43] Although these months are largely outside of Manomin's growing season, a significant increase in April could negatively impact its initial growth. These trends were observed in the downstream reaches of the Winnipeg River, which are heavily regulated, and in the unregulated headwater streams in the drainage basin, which suggests a climatic influence on streamflow. But it could also be a result of land use changes in the watershed.[44]

St. George also investigated precipitation records in Kenora, Ontario, and discovered significant precipitation increases in the summer and autumn months.[45] Increased intensity of precipitation during storm events means water levels will rise faster, increasing the risk of uprooting Manomin.[46] But Manomin is also sensitive to high winds and hail, which can shatter unripe seeds or lead to the loss of ripe Manomin seeds before they can be harvested.[47] Elder Danny Strong recounted that in 1979, they "had a storm that came in and just wiped out the whole [Manomin] field."[48] The Manomin harvest in 2021 was similarly affected by a severe storm. Occasional severe storms, which occur between ripening and harvest, can return a large amount of ripe seed to the sediment, benefitting future crops. If they occur frequently, however, there will be serious consequences for the humans and other-than-humans that rely upon Manomin.

Just as Manomin has adapted to natural hydrological patterns, it and other native species have adapted to temperature patterns. For example, ripened Manomin seeds must lie dormant in near or below-freezing temperatures for about eight months (through the fall and winter) before they will germinate.[49] Increasing annual temperatures will bring shorter periods of near or below-freezing conditions, which is expected to impact the rate of germination of Manomin seeds.[50] Hotter temperatures are also expected to improve conditions for brown spot disease.[51] Brown spot is a fungal disease that can restrict photosynthesis and impede seed production.[52] Carp prefer warmer waters and have been found near the southerly reaches of Anishinaabe-Aki. While carp do not eat Manomin, they are known to uproot the plant and stir up sediment, which influences the water's turbidity (i.e., clarity) and, thus, Manomin's ability to photosynthesize while in its submerged life stages.[53]

Vulnerability assessments in what is currently known as Minnesota and Wisconsin reveal that Manomin is one of the species most sensitive to the impacts of climate change.[54] The reports also reveal that there are numerous other beings vulnerable to climate change, including walleye, lake trout, cranberries, blueberries, snowshoe hare, and many species of waterfowl.[55]

There are other human activities that upset natural conditions and Manomin growth. For example, increased human development near Manomin fields means increased pollution. Whether the source is industrial discharges from mining operations or pulp and paper mills, nutrient loadings from agricultural runoff or municipal wastewater, or a variety of pollutants running off impervious urban surfaces, changes in water quality (and sediment quality) can drastically influence wetland and river systems.[56] The negative consequences of pollution may be better appreciated than those of dams, but the complexity of the relationships between pollutants and biota are no simpler than the relationships between flow patterns and biota.

When natural water-level, temperature, and water-quality patterns are disrupted, introduced species can outcompete Manomin.[57] Early in our work with Niisaachewan Anishinaabe Nation, Elders communicated that a "bog" was displacing Manomin. This bog includes *Typha* species, also known as cattail. *Typha* is a perennial. Once established, it has a competitive advantage over Manomin, which grows from seed each year. Manomin has a greater depth tolerance than *T. latifolia*, but *Typha* is more tolerant of environmental change, reinforcing its ability to take over wetlands.[58]

Further, other introduced species, such as *T. angustifolia* and the hybrid of *T. latifolia* and *T. angustifolia, T.x glauca,* have much greater depth tolerances than species native to Turtle Island.[59] The hybrid can grow in depths up to 1.5 metres, beyond the range of most healthy Manomin stands.[60] *Typha* can also form floating mats, making it more resilient to rising water levels.[61] It is difficult for Manomin to compete. *Typha* species outcompete Manomin in its historic habitat, leaving Manomin sparse or nonexistent.

Manomin has shown us that it is sensitive to changes caused by settler development. It has taught us that it is experiencing too much stress and needs more care. But is sparse growth caused by introduced species, river regulation, pollution, climate change, or the cumulative effects of many pressures? Too much environmental change will undermine the plant's ability to adapt. It will undermine the resilience of the ecosystem. Can we learn Manomin's lessons quickly enough to provide the care Manomin needs to continue to provide for humans and other-than-humans?

Resilience

Caring for Manomin means increasing the resilience of its ecosystem. Resilience has been defined as "the capacity of a system to absorb disturbance and reorganize while undergoing change so as to still retain essentially the same function, structure, identity, and feedbacks."[62] The system in which Manomin is embedded is socio-ecological: people and nature are too intertwined to separate. It has different organizational scales— the Manomin plant, the community of organisms, the river ecosystem, and the watershed. Such self-organizing systems are governed by feedbacks, whereby a change in a living or non-living component of a system causes changes in other components, which propagate through networks of connections and ultimately cause a change in the initial component. If the eventual change is in the same direction as the initial change, the feedback is positive or self-reinforcing. Net changes in the opposite direction indicate negative feedbacks, which help to keep different parts of the system within the boundaries necessary for the whole system to continue to function.

It is important to recognize feedbacks between social and ecological components and across scales.[63] The resilience of a system at a particular scale will depend on influences from the scales above and below. Thoughtful management by human actors in a socio-ecological system can build resilience, helping the system to retain its function, structure, and feedbacks. In spite of Manomin's sensitivity to environmental change, it has taught us that when we understand the importance of dynamic conditions, limits to disturbance, feedbacks, and diversity, we can improve its resilience.

Rivers, lakes, and wetlands are highly dynamic ecosystems. Even without anthropogenic changes to the environment, weather is inherently variable and, therefore, so are the aquatic systems influenced by it. High water levels are associated with wet periods and uncommonly heavy rainfall, especially when such conditions coincide with the snow melt. Both flood and drought conditions stress flora and fauna; there is either too little water or too much. "Testing the boundaries" of the system periodically promotes resilience. Manomin has adapted to the natural variability of the aquatic system. In deeper water conditions, it elongates the internodes[64] of the stems to reach the water's surface.[65] Although the taller growth may be at the expense of tillering and seed production, the plants can survive to produce some seed.

Further, Manomin seeds can lie dormant for several years. This means if a crop fails, there will still be seeds from previous years ready to germinate the following spring. Botanist Taylor A. Steeves shared his observations that if a spring freshet (i.e., high water conditions due to snow and ice melt) was unusually long and drowned the entire year's crop, leaving no new seeds, a healthy stand of Manomin could still appear the next year. This illustrates that the seeds can lie dormant for at least eighteen months.[66] Steeves acknowledged this unique adaptation: "This is a rather striking adaptation to an uncertain environment."[67]

More recent studies suggest Manomin seeds can lie dormant for several decades, providing seed reserves in the case of several sequential years of poor crops.[68] While dynamic conditions promote resilience, extreme conditions that stress biota (which occur more frequently and last longer as a result of alterations to the climate, watershed, or river) may exceed the biota's tolerance and the amount of change that the system can absorb while retaining similar structure and function.

A key feature of resilience is that there are limits to how much a system can be disturbed and continue to function in a similar way. Beyond these limits, change is often rapid and unpredictable. It is desirable to help steer the system away from known thresholds. The capacity of human actors to influence resilience and the trajectory of a system indicates adaptability in a socio-ecological system.[69]

Analysis of water-level data for the Upper Winnipeg River suggests that mean water levels through most of the Manomin growing season have increased since Whitedog Falls Generating Station (a hydroelectric dam) was installed downstream in 1958. Operations of upstream and downstream dams can further alter water-level conditions (e.g., rates of change) outside the preferred range for Manomin. It seems likely that water-level alterations have caused a major disturbance from which the system is attempting to recover. The system may not be resilient enough to absorb ongoing disturbances caused by frequent extreme conditions and rapid water-level changes. Reorganization of the system may, ultimately, include a shift in plant communities—and loss of Manomin.

However, Manomin would benefit from the following: reduced water depths, especially in spring; avoiding rapid water-level rises at any time during the growing season; and avoiding water-level drops in late summer. Further, wetland plant communities may be better able to withstand hydrologic conditions outside preferred ranges if other stressors acting at the same time are minimized. If optimal water patterns are not possible because of the complexity of river sharing or the presence of dams, managing for optimal nutrient conditions and alleviating the stress associated with intro-duced species may be even more important.

Nicholas Reo and Laura Ogden found that "Anishinaabe elders often feel strongly that nature finds its own balance, and people should not inter-vene using . . . drastic management techniques."[70] Our understanding is that gentle intervention to restore balance would be a culturally appropriate way to fulfill our responsibilities toward Manomin. Manomin at Pine Portage showed us that it is resilient but needs a little help. Where the encroaching mat of floating vegetation was removed by the storm, Manomin seeds that lay waiting in the substrate grew and re-established a Manomin field. If the removal of the floating vegetation by storms does not occur often enough to maintain space for Manomin, human caretakers could mimic the effect of a storm and intentionally remove sections of the floating mat.

Reseeding may be needed in some locations where the reserve of viable seed within the substrate has been depleted. Seeding more broadly could also build resilience if the seeds used help to increase the natural variability of Manomin. Different plants would respond differently to certain condi-tions and might help to avoid years with very poor crops.

The intent would not be to introduce drastic management but rather to restore healthy processes. Consider that the decline in Manomin has resulted in reduced populations of waterfowl and fewer Anishinaabe harvesters moving between Manomin fields to spread seed. The manage-ment intervention could simply restore the function of seed dispersal to support Manomin. Further investigation of historical seeding practices could provide insight into the cultural appropriateness of promoting resil-ience by using seeds with natural variability from different nearby sources.

Acting to move the system and known thresholds away from each other is a sound approach. However, in a complex system, it is unreasonable to expect to know all of the important feedbacks and thresholds. So, building the system's capacity to withstand any impact is also needed. When responding to a disturbance, a system needs to be able to reorganize to retain the same function and structure. Dynamic conditions, tight feedbacks, and diversity are attributes of self-organizing systems that contribute to general resilience.

Cues from Manomin at Pine Portage suggest that the plant and community-level systems can recover from disturbance if natural events or support from human caretakers can help limit the magnitude of the change. At the river scale, flow management that considers the needs of Manomin will help shift the system away from thresholds beyond which changes in structure and function can be expected. Care is needed so that Manomin can continue to sustain humans and other-than-humans in the Upper Winnipeg River. Building resilience may help to improve the system's ability to retain its structure and function with new disturbances, such as climate change.

Conclusion

It has been our great privilege to experience this place on the Upper Winnipeg River at Niisaachewan Anishinaabe Nation and to learn directly from Manomin and the Elders. We have seen firsthand the diversity of living things in Manomin habitats. We have seen Manomin's sensitivity to changes in water levels and storms. We have also seen how Manomin recovers when pressures from competitors are removed.

This is our first time learning from Elders' stories and from a spirited being—Manomin—who does not communicate with words. We cannot be sure that we have appropriately interpreted the lessons. But, we have also referred to Manomin teachings documented by others. We feel that our understanding has been deepened and extended.

The cumulative effects of settler development and global climate change are manifesting in the Upper Winnipeg River. Traditional knowledge may not be enough to care for Manomin in this place, where conditions have changed so dramatically. But traditional teachings instruct this generation to observe and to adapt. We share our understanding to help fulfill our responsibility to reduce stresses and restore care to Manomin so that it may continue to sustain the people and other-than-humans that are a part of this special place.

IMAGES FROM
ANISHINAABE-AKI:
THE SEASONS

by Andrea Bradford

———

Over the winter, Manomin seeds lie dormant in the mucky substrate below the water which contains the remains of Manomin from the previous crop. Rising temperatures in the spring trigger germination and the cycle of this annual plant begins anew.

FIGURE 20A: Nutrient Cycling. When Manomin dies in the fall, the plants fall back into the water. The accumulation of plant material can be seen in the spring after the ice melts. It provides places for aquatic organisms to live and hide from predators. Eventually, the organic material will decompose, releasing nutrients for future crops. Photograph by Samantha Mehltretter, 26 May 2022.

FIGURE 20B: Submerged Leaf Stage. Ripened seeds that fall into the water lodge themselves into the bottom sediments. Seeds germinate in the spring, and the shoots must reach the sunlight penetrating through the water before the energy stored in the seed is used up. Photograph by Samantha Mehltretter, 21 May 2021.

FIGURE 20C: Floating Leaf Stage. In the next stage of Manomin's life cycle, ribbons of floating leaves spread across the water surface. At this time, the buoyant leaves make the plants vulnerable to being uprooted by rising water levels. Photograph by Brittany Luby, 5 June 2018.

FIGURE 20D: Aerial Shoot Stage. Closer to shore, the aerial shoots are beginning to rise above the surface of the water. Later in the season, Manomin plants can tower over observers in canoes. Plants may have a single emergent stem or multiple stems (tillers). Photograph by Brittany Luby, 9 July 2020.

FIGURE 20E: Pistillate Flowers. The plants soon begin to flower. The pistillate (female) flowers are found closely pressed to the upper part of the stem. They open a few days before the male flowers on the same plant, which encourages cross-pollination. Photograph by Brittany Luby, 7 August 2021.

Images from Anishinaabe-Aki: The Seasons

FIGURE 20F: Damselfly. Clusters of staminate (male) flowers, on the lower branches are loosely arranged. Many other living organisms can be found living among the Manomin plants when you look more closely. Photograph by Brittany Luby, 24 July 2018.

FIGURE 20G: Rice Worm. Adult moths of the species *Apamea apamiformis* lay their eggs in July inside the florets. The larvae (commonly referred to as rice worms) gorge themselves on both seed and stalks over the growing season. Photograph by Manomin Project, 15 August 2021.

FIGURE 20H: Sun-kissed. In August and September, the seeds develop and ripen. The seeds on a Manomin plant reach maturity at different times. Where traditional harvesting methods are used, harvesters can return to the same area multiple times to collect newly ripened seeds. Photograph by Brittany Luby, 19 August 2018.

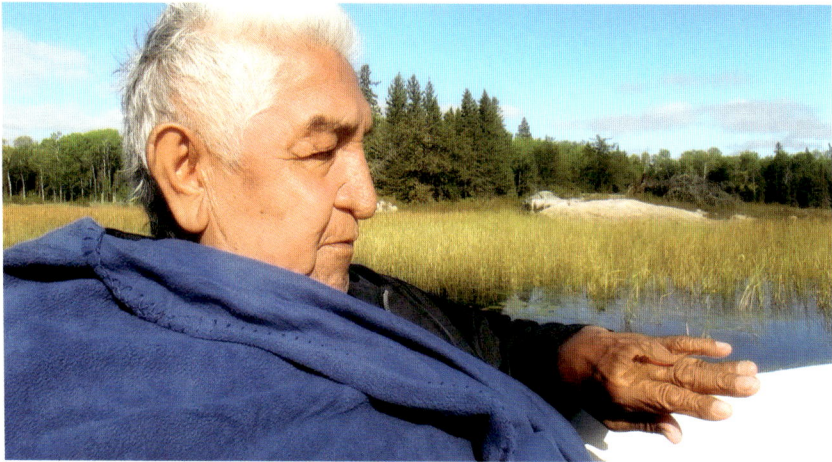

FIGURE 20I: Elder Larry Kabestra. Elders have so much to share. It is not just their knowledge, but also their perspectives and values that can help us become caretakers of the lands and waters. They—like Elder Larry Kabestra—are patient with those of us willing to learn with open hearts and minds. Photograph by Brittany Luby, 19 September 2019.

MANOMIN

FIGURE 21: A Moment of Reclamation. In this photograph, Ginnifer Menominee threshes Manomin. She writes: "Menominee is my family name. We are people of the wild rice, Manomin. As an Anishnawbe woman, I grew up hearing our Anishnawbe migration story which prophesied of a food that grew on water 'Manomin,' the good seed, and how it led Anishnawbe from the east into the interior of what is now the Great Lakes regions of Turtle Island. Unfortunately, in my community of Wasauksing, there has not been Manomin for generations now. The reasons for that loss are still not clear to me. I grew up not having or knowing my traditional food, Manomin, as a staple of my diet or learning the harvesting practices that would be shared throughout my community. . . . Presently I am reclaiming these practices in community and it's brought me healing, a deeper understanding of my gifts, my role in my family and community." Photograph by Ginnifer Menominee, 2020.

114

7

Disconnection

by Hannah Neufeld

Manomin is an Indigenous food that forms part of a larger food system developed and maintained by Nations like the Anishinaabeg and the Dakota (among others).[1] Foods like Manomin embody cultural and spiritual values, along with enhanced nutrition and well-being, food security, ways of knowing, and an ongoing connection to land and water,[2] yet only a quarter of First Nation adults consume wild meats from their local environments, and even fewer (18.6 percent) include wild plants and berries as part of their diets.[3] According to the final report of the First Nations Food, Nutrition and Environment Study (FNFNES), traditional food access does not meet current needs in First Nation communities within what is currently known as Canada.[4] This chapter invites readers to consider the environmental challenges urban Indigenous Peoples face in participating in their food systems. Readers are asked to consider Manomin as central to Indigenous food environments that also include forms of sustenance that are cultivated, foraged, and hunted.

Colonization has been recognized as the single most significant social determinant of health among Indigenous Peoples worldwide.[5] Indigenous communities are impacted to a greater degree by food insecurity and malnutrition than the general population and are disproportionately affected by chronic conditions such as type 2 diabetes.[6] Nationally, close to 50 percent of First Nation families struggle with putting enough food on the table,[7] compared to the Canadian average of just 12 percent.[8] The diets of many First Nation adults tend to be nutritionally inadequate, which is strongly tied to limited access to healthy food options, namely Indigenous foods.[9] These revered foods originate from the natural environment, either from farming, foraging, or hunting, and make up complex Indigenous food systems that are foundational to Indigenous Peoples' ways of life. Settler land encroachment and settler law have compromised Indigenous access to Indigenous foods, triggering disparities in health and well-being.

Beyond addressing individual and household barriers to accessing high-quality foods from both market and Indigenous food systems, it is imperative to reduce threats to the health of ecological and knowledge environments required to support the access, availability, quality, and sustainable use of Indigenous foods. Recent studies highlight the need to continue to build upon multi-jurisdictional efforts at community, regional, provincial, and national levels to reduce rates of food insecurity and improve nutritional status in First Nations and other Indigenous communities using a determinants-of-health approach.[10] Indigenous priorities and values also need to be recognized and included within relevant frameworks impacting food environments. Improving access to Indigenous food systems can help ensure that local ecosystems are healthy and can sustainably support Indigenous Peoples' rights to self-determination, including food sovereignty, which refers to the right to control food production (e.g., harvesting), distribution (e.g., sharing), and consumption (e.g., feasting).

Environmental Contexts

The health of the land and community for Indigenous Peoples are synonymous, nurtured through relationships and providing a healthy basis for overall well-being.[11] The concept of environmental dispossession is informed by a critical population health perspective to include processes that have reduced Indigenous Peoples' access to the land and resources of their traditional environments. As Indigenous communities experience physical dislocation, its members may experience greater barriers to participating in Indigenous food systems. Although the origins of these structural determinants may reflect global food trends, such as the overall environmental health of these food systems, the mechanisms or determinants by which access to Indigenous foods has been reduced are unique. The impacts of forced assimilation associated with urbanization have eroded relationships and disrupted the transmission of knowledge to subsequent generations.[12] These influences have not only reduced physical access to foods available on the lands and waters,[13] but they have also continued to put pressure on interpersonal and human-with-other-than-human relationships and wider socio-ecological environments.[14]

The Truth and Reconciliation Commission of Canada explicitly calls for actions that close these gaps in health equity.[15] To restore sustainable relationships to the land, culture, and communities, pathways to reconciliation, health, and well-being include re-establishing Indigenous food systems, including community roles and responsibilities to protect food environments; these are necessary acts of resurgence and reclamation.[16] While a broad body of research has investigated the roots of cultural change and environmental contamination among rural and northern Indigenous communities,[17] there is a significant gap in research exploring the mechanisms linking processes of environmental dispossession with Indigenous food systems among populations within southern regions of Canada, especially in urban settings and across generations. Indigenous communities are not only becoming more urban, but also overrepresented by youth and children.[18] Research that informs policies to address the health, social, and cultural needs of these unique and diverse populations is critically necessary as urban demographies continue to change.[19] Determinants of health and well-being must also be viewed from a more structural perspective, taking factors such as colonization, racism, loss of cultural practices, and patterns of urban migration into account.

Over 80 percent of Indigenous Peoples within the province of Ontario live off-reserve, with 62.1 percent living in urban areas.[20] The western cities with the largest proportion of Indigenous Peoples include Winnipeg, Manitoba; Edmonton, Alberta; and Vancouver, British Columbia. Toronto, Ontario, ranks fourth with an estimated Indigenous population of 55,000 to 70,000.[21] According to a study by the Ontario Federation of Indigenous Friendship Centres (OFIFC), Indigenous families within Ontario experience poverty at a rate of 18.4 percent compared to 11 percent of the non-Indigenous population and are one-third more likely to be unemployed and live in lower-income neighbourhoods.[22] These challenging socio-economic environments have received less attention from Indigenous health researchers over the last several decades than those in remote communities, even though these patterns of steady growth are continuing in southern Canadian cities. One significant trend among Indigenous populations within southern Ontario, and more broadly across southern Canada, is urbanization. For Indigenous families, urbanization has been accompanied by a nutrition transition characterized by decreased dietary diversity, declining access to Indigenous foods, and the increased tendency toward highly or ultra-processed foods that contain greater proportions of sugar, salt, and other preservatives.[23] Indigenous Peoples living away from their home communities and environments are more likely to experience food insecurity compared with the general population.[24] The Southwest Ontario Aboriginal Health Access Centre (SOAHAC) Food Choice Study published evidence that both reserve- and urban-based First Nation families experience significantly higher levels of food insecurity, with 35 percent of reserve-based and 55 percent of urban-based participants describing themselves as food insecure.[25]

Members of the Friendship Centre Movement founded the OFIFC in 1971 to provide cultural supports and connection for urban Indigenous Peoples and build the capacity of member Friendship Centres across Ontario.[26] The OFIFC emerged from a nationwide, grassroots movement dating back to the 1950s, when founding members established community hubs where Indigenous Peoples living in towns and cities could access cultur-ally-based programming and services. Residential School experiences have been identified as a significant factor pushing Indigenous Peoples toward cities.[27] The Toronto Council Fire Native Cultural Centre, along with six other Friendship Centres in Ontario, recently participated in a research project that explored some of the unique determinants of health that Indigenous urban communities continue to face in establishing community priorities.[28] One of the most challenging aspects for Indigenous Peoples living in urban centres is establishing a sense of belonging and connection in their often new urban environments.[29] Particularly for individuals and families who are regularly moving to and within cities, feeling a connection to place, which is so important for Indigenous Peoples, can be very challenging.[30]

In addition to place, social environments or networks are critical for Indigenous families to provide support and create a sense of solidarity. Families and communities possess sharing and caring values that can help to maintain one's identity, which unto itself is a determinant of health and well-being.[31] Bringing members of extended family and community together also provides opportunities to share knowledge and other gifts to build confidence and self-esteem while maintaining intergenerational connections. Indigenous Peoples in urban areas commonly embrace broader views of their physical and social environments and "community" to include members of different Nations and Territories, often resulting in a "three-way equilibrium" between the land, community, and city for those who travel to and from these spaces and places to maintain balance.

Urban Food Environments

Those who move or relocate frequently experience greater food insecurity, as resources are spent moving from reserve to urban spaces, or within cities.[32] Women, children, lone parent families, along with Indigenous Peoples, have previously been identified as being most likely to be food insecure within Canada.[33] An examination of other influences on urban food environments, however, is severely lacking in the literature on these population groups. Distal and environmental determinants shape individual and interpersonal behaviours, including food choice and acquisition patterns.[34] For example, Indigenous women in urban food environments are additionally limited by their relative social and cultural exclusion from their home communities. Indeed, many stories of urbanization are belied by uneasy truths about the politics of identity and Bill C-31 as the Indian Act has long separated Indigenous women from their communities and children from their maternal relations.[35] These processes of environmental dispossession have restricted access to traditional lands, water, and food resources,[36] with the health consequences of environmental dispossession occurring almost exclusively through disrupted food systems.

Both external and personal domains and dimensions of food environments, particularly in urban Indigenous contexts, therefore, need to consider the structural determinants of health.[37] Food environment frameworks need to be adapted to recognize that Indigenous food use is a central link between Indigenous Peoples, the land, and social networks regardless of physical space. Non-market-based food sources, including the harvesting of wild and locally cultivated foods, necessitate expanding these knowledge pathways to design targeted interventions and policies to support these unique food environments in urban settings. Food environments include a range of elements such as geographic food access, food availability, food affordability, and food quality.[38] Urban Indigenous Peoples interact with these elements in ways that are unique compared to those living on reserve.[39] Urban families within southwestern Ontario, for example, have reported being challenged to find sufficient time and access to teachings necessary to prepare traditional recipes like corn soup, without consistent access to Elders and extended family in the city.[40] It can also be challenging to access a consistent supply of locally sourced animals when immediate family members do not possess the skills or knowledge to hunt and prepare wild foods. These urban Indigenous food environments, like the communities that comprise them, are diverse.

Communities may consist of individuals new to urban environments and those who have made an urban location home for many years or generations.[41] Some have close connections to their home community, while others have adapted stronger ties to an urban social network.

Access to knowledge, land-based activities, contact with Elders, and cultural capacity around food are integral to the health and maintenance of Indigenous food systems.[42] Challenges regarding access to Indigenous foods have also been associated with an increased emphasis on the monetary culture in the city, which also serves to reduce food-sharing practices.[43] Sharing food through social networks is highly valued in urban centres where Indigenous foods are less prevalent.[44] Sharing practices are widely documented in the literature, even though only 27.9 percent of First Nation adults within Canada report sharing traditional foods on a yearly basis.[45] The majority of these studies have found that community sharing occurs as an adaptation to food shortages in more remote environments.[46] Unique challenges exist in accessing and harvesting foods like Manomin in an urban setting. Due to distance and disconnection, harvesting practices are limited in the city.[47]

Urban locations have, therefore, created significantly greater challenges for Indigenous Peoples to fully engage in diverse and sustainable Indigenous food systems because of their physical and social distances from land and Elders, limiting access to foods as well as knowledge. Geography presents some practical limitations, such as resource availability, as well. Consider that environmental modifications such as urban development can displace native species, whereas environmental contamination by industry can increase the risk of consuming Indigenous foods that are available in urban environments.[48]

Urban Experiences

In 2014, a community-based study was designed to advance knowledge of local food sovereignty efforts with urban and reserve-based First Nations communities within southwestern Ontario.[49] Study objectives included investigating current knowledge surrounding access, availability, and Indigenous food practices among urban and rural First Nations families; describing and comparing the historical context of present-day urban and rural food environments; and exploring SOAHAC's concerns that circumstances of food insecurity in these communities may be associated with knowledge loss resulting from the intergenerational impacts of Residential Schools. Two generations of First Nations women, aged twenty-three to seventy-six, were interviewed. Some of the main themes discussed by the younger generation of twenty-five women included knowledge, sharing, food preferences, and access.[50] Those living in the city frequently discussed knowledge limitations around the preparation of Indigenous foods, hunting, and harvesting practices.[51] Cindy made reference to barriers negatively impacting knowledge transfer due to families becoming increasingly "urbanized," along with "[not] knowing your Elders, because they're the ones that pass down all this tradition." Cindy was aware of the legacies of Residential Schools and their structural impacts on knowledge transfer from Elders to younger generations. She empathized with her sister, who did not have access to transportation to travel to speak with her Elders in her home community and learn how to prepare traditional foods. As Cindy said, "My sister, she doesn't even make bread." Substantially fewer urban-based participants talked about the concept of sharing foods and knowledge within the family and the wider community.

Transportation to and from their home communities was frequently mentioned as time consuming and costly, yet necessary to access locally harvested meats, fish, and other ingredients used to prepare Indigenous foods. As many live at a distance from family, accessing these ingredients meant increased transportation costs to obtain these foods from within their home communities or to participate in extended family meals. Chantal complained, "It's hard to have the money when you want to find the foods. Sometimes you hear about it in the city, you want to go but don't have the money to do it." Many young women were motivated and interested in preparing foods like deer meat for their families in London, yet their children preferred store-bought foods that are more common in urban environments. Over 70 percent of the young women interviewed were single parents living on fixed incomes in the city. They did not want to waste precious funds or time on foods their children would not eat. Celine described the frequency of Indigenous foods she prepared at home as "not something that happens all the time because my children won't eat them." She went on to say, "Because it takes a lot of work to cook them and make them and everything like that. It's something I always buy. I don't make corn soup and I won't make fry bread." Mothers in the city tended to associate Indigenous foods with celebratory occasions involving extended family, fostering a sense of belonging and identity. As Celine described: "It's a celebration. We all enjoy it, my extended family. So it's like a delicacy. So I think it's important. It's part of who I am. I grew up eating corn soup and having it at my grandma's and we always had fish [too]. And so it's just part of who I am."

Life history interviews with eighteen female Elders living within the city of London also illustrated these intergenerational impacts that have disconnected Indigenous women, especially those living in urban centres, from the land. Various mechanisms of displacement, loss of land, and community shifted the social construction of families, according to participants.[52] Elder women discussed painful circumstances of physical dispossession from the land and social disconnection from their families and communities. Ten participants were Residential School survivors, and talked about the ongoing, intergenerational effects of loss, responsibility, lack of support, and an altered sense of identity. Six had moved away from their home communities, which created significantly greater challenges to engage fully in traditional food procurement and sharing practices. Shifting from subsistence farming on reserves to wage economy pursuits in the nearby United States divided extended families from each other and the land.

Teachings associated with the harvesting and preparation of Indigenous foods were conveyed by observation but, according to Violet, were not as commonly practised in the city. She recalled how she learned traditional teachings from her grandparents by visiting them regularly and learning through "everyday talk" when she was younger and living in her home community. She would sit down with her grandmother and start "learning by just observing, even, too. It wasn't even necessarily that they were telling you things. It was just, you watched how they lived their life." Rose, who spent much of her early life away from her community, expressed these sentiments strongly and felt knowledge should only be shared in the home in the traditional way. As she expressed, "We stayed with our father's mother, our grandmother, but our mother's mother, she used to make baskets, too. And then she'd make oven bread outside. That's how I learned, from watching your auntie or your grandma cook."

I learned from the time spent with women in these communities that the determinants impacting the health of Indigenous Peoples in urban environments are unique and complex. The impacts of colonialism and forced assimilation associated with Indigenous Peoples moving to urban areas continue to impact the relationships that have existed between Indigenous Peoples and their ecosystems, with women most affected.[53] Indigenous women living in cities tend to carry an extra burden of stress, engage in fewer physical activities, and have compromised diets.[54] As mothers, women tend to have fewer opportunities than men and less access to resources such as land, credit, and education.[55] They are responsible for gender-determined labour that often includes taking care of children and Elders and completing tasks in the home when men migrate for work.[56] Women are also the ones who balance their families' meals on restricted budgets, without sufficient financial or social supports, often as single parents living away from their home communities. Urban families also tend to be food insecure and are more likely to rely on emergency food assistance.[57]

Other regional studies have similarly illustrated how physical distance and disconnection from family and one's home community can influence the dietary erosion of Indigenous foods in urban settings,[58] with social supports tending to help buffer against household food insecurity.[59] Food-insecure households are more likely to lack these social networks.[60] All of these complex life situations, compounded by circumstances of dislocation, amount to circumstances of structural violence that limit opportunities because of an unequal power balance.[61] These conditions can compromise one's self-determination and human rights, ultimately negatively impacting pathways toward Indigenous food sovereignty (IFS).

Creating Community

To address community needs identified in southwestern Ontario, a collaborative research project was initiated by myself along with academic colleagues and community research partners such as White Owl Native Ancestry Association (WONAA). Together, we worked to help bridge connections with the land for urban Indigenous Peoples and encourage sharing knowledge and developing relationships. The project was based on an emerging area of research exploring the relationships that Indigenous Peoples have with the land to encourage practices that perpetuate healthy families and communities.[62] In conjunction with this community-based research program, engagement efforts began in 2017 to support urban Indigenous communities within the wider Grand River Territory, providing increased social and physical connections to the land.[63] Four communal garden sites were established on campus at the Universities of Guelph and Waterloo, along with an urban farm in Kitchener and at the Blair Outdoor and Environmental Education Centre, with the aims of addressing food access and knowledge barriers and developing land-based education programming. These urban and campus-based gardens are known collectively as Wisahkotewinowak, which means "green shoots that grow after a fire," and include edible and medicinal plants that have been planted and nurtured by a group of committed community members, faculty, and students. The garden situated at the University of Waterloo's Environmental Reserve grows a wide variety of fruits and vegetables that are shared with the local urban Indigenous community through a weekly food sharing program coordinated by WONAA. The plots of land located at the Steckle Heritage Farm in Kitchener are used primarily for growing tobacco and sunflowers, along with Haudenosaunee white corn, beans, and squash. The Blair Garden, along with the Tea Garden at the University of Guelph's Arboretum, are utilized primarily by students and local youth to provide experiential learning opportunities. Using food as a starting point, community members find themselves rekindling relationships with each other across species, territorial, and generational lines.

Some of the research that has taken place to learn more about the ways the project is supporting Indigenous students and families has pointed to the importance of finding community on campus and within cities. During sharing circles that were held by University of Guelph students with members of the Collective, each participant within the circle spoke about how the land-based practices and teachings associated with the gardens bring about "a sense of community."[64] Community was discussed and described as being a part of the foundation, utilization, and perception of the garden sites. Each participant shared their experiences about how the gardens have grown to become a collective community and ways they hope to see the local Indigenous community use the gardens more as a common sharing space. One of Wisahkotewinowak's founders, for example, talked about his thoughts on how the gardens have the potential to be the community hub: "using the gardens to create community and having a different kind of space in place for Indigenous People to connect with . . . it was the idea of creating a community and now it's become . . . a part of our communal expression including land into the aspect of community."

Another member of the Collective discussed her hopes for the gardens to become a safe space for sharing Indigenous knowledge: "I'd like to see

Disconnection

[the gardens] as more of a hub for both community and students to interact together and engage together as a center for knowledge like transferring Indigenous knowledge or sharing Indigenous knowledge." The theme of knowledge related to the land and its history were also discussed as being integral to "build on to our knowledge of the land," and inform what can be grown at the various urban garden sites. Successful harvests in the years to come will support the wider urban Indigenous community by providing a deeper connection to the land and history of the wider Grand River Territory.

In building these connections, others in the sharing circle brought up the importance of relationships. As another founding member stated, "I think about how we encourage people to have relationships with all our relations: the land, but also spirit and each other . . . that's what the gardens I think have offered me." Recognizing these personal connections to the gardens was also discussed by another participant—how this sense of identity and relationship to the land helps to provide a better sense of community, "as we all reconcile our relationship to the land settler culture and Indigenous cultures then we will reconcile ourselves to each other." I am, too, a member of this garden community and the Wisahkotewinowak Collective. As with others who live in urban settings, I am disconnected from the lands of my ancestors. I was adopted before open communication with birth families was common, and I grew up knowing very little about my background. As an adult, I connected with urban Indigenous Peoples through my scholarly research. We found common ground as part of Wisahkotewinowak with many of us living away from blood kin and finding family. Together, we have worked toward creating safe spaces and a sense of belonging on the land by reconnecting with some of our Elder relatives: plant beings.

The garden spaces that make up Wisahkotewinowak have the potential to build and strengthen relationships, to be a part of sharing knowledge, along with imparting a sense of identity that is rooted in a safe and welcoming community where belonging, connection, and responsibility can flourish.

Strengthened relationship to land has also led Indigenous families in the Grand River Territory to begin asking questions about seeds that grow in the water and kindled a regional interest in Manomin care and consumption.[65]

Final Thoughts

The concept of food sovereignty or self-determination around food practices is not exclusively dependent on resurrecting Indigenous food practices.[66] My experiences working with Indigenous communities in cities draw attention to the importance of supporting the social structures as well as rebuilding and reconnecting to the physical landscapes that constitute Indigenous food systems and thereby cultivate community. It is the land that brings us together, the land that teaches relationship-based ways of knowing about the natural world and its food systems and environments.[67]

The dimensions that constitute urban-based food environments contribute toward the holistic health of individuals, families, and communities. Indigenous food systems are complex and holistic. They are valued from a physical health perspective, and the activities involved in their acquisition and distribution allow for the practice of cultural values, such as sharing and cooperation.[68] There is urgency in promoting knowledge sharing through increased social support within families and the larger community living within cities. Elevating these pathways toward self-determination also reinforces both dietary and biocultural diversity.[69] Diversity in both forms improves health and well-being, and continues to build resilience and connection toward traditional food systems in these complex and ever-evolving food environments.[70] Conditions for establishing Indigenous food systems within urban settings include diverse and complex relationships to the land, along with urban influences on food skills and knowledge. These differences must always be considered.[71]

The research findings making up this chapter suggest there is a need to gather additional community-led evidence on this growing population segment to develop interventions specifically designed to meet the unique needs of urban Indigenous communities. Environmental repossession refers to the social, economic, cultural, and political processes through which Indigenous Peoples are reclaiming land and knowledge systems and asserting their sovereign rights to improve health and well-being.[72] Gardens—whether on the land (like the Three Sisters) or in water (like Manomin fields)—can provide a critical space for sharing and learning[73] and a practical location for cultivating social connections. These processes within urban contexts may encompass a variety of self-determining actions and ideals, such as those held by the Wisahkotewinowak Collective to practise knowledge transfer. By acquiring access and developing connections to land and building identity through relationships, physical and social connections can continue to nurture community and belonging in the city.

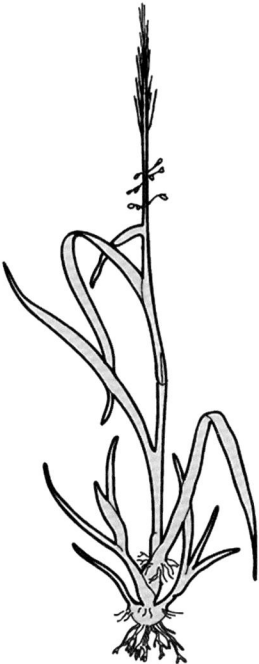

130

MANOMIN WITH MUSHROOMS

by Shane Chartrand

———

I was adopted by my family when I was almost seven years old. My mom is a Mi'kmaw-Irish woman, and my dad is Métis. My biological mother was from the Enoch Cree Nation. And I learned European, mostly French, cooking and recipes in culinary school. I also love Japanese food. I have been a chef at a Lebanese restaurant. And I have been able to travel to a dozen or so other Nations to learn about ingredients and foods from cooks and Elders there. And with every new day, my cooking changes because of all these influences. This is why I call my personal cooking style "progressive Indigenous cuisine." It is ever evolving.

Serves: 4 | *Prep time:* 20 mins | *Cook time:* 65 mins

Salt

Vegetable Oil

Pepper

Chicken Stock

Garlic

Manomin

Shallots

Chives

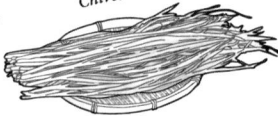

Butter

Grainy Dijon Mustard

Water

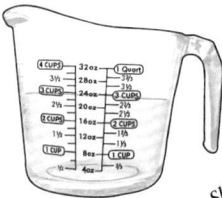

Sliced Brown Mushrooms

INGREDIENTS

1/2 cup Manomin

2 tbsp vegetable oil

1/2 cup brown mushrooms, fresh and sliced

1 1/2 tsp shallots, minced

1 1/2 tsp garlic, minced

1 1/2 tsp chives, minced

1 1/2 cups chicken stock

1/2 tsp grainy Dijon mustard

1 tbsp butter

Salt and pepper, to taste

Soak Manomin in about 2 1/2 cups of water overnight. Drain the Manomin and rinse.

Manomin with Mushrooms

This recipe is rooted in Indigenous ingredients, the lakes and forests, but then it has butter and a hit of Dijon. It is about conversation and collaboration, people talking back and forth, and trying new combinations. We do not need to be thinking about the "most Indigenous" way to do things. Get that out of your mindset and just try something new. That, to me, is the future that I see: acknowledge ingredients that have been around for thousands of years, and use them today and tomorrow in a new, exciting way.

PREP

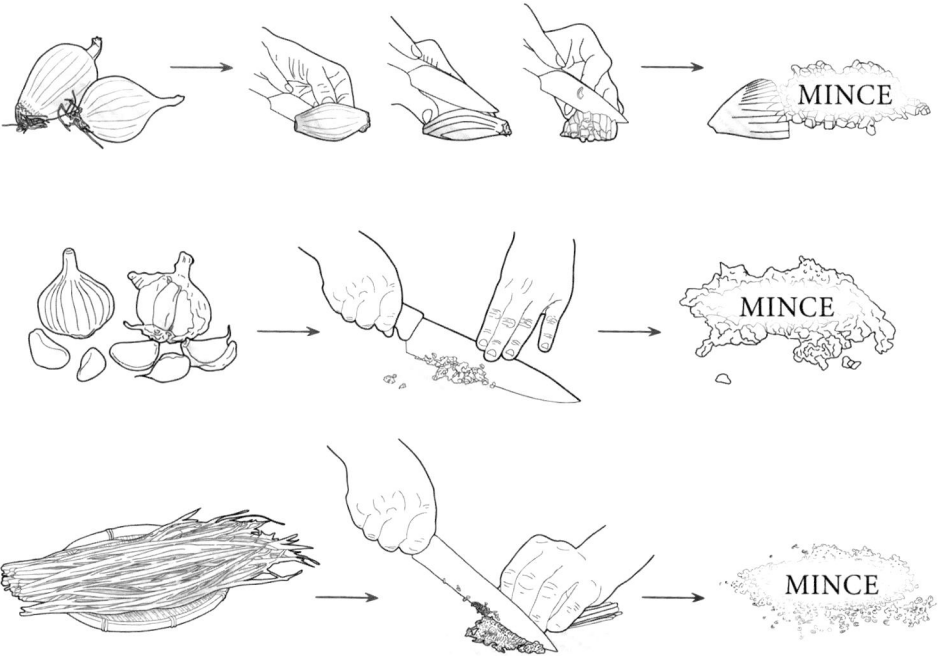

133

INSTRUCTIONS

1 In a medium saucepan, cook the Manomin in 3 cups of water at a gentle boil on medium heat. Cook until the grains are tender, about 30 minutes. You will see the white insides of some of the grains.

2 Strain the Manomin and set aside to cool.

3 In a sauté pan, add oil and sauté the mushrooms, shallots, garlic, and chives on medium-high heat for about 3 minutes.

4 Add the cooled Manomin and cook for another few minutes, stirring.

5 Add the stock. Turn down the heat to minimum and let it gently cook until most of the stock has evaporated, about 20 minutes.

6 To finish, stir in Dijon and butter. Season with salt and pepper to your taste.

FIGURE 22: A Moment of Connection. This photograph features Tewashutyaks, aged five. Her mother, Stephanie Stevens, writes, "This photograph was taken at the Oneida Nation of Indians of Wisconsin's first Wild Rice Camp. . . . When we made our knockers, we carefully shaved down the cedar. The perfect shavings curled on their own and laid on the ground next to the shave horse. My daughter was there, a part of the camp. When she saw the shavings, she put them in her hair and wore them proudly, a symbol of the beauty of the process. My daughter also helped . . . parch the Manomin, she danced on it, she winnowed it, and she sorted it. . . . Her spirit was connecting to something ancestral she had now inherited." Photograph by Stephanie Stevens, 2020.

⑧

Treaty and Mushkiki

by Jana-Rae Yerxa and Pikanagegaabo William Yerxa

Debwetaan manoomin, giiwiijiigoowing mushkiki gosha aye.
I believe manoomin will help us because it is medicine.

My relationship with manoomin has been an unexpected love affair. It is a relationship that caught me by surprise in terms of its depth and the power it holds for Anishinaabeg to reconcile with themselves, each other, and the land. What initially drew me to manoomin was the old man, my grandfather Willie Yerxa. He can be found every Manoominike Giizis sitting by the fire roasting the grain—a modern-day Rice Chief. Manoomin is many things. For my grandfather, I have come to see that passing on his knowledge of harvesting the grain, along with the philosophies embedded in the process, is his love song to our family.

As mass graves and unmarked graves of Indigenous children at the old sites of Indian Residential "Schools" are being revealed to the world, I think about him more than I already was. I reflect on the miraculous nature of my grandfather as a little boy, who attended those nightmare places, growing into the old man he has become. He carries the teachings manoomin provides to us, as Anishinaabeg, so we have opportunities to walk firmer, understanding more of who we are as Anishinaabeg—something that those schools and settler colonialism, in general, seek to destroy within us. In this way, my grandfather is also a lifesaver, even though he never intended to be.

Like many Indigenous families, mine is no different when it comes to colonial impacts playing out through disconnections, be it with ourselves, our families, our communities, or our traditional territories. My relationship with my grandfather was overshadowed for many years by distance birthed out of colonial violence. Over the years, my grandfather and I invested in reconciling our relationship. Manoomin has played and continues to play an important role in strengthening our relationship with one another. My grandfather's knowledge has significantly shaped my relationship with manoomin, and like-wise, manoomin has grown my understanding of the medicine it carries for Anishinaabeg reconciliation, governance, and nationhood. This is why, to me, manoomin sits at the intersection of the "personal is political" and vice versa.

It is the centring of and putting into motion reconciliation, on Anishinaabeg terms, which carry meaningful pathways for our healing and liberation from colonial harms. This is an important distinction to make because reconciliation often gets usurped by Western institutions to absolve settler guilt and shape-shift settler colonialism to appear more innocuous. However, Anishinaabe forms of reconciliation are about coming together with one another, picking up our ways that have always sustained us in our homelands, and being accountable to our places and one another. When we do this, we are accessing intricate systems of knowledge that guided our ancestors. Our systems embodied Anishinaabe governance and nationhood, collectively, and accounted for wellness, personally. These are necessary and powerful acts of turning away from settler-colonial logic.

Through my relationship with my grandfather and manoomin, my understanding of self, Anishinaabe governance, and nationhood continues to evolve. Because it began with something simple, but not necessarily easy, amidst colonial disarray—a granddaughter sitting beside her grandfather at a fire, accompanied by a curiosity and a craving for connection that was reciprocated—I now understand it is Anishinaabe forms of reconciliation, of reconnecting, that matter first and foremost. This is where Anishinaabe governance and nationhood exist and can flourish: within our relationships. This chapter is a story of how Anishinaabe reconciliation was made possible with the help of manoomin.

Centring Anishinaabeg Treaty Making

I have come to understand the relationship between Anishinaabe and manoomin as one of treaty. "Anishinaabeg's treaty with manoomin is one of our most significant and oldest treaties. We revisit and renew our treaty with manoomin every harvesting season."[1] By centring Indigenous perspectives of treaty, drawing on Anishinaabemowin to further understand an Anishinaabe perspective, deepening my own relationship with manoomin, and hearing stories of my grandpa's early memories of manoomin harvesting, my conceptualization of Anishinaabeg's relationship with manoomin has evolved to one of treaty.

Treaty making for Anishinaabeg is a practice of diplomacy that predates the creation of the Canadian state. Our ancestors engaged in treaty making with other Indigenous Nations and other beings long before engaging in treaty negotiations with European settlers. Stark reaffirms that "treaty making was a long-standing tradition" among the Anishinaabeg who have always been about maintaining peace through "healthy collective relationships."[2] Therefore, Anishinaabeg have always "had their own [treaty making] processes for making and maintaining peaceful diplomatic relationships." These relationships were sanctioned in front of Gitchi Manidoo because the Anishinaabeg understood that the treaty making process was "also sacred [and to be] made in the presence of the spiritual world and solemnized in ceremony."[3]

Simpson summarizes the Anishinaabeg concept Bimaadiziwin (the Good Life) as the foundation for Anishinaabeg living a life of balance and peace:

"This was the foundation of a set of ethics, values, and practices known as Bimaadiziwin. . . . [It] is a way of ensuring human beings live in balance with the natural world, their family, their clan, and their nation and it is carried out through the Seven Grandfather teachings, embedded in the social and political structures of the [Anishinaabeg]."[4] Bimaadiziwin is the goal of treaty making.

Anishinaabeg treaty making extended to other life forms. Our stories provide us with insight which can continue to guide our people in maintaining peaceful coexistence with all life forms. For example, Stark shares an Anishinaabeg story about the woman who married a beaver and highlights how the story represents the forging of a new relationship. Because significant Anishinaabeg treaty making principles such as mutual respect, responsibility, and renewal are present in the negotiation of the new relationship, between Anishinaabeg and the beaver, it is one of treaty. The "beaver offer themselves up to the [Anishinaabeg] as food, and in exchange the [Anishinaabeg] agree to return the bones of the beaver and make offerings so that the cycle can continue."[5]

Anishinaabemowin also reveals how our ceremonial ways were not separate from politics. For Anishinaabeg, it was an important part of how we prepared and engaged in political matters. It is through ceremony that our ancestors ensured our philosophies were brought forward in the political realm, in the practice of spirituality.

Zagaswe means to offer a smoke, especially in a pipe ceremony, or to invite to council. Zaagaswe'idiwag means they are "offering smoke to each other."[6] It means they have a council meeting. It means they have a ceremony. The root word, zagaswe, tells how making our offering and to smoke together was part of the process when Anishinaabeg had "a meeting or when we had to meet about an important decision coming up."[7]

When Anishinaabeg smoke, we call upon our ancestors to help us carry things out in a good way. Ceremony has always been an integral part of political practices and treaty making for the Anishinaabeg.[8] At the negotiations of Treaty #3, Treaty Commissioner Morris noted the drums, singing, and how he was offered the pipe of peace by the Anishinaabeg.[9] My grandfather also recalls ceremonies when he was out in the manoomin fields to harvest with his parents and other elders. "All these things that they were doing out there, before they did anything, was through a ceremony. They had a drum. They sang. Somebody always would say a prayer."[10] These are the practices we maintain to this day when engaging with manoomin.

Treaty Between Anishinaabeg and Manoomin

In *Decolonising the Mind*, Ngũgĩ wa Thiong'o discusses the importance of language. Language is a carrier of culture which holds "the collective memory bank of a people's experience in history" as well as "the entire body of values by which we come to perceive ourselves and our place in the world."[11] Anishinaabemowin reveals the sacredness of manoomin for the Anishinaabeg. Manito Gitigaan is an ancient term, older than the term manoomin, which means the "Great Spirit's Garden," and manoomin, when translated into English, means Spirit Food.[12]

In our sacred stories, Anishinaabeg are responsible for caring for Manito Gitigaan and in return, manoomin will care for us. Manoomin gifts us life by providing nourishment for our bodies and helps Anishinaabeg to understand our place in relation to the world. Manoomin, an other-than-human person, is deserving of respect and care and has always been an important part of our society: "It is through the exchange of gifts that one maintains its membership in Ojibway society. Are not these other-than-human persons with whom they exchange gifts members of that society and entitled to the same respect and help accorded to any other member of the community? There is, we suggest, a moral obligation to protect the habitat of the moose, the beaver, the muskrat, and the lynx; the habitat of the geese, ducks, grouse, and hare, not just because of the Band's wish to continue hunting and trapping, but because these other-than-human persons are also members of Ojibway society."[13] Our stories reaffirm the sacredness of manoomin to our Nation, governance, and existence as people. We are told manoomin was gifted to Anishinaabeg by Gitchi Manidoo. My great-grand-father, the late Bert Yerxa, acknowledged that manoomin was "the spiritual foundation of [Anishinaabeg] people and government."[14]

In our treaty with manoomin, we are to care for and respect manoomin, which will ensure it grows in abundance. In return, manoomin will care for the Anishinaabeg and be a plentiful source of nourishment for our bodies. Throughout many hard winters, manoomin has sustained our people, making sure we did not starve. When I speak with my grandfather, he reminds me of the spiritual responsibilities we carry: "It's a spiritual food. It was given to us from the Creator. We have to take care of it. Watch over it. You have to keep manoomin in good water and in good soil. You have to keep it healthy. It is alive. That's your responsibility because if you don't, it won't look after you."[15] Our treaty with manoomin is based on respect, care, reciprocity, and interdependence.

When we situate the relationship within an Anishinaabeg treaty frame-work, there is a re-emergence of Anishinaabe philosophy that recognizes the interconnectedness between our spiritual and political practices. From an Anishinaabe perspective, treaty is a living relationship, as is my relationship with my grandpa, as is my relationship with manoomin. So, if you do not take care of it, how good is that relationship going to be? This is what our teachings tell us.[16]

Nindinawemaa. I Am Related.

Yes, Anishinaabeg's relationship to manoomin is one of treaty. Like I said earlier, it is many things. I have also come to understand my relationship with manoomin as a birthright I inherited being Anishinaabe, a birthright meaning that manoomin is a relation of mine—a relative. My grandfather reminds me every year during harvesting season, that when we are with manoomin, it is "not work": "We have to take care of it. Watch over it. To me, it isn't work. It isn't a job. If I thought about it as work, I probably wouldn't do it or enjoy it. I just love doing it. I love doing it." It took me years to understand what the old man was communicating to me. It finally occurred to me that waking up and realizing that manoomin is our relative, someone we care for and cares for us, is the only way harvesting manoomin is not conceptualized as work. When we know manoomin as our relative, part of our kinship relations, we can see our caring as our responsibility that is linked to our own wellness. This is similar to how mothers care for their children or how any of us care for those we love. Our care ensures a collective well-being. Reciprocity. When those we care for are well, we are well.

I also have agency, as does manoomin, which brings about the normal ebb and flow of relations. Despite what the practice of agency may look like in our relationship, at any given time, what remains consistent is this—the teachings manoomin carries is medicine that can help me navigate life at any given time, and this was determined a long time ago. The migration story of the Anishinaabe and our language, Anishinaabemowin, let me know how deep, far back, and significant this relationship is and how it was brought into existence for me, hundreds of years before my human birth.

In the Seven Fires Prophecy of the Anishinaabeg, the story of the great migration of our Nation, from east to west, is told. Our ancestors were told by the prophets, who came to visit, that they were to keep travelling west until they came to the place where the food grows on the water.[17] Manoomin is "the sacred gift of their chosen ground."[18] It is estimated that the migration of the Anishinaabe took five hundred years to complete, spanning generations and vast distances. The beginning of the migration story and the instructions that were provided to my ancestors let me know that my relationship with manoomin was a long time in the making. Before my existence, this relationship was already thought about for me, and my ancestors helped bring it forward. My grandfather, playing a vital role, reminds me of these careful thoughts and purposeful, loving acts, that we must continue:

JY: Our migration story talks about manoomin. It got me thinking about how we, too, are part of that story—the migration story.

WY: Yes, because it goes way back. Way back. See, somebody was thinking about you a long time ago and here, we are, thinking of someone again. [Manoomin] will keep going forward. It won't die. It's a big picture.

Nimishomis Minowaa Niin. My Grandfather and I.

My grandfather was fifteen years old when he began to search for answers, as he puts it, with manoomin. As I write this, he is eighty-two years old. That is sixty-seven years of knowledge and experience he carries with manoomin. He is forty years my elder.

> *JY: What do you remember about our relationship before manoomin?*
>
> WY: I don't remember much. Very little about any conversations with you.
>
> *JY: That makes sense that you don't remember too much because remember when I came to see you that day and we sat on the blanket and talked for a long time.*
>
> WY: Yeah.
>
> *JY: I said I wanted to know you. Know about your life. That you were my grandpa and I didn't know you and I suspected it was because of stuff with Residential Schools.*
>
> WY: Yeah.
>
> *JY: We didn't have too many interactions before then.*
>
> WY: No, we didn't. And it was kind of a shock for me that you wanted to know who I was because no one asked me that before.

That day we sat on the blanket and talked was the beginning of a new relationship for my grandpa and me. I had called him two weeks prior and told him I was coming home from the city and asked if I could speak with him. He asked if it was serious. I told him yes.

Treaty and Mushkiki

When I got to his house that day, he was on the phone. I overheard him saying, "My oldest granddaughter is here. She never comes over. I have to go." When he hung up the phone, he told me to wait. When he returned a few minutes later, he led me upstairs, where he had a blanket laid on the floor, his feather out, and his medicines so we could smudge. My grandpa told me he had been praying the last two weeks, preparing for our visit, and that he hoped he could understand me.

When he handed me the feather, I was shaking and holding back tears. I admitted that I felt as though I did not know him and suspected it was because of Residential Schools. I told him that I cared about what happened to him in there and wondered aloud where I had learned that it was not okay for me to speak about Residential Schools, let alone acknowledge that he spent nine years of his life there, from five to fifteen years old. I told him that as long as he was still here, I did not want us to miss out on each other. He shared so much about his life with me that day. We cried, hugged, and laughed. From that day forward, I took every chance I could to visit with him at the fire, as he prepared manoomin, and I learned more about the three of us.

JY: *From that time, I came and saw you that day, and asked you about your life and wanting to know you more, manoomin has been really present in our relationship. What role do you see manoomin has played in your relationship with me?*

WY: *Smiles* That part of manoomin, was me, from a long time ago. I was a kid when I went out there with my mom and dad, in the canoe, and helping them when they went and harvested—when they made manoomin—our food. I was still in Residential School. I saw a lot of things out there, from the Elders, from the people that were around there, and my mom and dad. I saw a lot of things I didn't understand. I was confused that there was something wrong. I didn't know because all these things that they were doing out there, before they did anything, was through a ceremony. . . . It was very confusing because I was being brought up in a Residential School where that teaching was the only way and there was no other way. Where if it wasn't done that way, the way that they said in boarding school, it was not good. They didn't tell me "Oh, we are going to do a ceremony now. Come and sit over here and kneel down." Or anything like that when I went to Residential School in their services. You walked in there and you were scared to move or scared to look. You would get a big slap in the head. But it wasn't like that with what I seen here (manoomin fields). They would make the rice. I would dance on it for them. They would give me some. My mom would cook it and eat it. Holy man, it was awesome. I knew I was eating something that was so special. It was alive and it nourished me too. That was my first memories with manoomin. I was young and starting to get a taste of our ways of life. Rather than how they were saying it was in Residential School. How they were saying it was no damn good with our traditional ways.

When my grandfather speaks of manoomin, it is clear he loves the grain. Yet, when he speaks of manoomin, it is never in isolation. He also speaks of his family—his parents who are in the Spirit world, all of us, and our relations to come. He speaks of all the life that is connected to manoomin, that live with manoomin in its home. "The Ojibway narrative tradition is bound to have an attitude of respect toward nature, toward plants and animals and their shared homeland . . . such values, such attitudes, 'make a home of the land' by providing the deeper meaning which attaches to everything."[19] The interconnectedness of Anishinaabe worldview transcends Western boundaries of time, including life and death.

JY: Is part of the medicine of manoomin how it brings us together? Like when we collectively come together—that's the medicine, right?

WY: It is medicine. It is that strong. That is how powerful manoomin is. It's all a gift from the Creator. How can I explain it? To me, sitting with the fire, and seeing you come sit by the fire, you watch for a bit. You watch. You watch. And then, all of a sudden, you take the paddle. You see, by you taking the paddle, it is part of me. And now, you are also taking part. It is all connecting. We come in the circle of life together with manoomin and everything else.

JY: I do see. It is also your mom and dad, grandma and grandpa, when we are roasting.

WY: Yes.

JY: And their mom and dad. And who knows who else.

WY: Yes. That's exactly it! That is the healing and the gift manoomin offers us. And then . . . it goes back to Residential School.

JY: Of what they tried to take?

WY: Yeah. How they tried to cover it up with their things. But manoomin was too powerful because it had to come from mother earth, the water, the sun. It is all the life. You see?

JY: Yes. You are powerful too, Grandpa.

When Anishinaabeg and manoomin come together, liberatory praxes from colonial harms occur because a recentring of Anishinaabeg selves and ways of life are inherently embedded in these living, intimate relationships, carrying endless space for "a return to self-determination and change from within rather than recognition from the outside."[20]

WY: So you go back into, what they call . . . settlers and all that . . .

JY: Which reminds me, Grandpa, I wanted to speak with you about reconciliation and how the government or settler institutions talk about and use the term. Sometimes I think we get too externally focused, say like on what the government says, does, or wants. And what I have found is important is for us to reconcile with ourselves and for us to reconcile with our family.

WY: That's right.

JY: And our ways that have always helped us.

WY: Yes. You shouldn't depend on the government.

JY: *To help us? To fix us?*

WY: Yeah, because they can't. It's ourselves.

JY: *Yeah, like the government couldn't come and fix the distance between us.*

WY: Uhmm hmm. (nods head in agreement).

JY: *Right? But manoomin helped us.*

WY: Yeah. See. That's the teachings and ways of life of who we are. You look at Residential School. It drove me crazy because I was always searching for the answers in the wrong place.

JY: *Gramp, what are the wrong places?*

WY: The wrong places was trying to go out there and sit in their places. In their places of worship and their places of doing things and trying to make connections and it was so frustrating. See?

JY: *Yes. So, if those were the wrong places, what were the right places that you found?*

WY: Our traditional ways of doing things and traditional ways of life and understanding how closely they are connected to everything. And that was awesome. But through that, I could start to understand them too. I went to a lot of services in different denominations. I made a few attempts, but I would always go back to going outside. In the bush. On the lake. I would make my connections there spiritually because there are so many things out there to connect with. Manoomin would always come back to me. I think of all the things I have learned and the things my family has learned from it. And how it brought us closer together.

JY: *So I guess when they talk about being a good relative, manoomin teaches us how we are connected to everything because it is the water, all the animals that live with manoomin, the sun, the wind, fire. Even how we make it, I see so much teamwork. We got to work together.*

WY: Manoomin set me free to be me and with the little bit I have and the little bit that I learned, I pass it on. I thought I never would be sitting here with my granddaughter talking about traditional ways of life, when I couldn't even say I was human or an Anishinaabe person. They always referred to me as a savage, a pagan, and a devil worshipper. So that's the healing part you see that helped me. When I think of what I started to pick up in life—of manoomin and how far it has come for me. I hope as a family, we can continue to move it forward so it will be there for those in the future. What they tried to do to me in that school for eight or nine years, you can't shut me up anymore, when it comes to Anishinaabe—manoomin—how it is made and how it is for us. It brought me a long ways, Jana. And I hope it does for you too. Someday when you are eighty years old and sitting by the fire, you will think, that old man is still sitting here with me.

JY: Do you ever get worried about our relationship with manoomin? Is it like other relationships, where it ebbs and flows? Where it may appear to weaken and get strong again?

WY: Yeah. That's where the connection comes in with spirituality. You have to have good things within you. And you always think that over time, that cycle will end. Manoomin will come here and there again. All the sudden, the fields will be just full and that manoomin will be hanging again just like how I used to see them when I was younger.

Reflections For Now

One of the most prolific feminist intellectuals, bell hooks, wrote of her desire to find a meeting place for theory, politics, and spiritual practice.[21] Manoomin exists at the intersection of the personal is political, and the political is personal, encapsulating education, politics, and spiritual governance through the Anishinaabeg worldview. These intimate webs of relationships, when activated, allow us to become part of the sophisticated systems of knowledge that motivated and sustained our ancestors for hundreds of years.[22]

When my grandfather Willie reflects on his early years of relationship building with manoomin, and his search for answers, I relate. I, too, was searching for answers when I went to sit with him by the fire, as he roasted the grain. I did not know what questions I was seeking answers to or what answers would come. What I found is love. And for Anishinaabeg, living under settler-colonial occupation, love is liberatory.

Treaty and Mushkiki

dear manoomin

you know how sometimes you don't see people right away? where it takes you a while to notice them. this is what it was like for me with you. i heard you always brought us together. i don't know how far this goes back but i know it is long before i took my first breath. yes, it's true i have been around you my whole life. just like my ancestors before me. but it took me a while to truly see you. to appreciate you. i feel embarrassed to admit that. i'm sorry. even though i know you carry no hard feelings toward me.

you are forgiving, humble, patient, generous and oh, so strong. our relationship, though, caught me completely off guard. and yet, i am so glad we are here today. to be honest, it wasn't even you that i wanted to get to know. i wanted to get to know the old man who was always spending time with you. he and i became disconnected much like how many of us became disconnected from you. this old man. he sure loves you. he is a big reason i fell in love with you too.

i learned about respect by watching you both together. i see how deeply he honours you in all the steps he takes to care for you. when he picks you. when he lays you down. when he turns you over. when he brings you water. when he covers you up. when he cleans you. how he wakes when the sun rises to greet you. how he remains with you until the sun goes down. how he waits patiently, from year to year, praying during those in between moments, till you are ready to reconnect again the following year.

he pays great attention to you for when you are ready to come home with us. because he knows it is poplar wood you prefer, he chops it, knowing it provides the perfect heat you like. he takes such good care of you. and you, in return, care for all of us. anishinaabeg.

i need to tell you that he is always so patient with me. but he is especially patient when he is teaching me about you. i am beginning to wonder if it is you that taught him patience during all those countless hours he sat with you by the fire. probably. miigwech for that.

so, by the fire i sat. beside him. wanting my relationship with him to grow. while he worked with you. unaware that not only would my relationship with him grow stronger. my relationship with you would evolve. through it all, i would be transformed. miigwech for that too.

like the flames that help you to become ready to nourish our bodies, the love burns in my heart for you, ever so strong, manoomin. always.

love jana

FIGURE 23: Jana-Rae Yerxa with her grandfather Pikanagegaabo William (Willie) Yerxa. Photograph by Jana-Rae Yerxa, 2015.

FIGURE 24: A Gift from the Creator. In this image, Elder Guy Henry holds Manomin seeds in his hand. Each seed reminds us that the ancestors prepared for our arrival. They harvested Manomin and reseeded the fields so that we might eat well today. It is our responsibility to care for Manomin and, by so doing, feed the next generation. We are born future-makers. Photograph by Jane Mariotti, 15 August 2023.

9

Promise[1]

by Kristi Leora Gansworth

For the Anishinaabeg Who Will Come to This Earth:

Being Anishinaabe is a beautiful gift. I am sharing today as a matter of responsibility and meegwaywin, gift-giving. There are also times of hardship and darkness in life. I know this intimately; many times, as a young person, I struggled. At times, my path got so messy and hopeless that I thought ceaselessly about death and even tried to end my own life. Days of accumulated time were spent reliving the mistakes I had made, berating myself, convincing myself of my own uselessness, drowning in misery. I was enveloped in consistent self-hatred and the powerlessness that comes from the many after-effects of grief. In one way, these are elements of genocidal assimilation targeting the self-perception of my ancestors and relatives. I came to live as if pieces of my spirit had been taken away and replaced with foreign behaviours, thoughts, and beliefs. At the time, I did not know that powerlessness had a source, structure, or name—all I knew was that it would come to me that I should hate myself. I was a horrible person. Life would not get better. This was the way it was.

I could go on and on describing this. Streaks of painful memory and the raised skin of bleak scars document those times. That life feels distantly related to me now, a fleeting memory that comes and goes, not an absolute truth. Recalling the presence of that person feels like a trip to the boundaries of our planet, a thick force of pressure pushing my body to the edge of the troposphere where humans can no longer breathe.

But today, I breathe. Perhaps the entire span of one's life can be spent trying to learn this basic and yet powerful action: to breathe. For today, I have survived the days where I could not. It may be unlikely in some respects if you begin to trace the streams through which my blood, and perhaps your blood, flows and moves through time. The disruptions and threats to that flow are well documented in our interactions with powers that have invaded our homes, our stories, and our generations. Being here today is a testimony, asserting the right to walk in the footsteps and places of my ancestors, the ones who watched for the integrity of the land in a way that humans cannot do alone.

It may have been that I did not make it here, that we would not be here now, that the deaths we have experienced were more than metaphors. It is by and for those ancestors that I am still here and write to you now, from this voice, from this concrete, from overgrown towers, from our dispossession manifest.

After all that has been enacted to destroy all that is Anishinaabe, this existence is a miracle. Your existence is a miracle. Please know that. Please know how valued you are. Please know yourself in a way other than what is written about you in some of the books and films and other materials you will encounter in the worlds that want to take from you but do not acknowledge the truth of you. Know that your words and your heart are stronger than even you can know yourself until you use them fully. Call upon your ancestors who will come to help you when you ask, and are present even when you do not.

Understand that a long time ago your life occurred as a thought. You were thought of, you were seen—and all that you would need, all that you would become, all that you would suffer was poured into a single moment of birth. That moment became everything that you are now. You have everything you need to experience the fullness of human experience, and you will never be without the guidance of those who dreamt you into life.

In the place where we come from, time does not sound like the accumulation of dollars and churning engines. Time exists more accurately as shared love that pours from Elders, grandparents, uncles, aunties—those who are human and those who are not. They remind us that the land is our ancestor, too. Because of the love that flourishes from this understanding, you will not be left alone.

Those who came before you put their memories into this Earth and thought of you as they made delicate steps and preparations, as they learned how to live. They stood up to the ones who knew only how to destroy, the ones who only knew to hurt and bring more harm into the world. They knew what you would encounter because they encountered danger themselves; they knew this walk; they knew all that we know and all that we become when we walk this trail of human existence.

And there are ways that it seems like you have been separated from your relatives: the life spirit of the waters, the food and medicine and berries that support your healing, the sway of ancient trees, which are libraries for all of our kin. From fur and scale to feather and branch, intertwined powers work together each day, constantly renewing this life that you belong to. As you exist, so do they; there is no separation.

At times, the pain of walking with the Earth becomes the only sound, the only sight, the only feeling that is real. It seems that pain is all there is, even when the sun brings a beginning that has not happened before and will never happen again in exactly the same way.

In this place, sometimes things look different from how we remember them or think they should be. In this place, we have entered a time when each of us is made to believe it is possible to walk alone. It is at this time when the ones with sharp, violent, contorted thoughts are the strongest. At this time, you can look at yourself and believe you did something wrong. You can look at yourself and believe that somehow you are deserving of punishment and blame. Those contorted thoughts are the energies that will try to take from you and pull you from the protection of beauty and grace, which is the truth of who you are.

No matter the obstacle—no matter—you have a purpose. You have a light that cannot be extinguished until your purposes on this Earth are fulfilled. No assimilations can take this from you; no human cruelties can dilute the essence of your being, your so-divine being. No one has seen, no one has had the best of you yet. Do not give up. As each dawn arrives, you walk in the light of new beginnings. Listen, hear the flowers as they sing for you. As you put one foot in front of the other and share gifts that only you can bring to life, you fulfill the vision of all the ones who came before and those who are quietly walking behind.

As for those of us who are already on this Earth, may we have something to offer. May we respect your dreams and wishes, and may we heal beyond our own injuries and pain in order to be the support and nourishment that you need.

Epilogue

by Andrea Bradford and Brittany Luby

Every organism—from microscopic bacterium to towering trees—emerges from and returns to the earth. The circles of humans, other beings, and Manomin intersect and influence one another. It is our responsibility to observe and decipher signs from the plant and animal kingdoms. They can teach us how to live well in this world. They can also warn us when our environment is under threat.

Manomin teaches us about the relationships with the other forms of creation that it interacts with. Bacteria, invisible to the human eye, degrade organic compounds—including Manomin leaves and stalks from previous years—and help to recycle nutrients, enriching the soil to support future Manomin growth. Manomin seeds who germinate in this carefully catered soil must possess enough stored energy to reach the sun as seedlings. Water that is too deep or other plants that intercept the sunlight can stop Manomin in its path. Seedlings that reach the sunlight pass into the floating-leaf stage, with ribbons spreading across the water's surface before stems emerge from the water and extend upward.

Animals like muskrat live among Manomin, using the plant for shelter and food. Rice worms eat the maturing crop, and waterfowl feed on Manomin and worms. There is a limit to the number of beings that

Manomin can sustain, but Manomin also relies on others to help the wind pollinate its flowers, spread its seeds to promote natural diversity, and provide other sustenance for species that it cannot sustain on its own. When Anishinaabeg harvest Manomin by canoe, they also contribute to its well-being. Human beings gently knock seed into soil crafted by microscopic organisms, allowing for regrowth. And, so it is that every creature—no matter how big or how small—influences the cycle of life.

While Anishinaabeg have cared for ancestral Manomin fields for many generations, they have not had sufficient opportunity to share their knowledge and influence the activities of settler-colonists that threaten the spirit berry. If you tend to the fields, you will observe that Manomin is susceptible to rapid fluctuations in water levels due to dam operations and other human activities—rising levels can uproot plants, and falling levels can topple the tall stems. Declining yields throughout Anishinaabe-Aki demand we take notice.

Manomin teaches us how we can provide care. We need to listen with ears, eyes, and heart and act in ways that respect the many gifts this being offers. May you use these teachings to feed a generation that will sustain our connections.

A Note on Copyright, Rights Reversion, and Indigenous Language Rights

by Brittany Luby and Jill McConkey

Elder Clarence Henry entrusted the editors of this anthology to carry Manomin teachings to publication. The Manomin Advisory Committee at Niisaachewan Anishinaabe Nation set conditions under which we could publish, requiring active negotiation with Canadian scholarly presses, including our partner, the University of Manitoba Press (UMP). We understood that any contract we signed could affirm or erode Indigenous Rights.

Until 1996, few Canadians were compelled to think about Indigenous representation (or lack thereof) in the publishing industry. Then, the Royal Commission on Aboriginal Peoples reported that "the emergence of a distinct Aboriginal literature has not, unfortunately, been met with much openness by Canadian publishing houses."[1] Thirty years later, Indigenous literature is flourishing, though there are still too few Indigenous-run publishers. In the wake of the Truth and Reconciliation Commission and commitments to reconciliation, Indigenous-authored books are now regularly featured on bestseller lists. But, while publishers have responded to these market trends, the industry has been less than eager to engage with Indigenous authors' key messages of decolonization and to reflect on publishing's long history of contributing to and sustaining settler colonialism, white supremacy, and Indigenous dispossession.[2] Without systemic change to publisher precedents and practices, Indigenous authors and allies will continue to encounter barriers to publishing their work in ways that meet their own and their community's cultural, social, and economic needs and priorities. Despite the clear demand for their work, Indigenous authors and allies may rightly remain wary of the traditional models of publication and dissemination.

For Indigenous authors and allies today, there is pressure to forfeit their intellectual property for job security. To quote Ms. Mentor, "a newly hired Wally at a research university has five or six years to get his first book published. If he fails, he's unlikely to get tenure, which means that he's fired."[3] The adage "publish or perish" has its own Wikipedia page, where readers learn that "in popular academic perception, scholars who publish infrequently . . . may lose ground in competition for available tenure-track positions."[4] Literature intended to help junior scholars navigate their careers generally focuses on how to identify potential publishers and how to pitch your research. Unfortunately, little information about the publishing process—beyond the incentive to secure a book contract—is available. Few academics are taught how to negotiate the terms of their book contracts or how to navigate and influence the editorial, production, and marketing processes that follow, focusing instead on securing their position on campus. This Note identifies a few key clauses in our contract for *Manomin: Caring for Ecosystems and Each Other* that we negotiated to help affirm Indigenous Rights. Our goal is to create precedent that others can cite to help decolonize Canadian scholarly publishing.

COPYRIGHT

It is common for scholarly presses to assert copyright over the books they publish. Originally developed to regulate and protect the publishing industry, copyright is traditionally assigned to publishers, securing their sole right to the publication in its various forms to protect both press and author against competing unlicensed editions in Canada and abroad.[5] Today, copyright is also understood to constitute the exclusive rights of the author or creator. While authors retain moral rights to their work, they may be asked to assign copyright to their publisher (or required to as a condition of publication should negotiations fail), ceding authority for their work to the press. Since a book contract also includes the author's licence of rights to the publisher to determine the most appropriate format and price at which to produce and sell their work, a publisher's assumption of copyright may be less a matter of cost-recovery and legal protection than a hangover of centuries-old tradition. As a declaration of ownership and control, it is worth asking what that really means in an era of reconciliation and restoration of Indigenous knowledges threatened by colonialism.

In 2021, the United Nations Declaration on the Rights of Indigenous Peoples Act received Royal Assent in what is colonially known as Canada. Section 5 of the UNDRIP Act demands that "all measures necessary [are taken] to ensure that the laws of Canada are consistent with the Declaration." Although there are laws to ensure contracts are fairly executed in Canada, publishers are not legally required to uphold UNDRIP. Thus, Indigenous academics and allies can still be expected to consent to the transfer of intellectual property, normalizing industry standards that ignore (at best) or reject (at worst) UNDRIP as a "framework for reconciliation, healing and peace."[6]

We reason that the tradition of vesting copyright with the publisher runs counter to Article 31.1 of UNDRIP, which clearly states that Indigenous

Peoples "have the right to maintain, control, protect and develop their intellectual property over [their] cultural heritage, traditional knowledge, and traditional cultural expressions."[7] When deciding on a publisher, we sought to negotiate a contract for this book that clearly recognized and respected the authors' authority over their intellectual and cultural property.

At no point did the University of Manitoba Press request copyright. Their offer, to which we consented, was as follows: "You grant an exclusive licence to the Press, during the term of copyright, for the full and exclusive right to publish, print, record, distribute (including online or in print) and sell this work, or to cause it to be published, printed, recorded, performed, distributed (including online or in print), or sold, throughout the world, in the English and French languages and in all forms, editions, and formats." The Press further agreed to register copyright in our names, which was key to our decision to publish with them. Under these terms, each author retains control of and moral rights to their intellectual property while authorizing the Press to produce and disseminate the work under agreed-upon terms detailed in subsequent clauses. In sum, our contract sets out respective rights and responsibilities that protect the interests of the press, our contributors, and our communities.

Such an agreement recognizes a collaborative relationship between author and publisher based on trust and reciprocity, rather than a property transaction based on ownership and control. We are trusting UMP to circulate our knowledge in a good way. UMP is trusting that we will allow them to market and manage sales of our book for a fee (i.e., a percentage of the sales). We are partners in this publishing relationship, wherein we each commit our experience and resources to share the knowledge given to us in our work with the Manomin Project while respecting the origins of that knowledge and rejecting a colonial history of extraction and dispossession.

Rights Reversion

Sometimes books do not sell as hoped. They can also fall into disuse over time. For this reason, it can be helpful to negotiate the reversion of your rights (e.g., "publish, print, record, distribute") should your publisher stop investing in what may seem to be a "failed" product. If you negotiate a rights reversion clause, you will want to ensure it is timebound. You will also want to clearly spell out any definition of "out of print." It is important to clarify questions like, "Is an audiobook considered print?" If you set conditions under which the publisher's license expires, you retain the power to find an alternate publishing partner (if desired) or to recirculate the material in a format of your choosing. UMP and the Manomin Project consented to the following:

> If, three years or longer after first publication, we [UMP] decide that sales do not warrant continued publication of the work, we may declare it out of print. . . . At that time, you may terminate this agreement and require us, in writing, to return to you all rights granted to us under this agreement, with the exceptions noted below.
>
> You may also so terminate the agreement if we fail to keep the work in print and if we do not, within three months of receiving a written request from you, undertake to issue a new printing within a further nine months or to license a new printing to appear in that time.
>
> (The work will be considered "in print" as long as copies are available from us or our licensee for sale through normal retail and wholesale channels in a hardback or paperback version and we have cumulatively sold at least 20 copies of the work in print or electronic form in the two consecutive periods immediately preceding the date you could elect to send a termination notice under this provision.)

On termination of this agreement, all rights to the work will revert to you, except that we shall have the right to sell any bound copies or sheets remaining in our hands. Also, any licences previously granted by us will continue in effect and royalties from them will continue to be collected by us and shared with you in accordance with the terms of this agreement.

Language Rights

To bring our contract further into alignment with UNDRIP, we negotiated to retain Indigenous Language Rights in addition to rights reversion. This clause ensures that each contributor (who retains copyright) can circulate their traditional knowledge in their ancestral tongue on their own terms. Permission to do so is not required from the editors or the press. Our contract reads: "In accordance with the United Nations Declaration on the Rights of Indigenous Peoples, we [UMP] recognize and affirm the authors' right to retain Indigenous language rights for this work." Retaining Indigenous Language Rights empowers our authors to share their work in the language of the communities from which their knowledge originated, to safeguard and protect language as an Indigenous Right, and to contribute to language revitalization efforts. The ability to build on community connections and respond to community needs with full control over how Indigenous knowledge and language is presented, shared, and used is especially important, as many academic presses do not have the staff or resources to produce Indigenous language translations.

Translation is a costly venture, and the markets for Indigenous language books are still relatively small. Yet, the production of Indigenous knowledge in its original language is essential to repairing the harms of its suppression in Canadian schools, courtrooms, and seats of government. Official recognition of Indigenous Language Rights in Canada has been slow, however. Just this week, as we finalized this text for typesetting, NDP MPP Sol Mamakwa delivered a "history-making speech" in Oji-Cree—the first time an Indigenous language was recognized by the Ontario legislature.[8] In academia, 2024 is the first year that the Federation for the Humanities and Social Sciences has designated funding to assist with Indigenous language translation for just one title per year.[9] The $12,000 grant, announced in April 2023, would cover about half the cost of translation. Where a publisher might not be able to afford to translate and publish on a large enough scale to recoup production costs, individual authors and community members working on a smaller scale could succeed.

Depending on the limited resources and language speakers in Indigenous communities is, however, not a sustainable option, and we remind readers of the Truth and Reconciliation Commission's Calls to Action regarding language and culture, specifically Call #14 for an Aboriginal Languages Act that incorporates the following principles:

i. Aboriginal languages are a fundamental and valued element of Canadian culture and society, and there is an urgency to preserve them.

ii. Aboriginal language rights are reinforced by the Treaties.

iii. The federal government has a responsibility to provide sufficient funds for Aboriginal-language revitalization and preservation.

iv. The preservation, revitalization, and strengthening of Aboriginal languages and cultures are best managed by Aboriginal people and communities.

v. Funding for Aboriginal language initiatives must reflect the diversity of Aboriginal languages.

As Sol Mamakwa affirmed this week, "language is identity."[10] Given the dismal record in both publishing and academia of excluding, appropriating, and misrepresenting Indigenous knowledge, it is incumbent on university presses especially to reflect on and rectify traditional publishing practices—like assuming copyright over an author's work or insisting on language rights they may never exercise—that sustain a model of colonial extraction, in many cases contrary to express commitments to recognition of Indigenous Rights, treaty relationships, and reconciliation.

A book contract is the basis for your relationship with your publisher, a partnership you have a role in shaping. If you require precedent to protect such rights for yourself or your allies, this document is yours to cite. If you require support interpreting your contract and finances allow, you can retain a copyright or intellectual property lawyer to advocate for you. Whether you have professional support or not, it is important to read the terms of your contract carefully, to ask the publisher to explain any clauses you don't understand, and to be aware of your rights and responsibilities as author. This is not legal advice. It is the last gift we can offer you here: precedent.

NOTES

A Note on Language

1   James D. Mauseth, "Introduction to Plants and Botany," *Botany: An Introduction to Plant Biology* (Burlington, MA: Jones and Bartlett Learning, 2017), 10.

2   Stefano Mancuso and Alessandra Viola, *Brilliant Green: The Surprising History and Science of Plant Intelligence* (Washington, DC: Island Press, 2015), 13.

3   Mancuso and Viola, *Brilliant Green*, 9–10.

4   Mancuso and Viola, *Brilliant Green*, 2.

5   Robin Wall Kimmerer, *The Intelligence in All Kinds of Life*, interviewed by NPR, *On Being,* YouTube video, 23 September 2019, https://www.youtube.com/watch?time_continue=1061&v=2YuB1iU6DQI&feature=emb_log.

6   Robin Wall Kimmerer, "Returning the Gift," *Minding Nature* 7, no. 2 (2014): 21.

7   Robin Wall Kimmerer, "Robin Wall Kimmerer: The Intelligence of Plants," 25 February 2016, in *On Being with Krista Tippett*, produced by The On Being Project, podcast, https://onbeing.org/programs/robin-wall-kimmerer-the-intelligence-of-plants-2022/.

8   Kimmerer, "Robin Wall Kimmerer: The Intelligence of Plants."

9   *The Ojibwe People's Dictionary*, s.v. "gi= (pf)," accessed 22 April 2024, https://ojibwe.lib.umn.edu/main-entry/gi-pf.

10   Erin Allen, "How Did America Get Its Name," Library of Congress Blog, 4 July 2016, https://blogs.loc.gov/loc/2016/07/how-did-america-get-its-name/.

11   Amanda Robinson, "Turtle Island," *The Canadian Encyclopedia*, 6 November 2018, https://www.thecanadianencyclopedia.ca/en/article/turtle-island.

12 Patrick Wolfe, "Settler Colonialism and the Elimination of the Native," *Journal of Genocide Research* 8, no. 4 (2006): 387–409, https://doi.org/10.1080/14623520601056240.

13 Lorenzo Veracini, "Understanding Colonialism and Settler Colonialism as Distinct Formations," *interventions* 16, no. 5 (2014): 626, https://doi.org/10.1080/1369801X.2013.858983.

Introduction

1 O.W. Archibold, "Wild Rice," in *Encyclopedia of Food Science and Nutrition*, eds. Benjamin Caballero, Luiz Trugo, and Paul M. Finglas, 2nd ed. (Cambridge, MA: Academic Press, 2003), 6183–89; E.A. Oelke et al., *Wild Rice Production in Minnesota* (Minneapolis: University of Minnesota, 1982), 6; William G. Dore, *Wild-rice* (Ottawa: The Queen's Printer for Canada, 1969), 20.

2 Elder Clarence Henry Jr., interview with Brittany Luby and Josh Rognvaldson, 22 June 2021, Manomin Project NAN Elder Interviews.

3 Canada, *Indian Act*, R.S.C. 1952, c. 149, s. 115.

4 Canada, *Indian Act*, R.S.C. 1952, c. 149, s. 118(3).

5 Although subject to climatic variations, Hard Red Winter Wheat is generally harvested toward the southeast of Anishinaabe-Aki (e.g., what is currently known as Minnesota) in July. Hard Red Spring Wheat, which is more common in the southwest of Anishinaabe-Aki (e.g., what is currently known as North Dakota), tends to be harvested in early to mid-August (U.S. Wheat Associates, "U.S. Wheat," n.d., https://wheatworld.org/wp-content/uploads/2016/12/usw-the-worlds-most-reliable-choice.pdf). Within what is currently known as Ontario, Anishinaabe children were forced to begin Residential School in September. Elder Danny Strong of Niisaachewan Anishinaabe Nation indicated school began in the first week of September (Elder Danny Strong, interview with Brittany Luby and translator Barry Henry, Niisaachewan Anishinaabe Nation, 21 August 2018). Federal administrators demanded Indigenous children begin Residential School elsewhere in Canada throughout the early to mid-20th century. Principal Nicholas Coccola, who oversaw an industrial school at Cranbrook, British Columbia, "complained of having spent the month of September [1922] 'collecting children from different camps from the school'" (Truth and Reconciliation Commission of Canada [TRC], "Canada's Residential Schools: The History, Part 1, Origins to 1939" [final report, Montreal-Kingston, 2015], 276). In the 1930s, John Gambler risked criminal persecution under the Indian Act from Indian Agent N.P. L'Heureux if he refused to send his children to Residential School in Desmarais, Alberta, by 1 September (TRC, "Canada's Residential Schools: The History, Part 1," 286–87). Isabella Knockwood,

who attended Residential School at Shubenacadie, Nova Scotia, testified that her first day began on 1 September 1936 ("Canada's Residential Schools: The History, Part 1," 193).

6   A.B. Campbell, "Wheat," *The Canadian Encyclopedia*, last modified 4 March 2015, https://www.thecanadianencyclopedia.ca/en/article/wheat.

7   John Douglas Belshaw, "Building the Wheat Economy in Upper Canada," in *Canadian History: Pre-Confederation* (Victoria: BCcampus Open Education, 2015), https://opentextbc.ca/preconfederation/chapter/9-5-building-the-wheat-economy-in-upper-canada/.

8   Eli Yarhi and T.D. Regehr, "Dominion Lands Act," *The Canadian Encyclopedia*, last modified 30 January 2020, https://www.thecanadianencyclopedia.ca/en/article/dominion-lands-policy.

9   Brittany Luby, "Treaty through a Planting Lens: A Study of Manoomin Harvesting Rights in Anishinaabe-Aki, 1873—Present," *American Indian Quarterly* 47, no. 4 (2023): 370–73; Canada, *Indian Act*, S.C. 1876, s. 11.

10   Luby, "Treaty through a Planting Lens," 370–73.

11   Taylor A. Steeves, "Wild Rice: Indian Food and a Modern Delicacy," *Economic Botany* 6, no. 2 (1952): 108. While it is now commonly accepted that *Zizania palustris* and *Zizania aquatica* are distinct species, up until and throughout most of the twentieth century, there were discrepancies in the taxonomic classification of *Zizania*. See Suzanne I. Warwick and Susan G. Aiken, "Electrophoretic Evidence for the Recognition of Two Species in Annual Wild Rice (*Zizania*, Poaceae)," *Systematic Botany* 11 no. 3 (1986): 464, https://doi.org/10.2307/2419083; R.L. Counts and P.F. Lee, "Patterns of Variation in Ontario Wild Rice (*Zizania aquatica* L.) 1. The Influence of Some Climatic Factors on the Differentiation of Populations," *Aquatic Botany* 28, no. 3–4 (1987): 373–92, https://doi.org/10.1016/0304-3770(87)90012-X.

12   Steeves, "Wild Rice," 127.

13   Ann Garibaldi and Nancy Turner, "Cultural Keystone Species: Implications for Ecological Conservation and Restoration," *Ecology and Society* 9, no. 3, http://www.ecologyandsociety.org/vol9/iss3/art1/.

14   Sarah Carter, *Lost Harvests: Prairie Indian Reserve Farmers and Government Policy* (Montreal: McGill-Queen's University Press, 1990), 21.

15   Carter, *Lost Harvests*, 16, 19, 21; Roxanna Dunbar-Ortiz and Dina Gilio-Whitaker, "Europeans Brought Civilization to the Backward Indians," in *"All the Real Indians Died Off": And 20 Other Myths About Native Americans* (Boston: Beacon Press, 2016), 52.

16 Dunbar-Ortiz and Gilio-Whitaker, "Europeans Brought Civilization to the Backward Indians," 52, 55; Paul Jentz, "Uncivilized and Unwanted: The Myth of the Ignoble Savage," in *Seven Myths of Native American History,* eds. Alfred J. Andrea and Andrew Holt (Indianapolis: Hackett Publishing Company, 2018), 23; Carter, *Lost Harvests,* 19.

17 Canada, Parliament, Sessional Papers [CSP], 1877, paper no. 11. Department of the Interior, "Annual Report of the Year ended 30th June, 1876," xiv.

18 Ron (Deganadus) McLester, "Seven Generations," Algonquin College, 15 June 2017, YouTube, 2:35, https://www.youtube.com/watch?v=PI-QMcXrMsY&ab_channel=AcademicAlgonquin.

19 Thomas Peacock and Marlene Wisuri, *The Four Hills of Life: Ojibwe Wisdom* (St. Paul: Minnesota Historical Society, 2011), 105.

20 Ogichidaa Francis Kavanaugh, "Receiving and Giving Gifts," Grand Council Treaty #3, YouTube, 26 June 2020, https://www.youtube.com/watch?v=zQAUKU7fzEw.

21 Peacock and Wisuri, *The Four Hills of Life,* 113.

22 Peacock and Wisuri, 113.

23 Elder Edward Benton-Banai, of Lac Courte Oreilles Band of Lake Superior Chippewa Indians, was from northern Wisconsin. This chapter is an excerpt from his longer book of teachings called *The Mishomis Book: The Voice of the Ojibway* (Minneapolis: University of Minnesota Press with Indian Country Communications, 1988). Other public variants of the migration story include: "A Ojibway Migration Story: Chief Deborah Smith & Elder William Ballantyne of Brokenhead Ojibway First Nation," YouTube, 2021; Michael Lyons, "The Story of the Ojibwe Migration," YouTube, 2018; William Warren, *History of the Ojibway People, based upon traditional and oral statements* (1885; St. Paul, MN: Minnesota Historical Society, 1984), 77–81; George Copway, *The Life, History, and Travels, of Kah-ge-ga-gah-bow (George Copway), A Young Indian Chief of the Ojebwa Nation, A Convert to the Christian Faith, and a Missionary to His People for Twelve Years* (Albany, NY: Weed and Parsons, 1847), 55–58.

Chapter 1: Manito Gitigaan, the Great Spirit's Garden

1 Eleanor Skead, the daughter of the late Doug Skead, gave her permission to share his teachings from the 1970s for this publication and gave the correct spelling of his Anishinaabe name. The detailed descriptions in each of the six seasons and Anishinaabe spellings are by Kezhii'aanakwat Ron Kelly and other knowledge keepers of Onigaming.

2 Grand Council Treaty #3 and Treaty and Aboriginal Rights Research (TARR) Centre, *"We Have Kept Our Part of the Treaty": The Anishinaabe Understanding of Treaty #3* (Kenora, ON: Grand Council Treaty #3, 2011), 23. In brief, Anishinaabeg have never accepted the history written by Alexander Morris, Treaty Commissioner for the Crown, as it is only in his book and the pre-written 1872 version of Treaty #3 that lands are said to have been "ceded" to the Crown. Indeed, it is not in the Anishinaabe oral tradition to conceive of "selling Mother Earth." Cession does not appear in the terms of the Paypom Treaty, nor in the Métis interpreter's notes of 1873, nor even in the reports of the Winnipeg journalist attending the several days of final negotiations in 1873.

3 Amanda Raster and Christina Gish Hill, "The Dispute Over Wild Rice: An Investigation of Treaty Agreements and Ojibwe Food Sovereignty," *Agriculture and Human Values* 34, no. 2 (2017): 271, https://doi.org/10.1007/s10460-016-9703-6.

4 The authors are forever grateful to Dr. Leroy Little Bear, Professor Emeritus, Lethbridge University, for his naming of the way the Government of Canada used Treaties as if they were "proof-of-purchase" of the land, rather than Nation-with-Nation sharing agreements that Anishinaabeg believed necessary for their future and continued way of life.

5 National Inquiry into Missing and Murdered Indigenous Women and Girls, *Reclaiming Power and Place: The Final Report of the National Inquiry into Missing and Murdered Indigenous Women and Girls,* vol. 1 (Canada, 2019), 5. Note this Inquiry also researched and witnessed testimony for findings regarding 2SLGTBQQIA people.

6 Truth and Reconciliation Commission of Canada, *Honouring the Truth, Reconciling for the Future: Summary of the Final Report of the Truth and Reconciliation Commission of Canada* (Montreal: McGill-Queen's University Press, 2015), 1.

7 United Nations Declaration on the Rights of Indigenous Peoples Act, S.C.2021, c.14, assented 21 June 2021.

8 The Paypom Treaty does not refer to any land removal but affirms Anishinabeg's right to be "free as by the past in hunting and rice harvest." It was the late Elder and Chief Allan Paypom who ensured that this document lives on. He purchased it from noted photographer C.C. Linde, who photographed Anishinaabeg in Lake of the Woods in the latter part of the nineteenth and early twentieth century. Linde stated that it was Powassin of Northwest Angle, the Treaty #3 Ogitchitaa (honoured Chief) and one of the lead negotiators, who had given him that original document. The wording concurs with notes by Métis interpreters August and Joseph Nolin 1873, which can be found in the Public Archives of Manitoba. Grand Council Treaty #3, *"The Creator Placed Us Here": Timeline of Significant Events of the Anishinaabeg of Treaty #3* (Kenora, ON: Grand Council Treaty #3, 2013), 18–20.

9   Onigaming First Nation has produced innovative videos (which have been posted through social media) to educate band members and others about our traditional teachings and the land. This 8-minute video has Onigaming male and female Elders demonstrate manoomin processing and cooking as well as cleaning and cooking fish and ducks. It also shows Elders encouraging Anishinaabe youth to celebrate the fall harvest. See Grand Council Treaty #3, "Ojibways of Onigaming Fall Harvest," YouTube, 7 July 2020, https://www.youtube.com/watch?v=W3eRWG-FYINE&list=PLp7FLwNvwwoPnqD5ZZ38xpCCk05B_0DXd&index=3; Sandra Indian, "Onigaming First Nations," 10 July 2021, video, 7:07, https://m.youtube.com/watch?v=sz-lQFq-IYU; and, Kezhii'aanakwat Ron Kelly, "History of Onigaming," 11 January 2022, video, 4:51, https://m.youtube.com/watch?v=vklZ1HCv4k4.

Chapter 2: Migration

1   This edited version of "The Migration of the Anishinaabe" is from *The Mishomis Book: The Voice of the Ojibway* by Edward Benton-Banai and is reprinted with the permission of University of Minnesota Press. The full-length version was originally published by Indian Country Communications, Inc. Copyright 1988 by Edward Benton-Banai. The first University of Minnesota Press edition was published in 2010. Ellipsis points have been used to identify omitted text. Square brackets have been used to identify other editorial interventions, including but not limited to the insertion of clarifying text. All footnotes are the original creations of the editors of this anthology.

2   "Band" refers to a grouping of families, from various clans, who forge a self-governing community together. It is currently used by the Canadian Government in the Indian Act to distinguish between members of different reserves. Each Band has its own governing council consisting of a chief and several councillors. "Clan" or "Clan System" describes traditional Indigenous governance structures. Clans are also an important element of social and spiritual organization. See Bob Joseph, *21 Things You May Not Know About the Indian Act: Helping Canadians Make Reconciliation with Indigenous Peoples a Reality* (Port Coquitlam, BC: Indigenous Relations Press, 2018), 109; Gregory Younging, *Elements of Indigenous Style: A Guide for Writing By and About Indigenous Peoples* (Edmonton: Brush Education, 2018), 53–54.

3   This passage appears later in Benton-Banai's original telling. It has been moved up for the purposes of clarity in this edited excerpt.

4   "Mide people" are members of the Midewiwin Society. Mide people work with medicines and the Spirit World. They can use their gifts for healing or to cause harm. As such, they can positively or negatively impact community well-being. See Michael Angel, *Preserving the Sacred: Historical Perspectives on the Ojibwa Midewiwin* (Winnipeg: University of Manitoba Press, 2002), 12–13.

5 "Gitchie Manito" is known as the Great Creator in English.

6 The Waterdrum is made from a hollowed-out log with stretched hide covering both ends and is partially filled with water. The water allows for changes in pitch and for sound to travel long distances. Songs performed with the Waterdrum are used by Mide people to ensure good harvests and hunting. See Angel, *Preserving the Sacred*, 93, 214, 233; Thomas Vennum Jr., *Wild Rice and the Ojibway People* (St. Paul: Minnesota Historical Society Press, 1988), 75.

Chapter 3: Seeds and Soils

1 M. Boyd et al., "Holocene Paleoecology of a Wild Rice (*Zizania* sp.) Lake in Northwestern Ontario, Canada," *Journal of Paleolimnology* 50 (2013): 366–68, 372, 374, 375; Matthew Boyd et al., "Wild Rice (*Zizania* spp.), the Three Sisters, and the Woodland Tradition in Western and Central Canada," *Midwest Archaeological Conference Inc. Occasional Papers* 1 (2014): 14.

2 K.C.A. Dawson, "The MacGillivray Site: A Laurel Tradition Site in Northwestern Ontario," *Ontario Archaeology* 34 (1980): 46; Boyd et al., "Wild Rice, the Three Sisters, and the Woodland Tradition," 17.

3 K.C.A. Dawson, "The Martin-Bird Site," *Ontario Archaeology* 47 (1987): 52; Boyd et al., "Wild Rice, the Three Sisters, and the Woodland Tradition," 17. See also K.C.A. Dawson, "The Mound Island Site: A Multi-Component Woodland Period Habitation Site in Northwestern Ontario," *Ontario Archaeology* 30 (1978): 47–66.

4 Paleoethnobotany is defined as the archaeological study of plant remains, often for the purposes of interpreting the plant-human interrelationship. See Patti J. Wright, "Methodological Issues in Paleoethnobotany: A Consideration of Issues, Methods, and Cases," in *Integrating Zooarchaeology and Paleoethnobotany: A Consideration of Issues, Methods, and Cases*, eds. Amber M. Derwarker and Tanya M. Peres (New York: Springer, 2010), 37–38; Amber M. VanDerwarker et al., "New World Paleoethnobotany in the New Millennium (2000–2013)," *Journal of Archaeological Research* 24, no. 2 (2016): 127.

5 "Wild rice" is a misleading term. Anishinaabeg have not only harvested Manomin for millennia, but they have also encouraged its growth and reseeded it so it could feed people in the future, making it a cultivated plant. In this paper, I use the term "Manomin" instead.

6 "Wild Rice," *Encyclopaedia Britannica*, 3 April 2019, https://www.britannica.com/plant/wild-rice; Gary W. Crawford and David G. Smith, "Paleoethnobotany in the Northeast," in *People and Plants in Ancient Eastern North America*, ed. Paul E. Minnis (Washington, DC: Smithsonian Books, 2003), 174, 202–203.

7   See, for example, A.G. Thomas and J.M. Stewart, "The Effect of Different Water Depths on the Growth of Wild Rice," *Canadian Journal of Botany* 47 (1969): 1531.

8   Constance Arzigian, "Middle Woodland and Oneota Contexts for Wild Rice Exploitation in Southwestern Wisconsin," *Midcontinental Journal of Archaeology* 25, no. 2 (2000): 246.

9   Charles R. Moffat and Constance M. Arzigian, "New Data on the Late Woodland Use of Wild Rice in Northern Wisconsin," *Midcontinental Journal of Archaeology* 25, no. 1 (2000): 51–52.

10 Cynthia E. Weir and Hugh M. Dale, "A Developmental Study of Wild Rice, *Zizania aquatica* L.," *Canadian Journal of Botany* 38 (1960): 719; Constance Arzigian, "Middle Woodland and Oneota Contexts," 247. For a contemporary context, see also G. Michael Haramis and Gregory D. Kearns, "Herbivory by Resident Geese: The Loss and Recovery of Wild Rice Along the Tidal Patuxent River," *Journal of Wildlife Management* 71, no. 3 (2007): 788–94, https://doi.org/10.2193/2006-350/.

11 Even macrobotanical evidence tends to be very small: for this reason, paleoethnobotanist Stephen G. Monckton refers to this field as "the archaeology of the invisible." Stephen G. Monckton, "Plants and the Archaeology of the Invisible," in *Before Ontario: The Archaeology of a Province*, eds. Marit K. Munson and Susan M. Jamieson (Montreal: McGill-Queen's University Press, 2013): 125.

12 Elden Johnson, "Archaeological Evidence for Utilization of Wild Rice," *Science* 163, no. 3864 (1969): 276–77.

13 David S. Brose, *The Dunn's Farm Site; 20LU22: A Late Middle Woodland Event in Northwest Michigan* (Kalamazoo, MI: Imprints from the Past, 2016), 13–14, 15.

14 M. Boyd et al., "Holocene Paleoecology of a Wild Rice," 365-366; C.L. Yost et al., "Detecting Ancient Wild Rice (*Zizania* spp. L.) Using Phytoliths: A Taphonomic Study of Modern Wild Rice in Minnesota (USA) Lake Sediments," *Journal of Paleolimnology* 49 (2013): 222.

15 Kerstin O. Griffin, "Paleoecological Aspects of the Red Lake Peatland, Northern Minnesota," *Canadian Journal of Botany* 55 (1977): 178.

16 See, for example, James Kenneth Huber, "Palynological Investigations Related to Archaeological Sites and the Expansion of Wild Rice (*Zizania aquatica* L.) in Northeast Minnesota" (PhD diss., University of Minnesota, 2001).

17 Clarence Leopold Joseph Surette, "The Potential of Microfossil Use in Paleodiet and Paleoenvironmental Analysis in Northwestern Ontario" (Master's thesis, Lakehead University, 2008), 118, 150, 173.

18 Moffat and Arzigian, "New Data on the Late Woodland Use of Wild Rice," 53. See also Wright, "Methodological Issues in Paleoethnobotany," 40.

19   Surette, "The Potential of Microfossil Use," 136.

20   For example, see Zicheng Yu, J.H. McAndrews and D. Siddiqi, "Influences of Holocene Climate and Water Levels on Vegetation Dynamics of a Lakeside Wetland," *Canadian Journal of Botany* 74 (1996): 1605–606.

21   For one such study, see Yu, McAndrews, and Siddiqi, "Influences of Holocene Climate."

22   Moffat and Arzigian, "New Data on the Late Woodland Use of Wild Rice," 53. Note that in archaeological dating, "BP" stands for "before present" (with "present" referring to the date ~1950 AD) and is used in radiocarbon dating. Radiocarbon dates are also sometimes shown with "calibrated" or "cal BP," meaning the dates have been corrected to associate with the calendar year.

23   Boyd et al., "Holocene Paleoecology of a Wild Rice Lake," 372.

24   Boyd et al., 374.

25   John P. Hart, Robert G. Thompson, and Hetty Jo Brumbach, "Phytolithic Evidence for Early Maize (Zea Mays) in the Northern Finger Lakes Region of New York," *American Antiquinty* 68, no. 4 (2003): 619.

26   Surette, "The Potential of Microfossil Use," 73.

27   Huber, "Palynological Investigations," 287–88.

28   This site was reoccupied several times over the centuries and includes components as old as 10,000 years old. As a result of the reoccupation, dating specific materials and activities at this site is very difficult. For more details, see Huber, "Palynological Investigations," 287–88.

29   Moffat and Arzigian, "New Data on the Lake Woodland Use of Wild Rice," 52.

30   Arzigian, "Middle Woodland and Oneota Contexts," 263–64.

31   Boyd et al., "Holocene Paleoecology of a Wild Rice Lake," 365.

32   Huber, "Palynological Investigations," 267, 277, 287.

33   Some other, older archaeological studies would seem to suggest that Manomin collection was eventually replaced by maize agriculture once maize became available, implying that the collection of "wild" food was somehow less desirable than the deliberate growth of crops like maize. However, it seems more likely that many peoples experimented with maize agriculture while also continuing to gather and consume Manomin. See Arzigian, "Middle Woodland and Oneota Contexts," 257.

34   Surette, "The Potential of Microfossil Use," 177.

35   Boyd et al., "Wild Rice, the Three Sisters, and the Woodland Tradition," 7, 27.

36 Boyd et al., 13.

37 Surette, "The Potential of Microfossil Use," 171.

38 For example, John McAndrews traced Rice Lake's (Minnesota) history, explaining that the changing conditions in the lake could determine how much Manomin grew from year to year. McAndrews also points to the correlation between the spread of pine and the spread of Manomin at the site and indicates the pines may have helped produce a stable environment for the Manomin. John H. McAndrews, "Paleobotany of a Wild Rice Lake in Minnesota," *Canadian Journal of Botany* 47 (1969): 1671, 1679.

39 Monckton, "Plants and the Archaeology of the Invisible," 124–25; Crawford and Smith, "Paleoethnobotany in the Northeast," 176.

40 Surette, "The Potential of Macrofossil Use," 78, 171.

41 Crawford and Smith, "Paleoethnobotany in the Northeast," 199. See also Moffat and Arzigian, "New data on the Late Woodland Use of Wild Rice," 60.

42 Arzigian, "Middle Woodland and Oneota Contexts," 258; Monckton, "Plants and the Archaeology of the Invisible," 125.

43 Christine Branstner, "Archaeological Investigations at the Cloudman Site (20CH6): A Multicomponent Native American Occupation on Drummond Island, Michigan 1992 and 1994 Excavations," submitted to the Consortium for Archaeological Research, Michigan State University (East Lansing: Michigan State University, 1995): 43, 46, 54.

44 Heidi A. Lennstrom and Christine A. Hastorf, "Interpretation in Context: Sampling and Analysis in Paleoethnobotany," *American Antiquity* 60, no. 4 (1995): 701–21.

45 Yost et al., "Detecting Ancient Wild Rice," 234.

46 Moffat and Arzigian, "New Data on the Late Woodland Use of Wild Rice," 54.

47 Crawford and Smith, "Paleoethnobotany in the Northeast," 202.

48 Crawford and Smith, 213.

49 Crawford and Smith, 177.

50 Huber, "Palynological Investigations," 57.

51 Huber, "Palynological Investigations," 47, 64, 232; Surette, "The Potential of Macrofossil Use," 15, 17.

52 For a detailed breakdown of the possibility of a longer use of Manomin without leaving behind archaeological evidence, see Huber, "Palynological Investigations," 290–93.

53 Brittany Luby, personal communication, 26 July 2020. See also: "While Indians did not subject the plant to thorough domestication, they intensively cultivated particular stands to ensure that they would regularly produce grain . . . in northern regions where stands were the most widespread and abundant, there is some limited archaeological evidence suggesting that Indians might have sown seeds." Anya Zilberstein, "Inured to Empire: Wild Rice and Climate Change," *The William and Mary Quarterly* 72, no. 1 (2015): 134.

54 See, for example, Roger C. Echo-Hawk, "Ancient History in the New World: Integrating Oral Traditions and the Archaeological Record in Deep Time," *American Antiquity* 65, no. 2 (2000): 267–90.

55 Shawn Adler and James Whetung, "Foraging for Wild Rice with Chef Shawn Adler," *CBC Life*, 10 December 2019, video, 6:30, https://www.youtube.com/watch?v=NRdVnJwgW1s.

Chapter 4: Manomin as Teacher

1 Edward Benton-Banai, *The Mishomis Book: The Voice of the Ojibway* (Minneapolis: University of Minnesota Press with Indian Country Communications, 1988), 94.

2 "Manoomin (Wild Rice): The Food that Grows on Water (Part 1 of 3)," *Native Earth: A Subdivision of White Earth Land Recovery Project*, 30 August 2017, https://nativeharvest.com/blogs/news/manoomin-wild-rice-the-food-that-grows-on-water-part-1-of-3 [https://perma.cc/Z7HU-B696]. See also *First Daughter and the Black Snake*, directed by Keri Pickett (Minneapolis: Pickett Pictures, 2017), DVD.

3 Library and Archives Canada (LAC), "Letter from Wemyss Simpson, S.J. Dawson, Robert Pither, Indian Commissioners to Joseph Howe, Secretary of State for the Provinces," 17 July 1872, RG 10, v. 1868, f. 577. Manomin is not explicitly identified in records of treaty negotiations until 1873. At this time, Anishinaabe negotiators ensured that "The Indians will be free as by the past for their hunting and rice harvest," as evidenced by the Paypom Treaty. See Ojibwa Chiefs of Treaty 3, *Paypom Treaty*, 4 October 1873 (Kenora, ON: Treaty #3 and Aboriginal Rights Research Centre).

4 Frances Densmore, "Uses of Plants by the Chippewan Indians," extract from the *Forty-Fourth Annual Report of the Bureau of American Ethnology* (Washington, DC: Government Printing Office, 1928), 316.

5 Densmore, "Uses of Plants," 316.

6 John B. Moyle, "Wild Rice in Minnesota," *Journal of Wildlife Management* 8, no. 3 (1944): 179.

7   Thomas Vennum Jr., *Wild Rice and the Ojibway People* (St. Paul: Minnesota Historical Society Press, 1988), 175.

8   Vennum Jr., *Wild Rice and the Ojibway People*, 127.

9   Amanda Raster and Christina Gish Hill, "The Dispute Over Wild Rice: An Investigation of Treaty Agreements and Ojibwe Food Sovereignty," *Agriculture and Human Values* 34, no. 2 (2017): 271, https://doi.org/10.1007/s10460-016-9703-6.

10 During a community workshop on 5 June 2018, Elders took Brittany Luby from the Department of History and Andrea Bradford from the School of Engineering at the University of Guelph on the Winnipeg River and identified ancestral harvesting sites. The Elders identified four sites to include in the study. On 6 June 2018, band members discussed interview questions drafted by Luby and Bradford. Questions were edited by band members to ensure clarity in English, accurate translation into Anishinaabemowin if required, and the protection of sacred knowledge.

11 "Ojibwe Moons," *Muskrat Magazine*, 14 August 2015, http://muskratmagazine.com/ojibwe-moons/ [https://perma.cc/WR7U-Y5K3].

12 Linda LeGarde Grover, *Onigamiising: Seasons of an Ojibwe Year* (Minneapolis: University of Minnesota Press, 2017), 92.

13 Raster and Hill, "The Dispute Over Wild Rice," 271.

14 Elder John Henry, interview with Brittany Luby, 15 August 2018, Manomin Project NAN Elder Interviews.

15 Elder Clarence Henry Jr., interview with Brittany Luby, 14 August 2018, Manomin Project NAN Elder Interviews.

16 Elder Terry Greene, interview with Brittany Luby, 16 August 2018, Manomin Project NAN Elder Interviews.

17 Moyle, "Wild Rice in Minnesota," 183.

18 Elder Danny Strong, interview with Brittany Luby, 21 August 2018, Manomin Project NAN Elder Interviews.

19 Elder J. Henry, interview, 15 August 2018.

20 Robert Aherin and Christine Todd, "Developmental Stages of Children and Accident Risk Potential," *Agricultural Safety and Health, University of Illinois Extension*, accessed 3 July 2020, https://web.extension.illinois.edu/agsafety/factsheets/devstage.cfm [https://perma.cc/TKW5-55HT].

21 Elder T. Greene, interview, 16 August 2018.

22 Aherin and Todd, "Developmental Stages of Children."

23 Elder T. Greene, interview, 16 August 2018; Elder D. Strong, interview, 21 August 2018; Elder Terry Greene, knowledge exchange at community feast, 18 September 2018, Manomin Project NAN Elder Interviews.

24 Kim Anderson, *Life Stages and Native Women: Memory, Teachings, and Story Medicine* (Winnipeg: University of Manitoba Press, 2011), 81.

25 Chief Lorraine Cobiness, knowledge exchange at community feast, 20 September 2019, Manomin Project NAN Elder Interviews.

26 Elder C. Henry Jr., interview, 14 August 2018.

27 Elder Theresa Jourdain (née Kabestra), interview with Brittany Luby, 21 August 2018, Manomin Project NAN Elder Interviews.

28 LeGarde Grover, *Onigamiising*, 94.

29 Elder J. Henry, interview, 15 August 2018.

30 Elder J. Henry, interview, 15 August 2018; Elder D. Strong, interview, 21 August 2018.

31 Elder D. Strong, interview, 21 August 2018.

32 Kathi Avery Kinew, "Manito Gitigaan—Governing in the Great Spirit's Garden: Wild Rice in Treaty #3" (PhD diss., University of Manitoba, 1995), 4.

33 Dorothy Dora Whipple, *Chi-mewinzha: Ojibwe Stories from Leech Lake* (Minneapolis: University of Minnesota Press, 2015), 23.

34 Heather Cardinal and Becky Maki, "Wild Rice," Using Native American Legends to Teach Mathematics, The College of Education and Human Services at the University of Wisconsin Oshkosh, accessed 3 July 2020, http://www.uwosh.edu/coehs/cmagproject/ethnomath/legend/legend6.htm [https://perma.cc/YM9T-Z37G].

35 Kimmerer, "Returning the Gift," 20.

36 William G. Dore, *Wild-rice* (Ottawa: The Queen's Printer for Canada, 1969), 51.

37 Kinew, "Manito Gitigaan," 93.

38 Kristi Leora Gansworth, "For Those Anishinaabeg Who Are Coming to This Earth," 3 August 2018, comment on *Center for Humans and Nature*, "What Kind of Ancestor Do You Want to Be?" https://www.humansandnature.org/for-those-anishinaabeg-who-are-coming-to-this-earth.

39 "Seven Generations," *Algonquin College*, 4 October 2017, https://www.algonquincollege.com/sustainability-toolkit/2017/10/seven-generations.

40 Joseph Bowron, *Transactions of the Wisconsin State Agricultural Society, with portions of the correspondence of the secretary,* vol. II (Madison, WI: Beriah Brown, State Printer, 1852), 288.

41   Elder Danny Strong, interview with Brittany Luby, 20 September 2019, Manomin Project NAN Elder Interviews.

42   Former Chief Allan Luby, knowledge exchange workshop, 5 June 2018, Manomin Project NAN Elder Interviews.

43   Elder T. Greene, interview, 16 August 2018.

44   Elder Danny Strong, interview with Brittany Luby, 1 August 2018, Manomin Project NAN Elder Interviews.

45   Elder D. Strong, interview, 20 September 2019.

46   Clay balls were also used to extend the area under cultivation. As I write elsewhere, "Clay drains slowly and retains water and shape longer than other soil separates like sand and silt. I speculate that clay balls helped to keep seed moist during transport. . . . Clay may also have been selected to reduce seed loss during transit—clay balls are less likely to fall apart than sand or silt" (Brittany Luby, "Treaty through a Planting Lens: A Study of Manoomin Harvesting Rights in Anishinaabe-Aki, 1873–Present," *American Indian Quarterly* 47, no. 4 (2024): 359–60).

47   "Manoomin: Food that Grows on the Water," *The Ways: Great Lakes Native Culture and Language*, Wisconsin Educational Communications Board, 2019, https://theways.org/story/manoomin.html [https://perma.cc/PVG4-Q8VA].

Chapter 5: Relational Vocabularies

1   The editors note that this is substantiated in the sixth edition of *Botany: An Introduction to Plant Biology*, which states that "plants produce the oxygen we breathe and the food we eat. We get cloth, paper, lumber and chemicals from plants." See James D. Mauseth, *Botany: An Introduction to Plant Biology,* 6th ed. (Burlington, MA: Jones and Bartlett Learning, 2017), 3.

2   These relationships are elaborated on by Indigenous scholar James Frideres, who explains that "people travel through life in a relational existence." Whether those relationships be with plants, humans, or other elements of the natural world—no distinction exists because everything is imbued with living spirit deserving of "respect, reciprocity, relationship and responsibility." See James Frideres, *Indigenous People in the Twenty-First Century,* 3rd ed. (Don Mills, ON: Oxford University Press, 2020), 51, 56.

3   Paul A. Keddy, "Wetlands: An Overview," in *Wetland Ecology: Principles and Conservation,* 2nd ed. (Cambridge: Cambridge University Press, 2010), 2.

4   M. Fedailaine et al., "Modeling of Anaerobic Digestion of Organic Waste for Biogas Production," *Procedia Computer Science* 52 (2015): 730–37.

5   Mauseth, *Botany,* 573.

6   Lanny Sapei et al., "Structural and Analytical Studies of Silica Accumulations in *Equisetum Hyemale,*" *Analytical and Bioanalytical Chemistry* 389 (2007): 1250, https://doi.org/10.1007/s00216-007-1522-6; Shigeru Yamanaka et al., "Roles of Silica and Lignin in Horsetail (*Equisetum Hyemale*), with Special Reference to Mechanical Properties," *Journal of Applied Physics* 111 (2012): 1, https://doi.org/10.1063/1.3688253.

7   Sapei et al., "Structural and Analytical Studies of Silica Accumulations," 1250.

8   Sandra Walker, *The Path to Wild Food: Edible Plants and Recipes for Canada* (Edmonton: Lone Pine Publishing, 2018), 147.

9   Walker, *The Path to Wild Food,* 142.

10   See also Merritt Lyndon Fernald, Alfred Charles Kinsey, and Steve William Chadde, *The New Edible Wild Plants of Eastern North America* (Sullivan, IN: Orchard Innovations, 2019), 371.

11   Mauseth, *Botany,* 624.

12   Mauseth, 234–36.

13   National Geographic Society, *Field Guide to the Birds of North America,* 3rd ed. (Washington, DC: National Geographic, 1999), 146.

14   Mauseth, *Botany,* 617–18.

15   Members of the family Nymphaeaceae have a long history of use in diabetes treatment, and compounds contained within the plants have been found to support glucose uptake. See Mabel Parimala et al., "*Nymphaea nouchali* Burm. F. Hydroalcoholic Seed Extract Increases Glucose Consumption in 3T3-L1 Adipocytes through Activation of Peroxisome Proliferator-Activated Receptor Gamma and Insulin Sensitization," *Journal of Advanced Pharmaceutical Technology and Research* 6, no. 4 (2015): 183–89, https://doi.org/10.4103/2231-4040.165013.

16   William G. Dore, *Wild-rice* (Ottawa: The Queen's Printer for Canada, 1969), 51.

17   Dore, *Wild-rice,* 51.

18   Moose have been found to act as ecosystem engineers in wetland habitats by modifying habitat structure, exporting nutrients, and acting as transport vectors for other plants and animals. Large herbivores have been noted to open new niches through sediment disturbance, which benefits annual species in particular. See Elisabeth S. Bakker et al., "Accessing the Role of Large Herbivores in the Structuring and Functioning of Freshwater and Marine Angiosperm Ecosystems," *Ecography* 39, no. 2 (2016): 169–70, https://doi.org/10.1111/ecog.01651.

19 Mak'akiimdaas (Pitcher Plant) is a small plant with tubular leaves that collect rainwater, which subsequently becomes mixed with digestive enzymes produced by the plant. Rising tall above short, pitcher-like leaves are the flowers, containing the structures where the seeds will eventually be formed. See "Pitcher Plant," *Nature Conservancy Canada*, 2020, https://www.natureconservancy.ca/en/what-we-do/resource-centre/featured-species/plants/pitcher-plant.html.

20 "Pitcher Plant."

21 *Sarracenia purpurin* is the main ingredient in the drug Sarapin®, which has been shown to relieve pain associated with lumbar facet joint nerve blocks. See Laxmaiah Manchikanti et al., "Therapeutic Lumbar Facet Joint Nerve Blocks in the Treatment of Chronic Low Back Pain: Cost Utility Analysis Based on a Randomized Controlled Trial," *The Korean Journal of Pain* 31, no. 1 (2018): 27, https://doi.org/10.3344/kjp.2018.31.1.27.

22 *Sarracenia purpurea* has been found to be effective in treating diabetes, inhibiting glucose toxicity in cells, treating a variety of pain-related ailments, and healing infection. See Cory S Harris et al., "Characterizing the Cytoprotective Activity of Sarracenia Purpurea L., a Medicinal Plant That Inhibits Glucotoxicity in PC12 Cells," *BMC Complementary and Alternative Medicine* 12, no. 1 (2012): 1–10, https://doi.org/10.1186/1472-6882-12-245.

Chapter 6: Environmental Change, Environmental Care

1 This chapter is written from the perspective of the first two authors (Mehltretter and Bradford) and their experiences learning from Niisaachewan Anishinaabe Nation Elders and Manomin. Niisaachewan, however, is listed as an author because not only are the vast knowledges of community members included in these pages, but also because the piece would not be possible without NAN, who initiated the Manomin Project.

2 Elder Terry Greene, interview with Brittany Luby, 16 August 2018, Manomin Project NAN Elder Interviews.

3 Kathi Avery Kinew, "Manito Gitigaan—Governing in the Great Spirit's Garden: Wild Rice in Treaty #3" (PhD diss., University of Manitoba, 1995), 4.

4 Nicholas J. Reo and Laura A. Ogden, "Anishnaabe Aki: An Indigenous Perspective on the Global Threat of Invasive Species," *Sustainability Science* 13, no. 5 (2018): 1445–46, https://doi.org/10.1007/s11625-018-0571-4.

5 Robin Wall Kimmerer, "Returning the Gift," *Minding Nature* 7, no. 2 (2014): 20.

6   "Seven Grandfather Teachings," *Seven Generations Education Institute*, last modified 3 February 2021, http://www.7generations.org/seven-grandfather-teachings/.

7   Manuel C. Molles and James F. Cahill, *Ecology: Concepts and Applications*, 2nd ed. (Whitby, ON: McGraw-Hill Ryerson, 2011), 417, 420.

8   A "niche" is the specific set of environmental conditions within which a species can live. See Molles and Cahill, *Ecology,* 225.

9   Thomas Vennum Jr., *Wild Rice and the Ojibway People* (St. Paul: Minnesota Historical Society Press, 1988), 16.

10 Elder John Henry, interview with Brittany Luby, 15 August 2018, Manomin Project NAN Elder Interviews.

11 Elder Terry Greene, interview, 16 August 2018.

12 Vennum, *Wild Rice and the Ojibway People,* 16.

13 Vennum, 17.

14 Elder Clarence Henry Jr., interview with Brittany Luby, 14 August 2018, Manomin Project NAN Elder Interviews.

15 William G. Dore, *Wild-rice* (Ottawa: The Queen's Printer for Canada, 1969), 58.

16 Dore, *Wild-rice,* 58.

17 James E. Meeker, "The Ecology of 'Wild' Wild-Rice (*Zizania palustris* var. *palustris*) in the Kakagon Sloughs, a Riverine Wetland on Lake Superior," in P*roceedings of the Wild Rice Research and Management Conference*, eds. Lisa S. Williamson, Lisa A. Dlutkowski, and Amy P. McCammon-Soltis (Carlton, MN: Great Lakes Indian Fish and Wildlife Commission, 1999), 74.

18 Dore, *Wild-rice,* 58; Meeker, "The Ecology of 'Wild' Wild-Rice," 58, 74; Vennum, *Wild Rice and the Ojibway People,* 16.

19 Kevin Aagaard et al., "Modeling the Relationship Between Water Level, Wild Rice Abundance, and Waterfowl Abundance at a Central North American Wetland," *Wetlands* 39, no. 1 (2019): 149, http://doi.org/10.1007/s13157-018-1025-6.

20 Dore, *Wild-rice,* 64.

21 Dore, 64.

22 Dore, 64.

23 P.F. Lee, "Ecological Relationships of Wild Rice, *Zizania aquatica.* 5. Enhancement of Wild Rice Production by *Potamogeton robbinsii," Canadian Journal of Botany* 65, no. 7 (1987): 1434, https://doi.org/10.1139/b87-198.

24 Robert W. Pillsbury and Melissa A. McGuire, "Factors Affecting the Distribution of Wild Rice (*Zizania palustris*) and the Associated Macrophyte Community," *Wetlands* 29, no. 2 (2009): 730, https://doi.org/10.1672/08-41.1.

25 Pillsbury and McGuire, "Factors Affecting the Distribution of Wild Rice," 730.

26 Wisconsin Department of Natural Resources (WDNR), *Wild Rice: Ecology, Harvest, Management*, (Madison, WI, n.d.), 1.

27 Reo and Ogden, "Anishnaabe Aki," 1446–47.

28 Reo and Ogden, 1447.

29 Elder C. Henry Jr., interview, 14 August 2018.

30 S.G. Aiken, P.F. Lee, D. Punter, and J.M. Stewart, *Wild Rice in Canada* (Toronto: NC Press Limited and Agriculture Canada, 1988), 39–40.

31 Elder Archie Wagamese, interview with Brittany Luby, 14 August 2018, Manomin Project NAN Elder Interviews.

32 Angela Arthington, *Environmental Flows: Saving Rivers in the Third Millennium* (Berkeley: University of California Press, 2012), 90.

33 N. LeRoy Poff et al., "The Natural Flow Regime," *BioScience* 47, no. 11 (1997): 769, https://doi.org/10.2307/1313099.

34 Arthington, *Environmental Flows*, 54–55.

35 Arthington, *Environmental Flows,* 113; FISRWG, *Stream Corridor Restoration: Principles, Processes, and Practices* (Washington, DC, 1998), 2–86.

36 Poff et al., "The Natural Flow Regime," 770.

37 Vennum, *Wild Rice and the Ojibway People*, 21. See also: Samantha Mehltretter and Niisaachewan Anishinaabe Nation, "Manomin Ecology: Environmental Factors That Impact Manomin Growth," Network in Canadian History and Environment, 19 June 2020, https://niche-canada.org/2020/06/19/manomin-ecology-environmental-factors-that-impact-manomin-growth/.

38 Aiken et al., *Wild Rice in Canada,* 39.

39 Vennum, *Wild Rice and the Ojibway People*, 21.

40 Xuebin Zhang et al., "Trends in Canadian Streamflow," *Water Resources Research* 37, no. 4 (2001): 995.

41 Scott St. George, "Streamflow in the Winnipeg River Basin, Canada: Trends, Extremes and Climate Linkages," *Journal of Hydrology* 332, no. 3–4 (2007): 401, https://doi.org/10.1016/j.jhydrol.2006.07.014.

42   A hydrometric gauge measures water level and/or streamflow.

43   St. George, "Streamflow in the Winnipeg River Basin," 401–2.

44   "Headwater streams" refers to streams formed from the first water that starts to collect at high elevations.

45   St. George, "Streamflow in the Winnipeg River Basin," 401.

46   Minnesota Department of Natural Resources (MNDNR), "Natural Wild Rice in Minnesota: A Wild Rice Study," submitted to the Minnesota Legislature by the Minnesota Department of Natural Resources (St. Paul: MNDNR, 2008), 31.

47   M. Stults et al., *Climate Change Vulnerability Assessment and Adaptation Plan: 1854 Ceded Territory Including the Bois Forte, Fond du Lac, and Grand Portage Reservations* (Duluth, MN: 1854 Ceded Territory, 2016), 40.

48   Elder Danny Strong, interview with Brittany Luby, 21 August 2018, Manomin Project NAN Elder Interviews.

49   Aiken et al., *Wild Rice in Canada,* 19; G.M. Simpson, "A Study of Germination in the Seed of Wild Rice (*Zizania aquatica*)," *Canadian Journal of Botany* 44, no. 1 (1966): 8.

50   MNDNR, "Natural Wild Rice in Minnesota: A Wild Rice Study," 30.

51   MNDNR, "Natural Wild Rice in Minnesota," 29; Aiken et al., *Wild Rice in Canada*, 60.

52   Hannah Panci et al., *Climate Change Vulnerability Assessment: Integrating Scientific and Traditional Ecological Knowledge* (Odanah, WI: Great Lakes Indian Fish and Wildlife Commission, 2018), 28–30.

53   Pillsbury and McGuire, "Factors Affecting the Distribution of Wild Rice," 732.

54   Panci et al., "Climate Change Vulnerability Assessment," 29.

55   Stults et al., *Climate Change Vulnerability Assessment and Adaptation Plan,* 11; Panci et al., "Climate Change Vulnerability Assessment," 5.

56   Few pollutants have been studied in relation to their impact on Manomin aside from sulfate and, to a lesser extent, copper. For details on pollutants in Manomin ecosystems, please see: A. Myrbo et al., "Sulfide Generated by Sulfate Reduction is a Primary Controller of the Occurrence of Wild Rice (*Zizania palustris*) in Shallow Aquatic Ecosystems," *Journal of Geophysical Research: Biogeosciences* 122, no. 11 (2017): 2736–53, https://doi.org/10.1002/2017JG003787; John Pastor et al., "Effects of Sulfate and Sulfide on the Life Cycle of *Zizania palustris* in Hydroponic and Mesocosm Experiments," *Ecological Applications* 27, no. 1 (2017): 321–36, https://doi.org/10.1002/eap.1452; Douglas J. Fort et al., "Toxicity of Sulfate and Chloride to Early Life Stages of Wild Rice (*Zizania palustris*): Sulfate Toxicity to Wild Rice,"

Environmental Toxicology and Chemistry 33, no. 12 (2014): 2802–9, https://doi.
org/10.1002/etc.2744; and Del Wayne R. Nimmo et al., "Effects of Excess Copper
on Growth of Wild Rice (*Zizania palustris*) Seedlings Tested in Reconstituted and
Natural Waters," *Environmental Management* 32, no. 4 (2003), 466–75, https://doi.
org/10.1007/s00267-003-2899-4.

57 MNDNR, "Natural Wild Rice in Minnesota," 30.

58 Sheel Bansal et al., "*Typha* (Cattail) Invasion in North American Wetlands: Biology,
Regional Problems, Impacts, Ecosystem Services, and Management," *Wetlands* 39,
no. 4 (2019): 647, https://doi.org/10.1007/s13157-019-01174-7.

59 Bansal et al., "*Typha* (Cattail) Invasion in North American Wetlands," 646.

60 Kristi E. Dysievick, Peter F. Lee, and John Kabatay, *Recovery of Wild Rice Stand
Following Mechanical Removal of Narrowleaf Cattail* (Windsor, ON: International
Joint Commission, 2016), 4.

61 "Floating mat" refers to a dense web of roots and stems forming a semi-solid
platform. A. U. Mallik, "Small-Scale Succession Towards Fen on Floating Mat of a
Typha Marsh in Atlantic Canada," *Canadian Journal of Botany* 67, no. 5 (1989): 1309,
https://doi.org/10.1139/b89-174.

62 Brian Walker et al., "Resilience, Adaptability and Transformability in Social-
Ecological Systems," *Ecology and Society* 9, no. 2 (2004): 2.

63 Walker et al., "Resilience, Adaptability and Transformability," 4–5.

64 An internode is a segment of the plant's stem between two nodes, which are the
points where leaves grow out from the stem. See "Stem," *Encyclopaedia Britannica,*
last modified 22 December 2020, https://www.britannica.com/science/stem-plant.

65 Cynthia E. Weir and Hugh M. Dale, "A Developmental Study of Wild Rice, *Zizania
aquatica* L.," *Canadian Journal of Botany,* 38 (1960): 720.

66 Taylor A. Steeves, "Wild Rice: Indian Food and a Modern Delicacy," *Economic Botany*
6, no. 2 (1952): 113, https://doi.org/10.1007/BF02984871.

67 Steeves, "Wild Rice: Indian Food and a Modern Delicacy," 113.

68 MNDNR, "Natural Wild Rice in Minnesota," 16.

69 Walker et al., "Resilience, Adaptability and Transformability," 3.

70 Reo and Ogden, "Anishnaabe Aki," 1448.

Chapter 7: Disconnection

1   Taylor A. Steeves, "Wild Rice: Indian Food and a Modern Delicacy," *Economic Botany* 6, no. 2 (1952): 108, 118.

2   Hannah T. Neufeld, Chantelle A.M. Richmond, and Southwest Ontario Aboriginal Health Access Centre (SOAHAC), "Impacts of Place and Social Spaces on Traditional Food Systems in Southwestern Ontario," *International Journal of Indigenous Health* 12, no. 1 (2017): 94.

3   First Nations Information Governance Centre (FNIGC), *First Nations Regional Health Survey (RHS) 2008/10: National Report on Adults, Youth and Children Living in First Nations Communities* (Ottawa: FNIGC, 2012), 86.

4   Laurie Chan et al., *First Nations Food, Nutrition and Environment Study (FNFNES) Final Report for Eight Assembly of First Nations Regions: Draft Comprehensive Technical Report* (Ottawa: Assembly of First Nations, University of Ottawa, and Université de Montréal, 2019), 8.

5   Myrna Cunningham, "Chapter V: Health," in *United Nations, Permanent Forum on Indigenous Issues, State of the World's Indigenous Peoples* (New York: United Nations, 2009), 159.

6   Hasu Ghosh, "Urban Reality of Type 2 Diabetes among First Nations of Eastern Ontario: Western Science and Indigenous Perceptions," *Journal of Global Citizenship and Equity Education* 2, no. 2 (2012): 159; Stefanie Lemke and Treena Delormier, "Indigenous Peoples' Food Systems, Nutrition and Gender: Conceptual and Methodological Considerations," *Maternal and Child Nutrition* 13, no. 3 (2017): 2.

7   Chan et al., *FNFNES Final Report*, 6.

8   Valerie Tarasuk, Andy Mitchell, and Naomi Dachner, *Household Food Insecurity in Canada, 2014* (Toronto: Research to Identify Policy Options to Reduce Food Insecurity, 2014), 2.

9   Harriet Kuhnlein and Oliver Receveur, "Dietary Change and Traditional Food Systems of Indigenous Peoples," *Annual Review of Nutrition* 16, no. 1 (1996): 418.

10 Chan et al., *FNFNES Final Report,* 9.

11 Chantelle A.M. Richmond and Nancy Ross, "The Determinants of First Nation and Inuit Health: A Critical Population Health Approach," *Health and Place* 15, no. 2 (2009): 403.

12 Brenda Elias et al., "Trauma and Suicide Behaviour Histories among a Canadian Indigenous Population: An Empirical Exploration of the Potential Role of Canada's Residential School System," *Social Science and Medicine* 74, no. 10 (2012): 1561.

13 Jennifer Organ et al., "Contemporary Programs in Support of Traditional Ways: Inuit Perspectives on Community Freezers as a Mechanism to Alleviate Pressures of Wild Food Access in Nain, Nunatsiavut," *Health and Place* 30 (2014): 251.

14 Hannah T. Neufeld, Chantelle A.M. Richmond, and SOAHAC, "Exploring First Nation Elder Women's Relationships with Food from Social, Ecological, and Historical Perspectives," *Current Developments in Nutrition* 4, no. 3 (2020): 2.

15 Truth and Reconciliation Commission of Canada, *Truth and Reconciliation Commission of Canada: Calls to Action* (2015): 2–3. More specifically, Call 19 focuses on: "infant mortality, maternal health, suicide, mental health, addictions, life expectancy, birth rates, infant and child health issues, chronic diseases, illness and injury incidence, and the availability of appropriate health services."

16 Jeff Corntassel, "Re-Envisioning Resurgence: Indigenous Pathways to Decolonization and Sustainable Self-Determination," *Decolonization: Indigeneity, Education and Society* 1, no. 1 (2012): 88–89.

17 Noreen Willows et al., "Associations between Household Food Insecurity and Health Outcomes in the Aboriginal Population (Excluding Reserves)," *Health Reports* 22, no. 2 (2011): 1.

18 Marcie Snyder and Kathi Wilson, "'Too much moving . . . there's always a reason': Understanding Urban Aboriginal Peoples' Experiences of Mobility and Its Impact on Holistic Health," *Health and Place* 34 (2015): 184–85, http://dx.doi.org/10.1016/j.healthplace.2015.05.009.

19 Neufeld, Richmond, and SOAHAC, "Impacts of Place and Social Spaces," 95.

20 Statistics Canada, *Aboriginal Peoples in Canada: Key Results From the 2016 Census*, last modified 25 October 2017, https://www150.statcan.gc.ca/n1/daily-quotidien/171025/dq171025a-eng.htm?indid=14430-1&indgeo=0.

21 Statistics Canada, *Aboriginal Peoples in Canada*; *Our Health Counts*, *Our Health Counts Toronto Report* (Toronto: Our Health Counts, 2018), 1, 5, http://www.welllivinghouse.com/wp-content/uploads/2019/10/OHC-TO-Adult-Demographics-.pdf.

22 Ontario Federation of Indigenous Friendship Centres (OFIFC), *Ganohonyohk—Giving Thanks: Understanding Prosperity from the Perspectives of Urban Indigenous Friendship Centre Communities in Ontario* (Toronto: OFIFC, 2020), 18, https://ofifc.org/?research=ganohonyohk-giving-thanks-indigenous-prosperity.

23 Neufeld, Richmond, and SOAHAC, "Impacts of Place and Social Spaces," 94–95.

24 Valerie Tarasuk, "Household Food Insecurity in Canada," *Topics in Clinical Nutrition* 20, no. 4 (2005): 304.

25 Chantelle Richmond et al., "First Nations Food Environments: Exploring the Role of Place, Income, and Social Connection," *Current Developments in Nutrition* 4, no. 8 (2020): 4.

26 Ontario Federation of Indigenous Friendship Centres, *Ganohonyohk—Giving Thanks,* front matter.

27 Heather A. Howard, "Canadian Residential Schools and Urban Indigenous Knowledge Production about Diabetes," *Medical Anthropology* 33, no. 6 (2014): 531.

28 Ontario Federation of Indigenous Friendship Centres, *Ganohonyohk–Giving Thanks,* 1–2.

29 Andrew R. Hatala et al., "Re-Imagining Miyo-Wicehtowin: Human-Nature Relations, Land-Making, and Wellness among Indigenous Youth in a Canadian Urban Context," *Social Science and Medicine* 230 (2019): 122.

30 Snyder and Wilson, "'Too much moving . . . there's always a reason,'" 181–82.

31 Véronique Landry, Hugo Asselin, and Carole Lévesque, "Link to the Land and *Mino Pimatisiwin* (Comprehensive Health) of Indigenous People Living in Urban Areas in Eastern Canada," *International Journal of Environmental Research and Public Health* 16 (2019): 6.

32 Snyder and Wilson, "'Too much moving . . . there's always a reason,'" 186.

33 Noreen Willows et al., "Prevalence and Sociodemographic Risk Factors Related to Household Food Security in Aboriginal Peoples in Canada," *Public Health and Nutrition* 12, no. 8 (2009): 1152, 1154.

34 Christopher Turner et al., "Concepts and Critical Perspectives for Food Environment Research: A Global Framework with Implications for Action in Low- and Middle-Income Countries," *Global Food Security* 18 (2018): 94.

35 Chantelle A.M. Richmond and Catherine Cook, "Creating Conditions for Aboriginal Health Equity: The Promise of Healthy Public Policy," *Public Health Reviews* 37 (2016): 3–4.

36 Chantelle Richmond et al., "First Nations Food Environments," 6.

37 Charlotte Reading, "Structural Determinants of Aboriginal Peoples' Health," in *Determinants of Indigenous Peoples' Health in Canada: Beyond the Social,* eds. Margo Greenwood, Sarah de Leeuw, Nicole Marie Lindsay, and Charlotte Reading (Toronto: Canadian Scholars' Press, 2018), 4–5.

38 Anna Herforth and Selena Ahmed, "The Food Environment, Its Effects on Dietary Consumption, and Potential for Measurement within Agriculture-Nutrition Interventions," *Food Security* 7, no. 3 (2015): 506.

39   Kelly Skinner, Erin Pratley, and Kristin Burnett, "Eating in the City: A Review of the Literature on Food Insecurity and Indigenous People Living in Urban Spaces," *Societies* 6, no. 2 (2016): 1; Neufeld, Richmond, and SOAHAC, "Impacts of Place and Social Spaces," 95–96; Richmond et al., "First Nations Food Environments," 2.

40   Neufeld, Richmond, and SOAHAC, "Impacts of Place and Social Spaces," 107.

41   Skinner, Pratley, and Burnett, "Eating in the City," 1.

42   Neufeld, Richmond, and SOAHAC, "Impacts of Place and Social Spaces," 106.

43   Skinner, Pratley, and Burnett, "Eating in the City," 9.

44   Neufeld, Richmond, and SOAHAC, "Impacts of Place and Social Spaces," 106.

45   FNIGC, *First Nations Regional Health Survey,* 75.

46   Kelly Skinner et al., "Giving Voice to Food Insecurity in a Remote Indigenous Community in Subarctic Ontario, Canada: Traditional Ways, Ways to Cope, Ways Forward," *BMC Public Health* 13, no. 1 (2013): 9.

47   Bethany Elliott et al., "'We are not being heard': Aboriginal Perspectives on Traditional Foods Access and Food Security," *Journal of Environmental and Public Health* 1 (2012): 4.

48   Skinner et al., "Giving Voice to Food Insecurity," 6–7; Nancy J. Turner and Katherine L. Turner, "'Where our women used to get the food': Cumulative Effects and Loss of Ethnobotanical Knowledge and Practice, Case Study from Coastal British Columbia," *Botany* 86, no. 2 (2008): 110.

49   The Southwest Ontario Aboriginal Health Access Centre (SOAHAC) Food Choice Study began in 2008 as a two-phase, community-based project collaboratively designed to examine the social and spatial processes underlying dietary practices, food security, and sources of food among urban and reserve-based First Nation households in southwestern Ontario (see: Neufeld, Richmond, and SOAHAC, "Impacts of Place and Social Spaces," 96; Richmond et al., "First Nations Food Environments," 3).

50   Neufeld, Richmond, and SOAHAC, "Impacts of Place and Social Spaces," 96. This chapter makes secondary use of data collected for "Impacts of Place and Social Places." Pseudonyms selected for the primary output have been honoured here.

51   Neufeld, Richmond, and SOAHAC, "Impacts of Place and Social Spaces," 100.

52   Neufeld, Richmond, and SOAHAC, "Exploring First Nation Elder Women's Relationships with Food," 5.

53   Neufeld, Richmond, and SOAHAC, "Exploring First Nation Elder Women's Relationships with Food," 7.

54 Ghosh, "Urban Reality of Type 2 Diabetes," 171.

55 Lemke and Delormier, "Indigenous Peoples' Food Systems," 3.

56 Food and Agriculture Organization of the United Nations, *The State of Food and Agriculture: Climate Change, Agriculture and Food Security* (Rome, Italy: Food and Agriculture Organization, 2016), 48.

57 Richmond et al., "First Nations Food Environments," 4.

58 Bethany Elliot and Deepthi Jayatilaka, "Healthy Eating and Food Security for Urban Aboriginal Peoples Living in Vancouver," *BC Provincial Health Services Authority* (Vancouver: Provincial Health Services Authority, 2011), 34–35.

59 Richmond et al., "First Nations Food Environments," 5.

60 Richmond et al., 5.

61 Lemke and Delormier, "Indigenous Peoples' Food Systems," 3.

62 Katie Big-Canoe and Chantelle A. M. Richmond, "Anishinabe Youth Perceptions About Community Health: Toward Environmental Repossession," *Health and Place* 26 (2014): 133.

63 For more information on the Collective, go to https://www.wisahk.ca/.

64 R. Delduco, "Land-Based Engagement for Building Community: Discussing Indigenous Gardens at the University of Guelph" (unpublished thesis report, University of Guelph, 2019).

65 Liz Miltenburg, email message to Manomin Research Project, 11 February 2020.

66 Treena Delormier et al., "Reclaiming Food Security in the Mohawk Community of Kahnawà:ke through Haudenosaunee Responsibilities," *Maternal and Child Nutrition* 13 (2017): 10.

67 Hannah T. Neufeld, Brittany Luby, and Kim Anderson, "Indigenous Researchers Plant Seeds of Hope for Health and Climate," *Conversation Canada*, last modified 12 February 2019, https://theconversation.com/indigenous-researchers-plant-seeds-of-hope-for-health-and-climate-106217.

68 Lynda Earle, "Traditional Aboriginal Diets and Health," *National Collaborating Centre for Aboriginal Health* (Prince George, BC: National Collaborating Centre for Aboriginal Health, 2011), 3.

69 Timothy Johns and Bhuwon R. Sthapit, "Biocultural Diversity in the Sustainability of Developing Country Food Systems," *Food and Nutrition Bulletin* 25, no. 2 (2004): 144.

70 Neufeld, Richmond, and SOAHAC, "Impacts of Place and Social Spaces," 109.

71   Jaime Cidro et al., "Beyond Food Security: Understanding Access to Cultural Food for Urban Indigenous People in Winnipeg as Indigenous Food Sovereignty," *Canadian Journal of Urban Research* 24, no. 1 (2015): 38.

72   Big-Canoe and Richmond, "Anishinabe Youth Perceptions," 133; Joshua K. Tobias and Chantelle A. M. Richmond, "'That land means everything to us Anishinaabe . . .': Environmental Dispossession and Resilience on the North Shore of Lake Superior," *Health and Place* 29 (2014): 28.

73   Laura Peach, Chantelle A.M. Richmond, and Candace Brunette-Debassige, "'You can't just take a piece of land from the university and build a garden on it': Exploring Indigenizing Space and Place in a Settler Canadian University Context," *Geoforum* 114 (2020): 118–19.

Chapter 8: Treaty and Mushkiki

1   Jana-Rae Yerxa, "Gii-kaapizigemin Manoomin Neyaashing: A Resurgence of Anishinaabeg Nationhood," *Decolonization: Indigeneity, Education and Society* 3, no. 3 (2014): 162.

2   Heidi Kiiwetinepinesiik Stark, "Respect, Responsibility, and Renewal: The Foundations of Anishinaabe Treaty Making with the United States and Canada," *American Indian Culture and Research Journal* 34, no. 2 (2010): 148; Leanne Simpson, "Looking after Gdoo-naaganinaa: Precolonial Nishinaabeg Diplomatic and Treaty Relationships," *Wicazo Sa Review* 23, no. 2 (2008): 35.

3   Simpson, "Looking after Gdoo-naaganinaa," 29.

4   Simpson, 32.

5   Stark, "Respect, Responsibility, and Renewal," 146–47.

6   Terry Copenace, personal communication with author, 2022.

7   Terry Copenace, personal communication with author, 2013.

8   Stark, "Respect, Responsibility, and Renewal," 148.

9   Alexander Morris, *The Treaties of Canada with the Indians of Manitoba and the Northwest Territories: Including the Negotiations on which They Were Based, and Other Information Relating Thereto* (Toronto: Belfords, Clarke and Company, 1880), 47.

10   Elder William Yerxa, interview with author, 2022.

11   Ngũgĩ wa Thiong'o, *Decolonising the Mind: The Politics of Language in African Literature* (1981; London, UK: James Currey, 2004), 15–16.

12   Kathi Avery Kinew, "Manito Gitigaan—Governing in the Great Spirit's Garden: Wild Rice in Treaty #3" (PhD diss., University of Manitoba, 1995), 4; Jason Jones, personal communication with author, 2013.

13   Dennis McPherson and Douglas Rabb, *Indian from the Inside: Native American Philosophy and Cultural Renewal*, 2nd ed. (Jefferson, NC: McFarland and Company, 2014), 91.

14   Kinew, "Manito Gitigaan—Governing in the Great Spirit's Garden," 152.

15   Elder William Yerxa, personal communication with author, 2022.

16   Stark, "Respect, Responsibility, and Renewal," 146–47, 153, 155–57.

17   Edward Benton-Banai, *The Mishomis Book: The Voice of the Ojibway* (Minneapolis: University of Minnesota Press with Indian Country Communications, 1988), 94–102; Leanne Simpson, *Dancing on Our Turtle's Back: Stories of Nishnaabeg Re-Creation, Resurgence, and a New Emergence* (Winnipeg: ARP Books, 2011), 65–67; Winona LaDuke, *Recovering the Sacred: The Power of Naming and Claiming* (2005; Chicago: Haymarket Books, 2016), 113–14; Jason Jones, personal communication with author, 2013.

18   Benton-Banai, *The Mishomis Book*, 101.

19   McPherson and Rabb, *Indian from the Inside*, 90.

20   Leanne Betasamosake Simpson, *As We Have Always Done: Indigenous Freedom through Radical Resistance* (Minneapolis: University of Minnesota Press, 2017), 22.

21   For further information, please consult bell hooks, *Teaching Community: Pedagogy of Hope* (New York, NY: Routledge Press, 2003).

22   Lucero, personal communication with author, 2022.

Chapter 9: Promise

1   "Promise" by Kristi Leora Gansworth has been updated and is republished with the permission of the Center for Humans & Nature.

Note on Copyright

1   Royal Commission on Aboriginal Peoples, *Report of the Royal Commission on Aboriginal Peoples: Volume 3: Gathering Strength* (Ottawa: Canada Communication Group Publishing, 1996), 598.

2   See, for instance, Catherine Larochelle, *School of Racism: A Canadian History, 1830–1915*, trans. S.E. Stewart (Winnipeg: University of Manitoba Press, 2023); Gregory

Younging, *Elements of Indigenous Style: A Guide for Writing By and About Indigenous Peoples* (Edmonton: Brush Education, 2018); and UMP's First Voices, First Texts series, https://uofmpress.ca/books/series/first-voices-first-texts.

3   Emily Toth, *Ms. Mentor's New and Ever More Impeccable Advice for Women and Men in Academia* (Philadelphia: University of Pennsylvania Press, 2009), 218.

4   Wikipedia, "Publish or perish," last modified 14 May 2024, https://en.wikipedia.org/wiki/Publish_or_perish.

5   By "abroad," we refer to roughly 180 countries that have signed the Berne Convention, an international treaty providing copyright holders with "the same protection in each of the other Contracting States as the latter grants to the works of its own nationals" ("Summary of the Berne Convention for the Protection of Literary and Artistic Works (1886)," World Intellectual Property Organization [WIPO], accessed 2 June 2024, https://www.wipo.int/treaties/en/ip/berne/summary_berne.html).

6   Department of Justice Canada, "Backgrounder: *United Nations Declaration on the Rights of Indigenous Peoples Act*," Government of Canada, 10 December 2021, https://www.justice.gc.ca/eng/declaration/about-apropos.html.

7   United Nations General Assembly, *United Nations Declaration on the Rights of Indigenous Peoples*, GA Res. 61/295, UN GAOR, 61st Session, 107th Plenary Meeting, UN Doc A/RES/61/295, 13 September 2007.

8   "Ontario Lawmaker Gives Historic Speech in Oji-Cree," CPAC Primetime News, 29 May 2024.

9   "Federation Announces Major Investments in Scholarly Books," Federation of Humanities and Social Sciences News, 4 April 2023.

10   Kerry Slack, "Sol Mamakwa Breaks a Language Barrier in Ontario," APTN National News, 28 May 2024.

GLOSSARY

by Jane Mariotti and Brittany Luby

Aquaculture: Aquatic animals and plants cared for by humans, and, in certain cases, harvested for food.

Anishinaabe-Aki: Territories inhabited and maintained by Anishinaabeg since time immemorial.

Anishinaabeg: Algonquian-speaking persons believed to share a common ancestor. Members of the Ojibwe, Odawa, and Potawatomi Nations may refer to themselves as "Anishinaabe" or "Anishinabe," which is the singular of "Anishinaabeg."

Biodiversity: The variety of plant, animal, and fungi relatives co-existing within an ecosystem.

Biota: All that is living (plant, animal or fungal) within a given area.

Cross-pollination: The pollination of a flower by pollen from a different plant of the same species—an alternative to self-pollination.[1]

Cultural keystone species: A species of cultural import with whom a peoples may have healing, nourishing, or other relations. For example, a cultural keystone species may be involved in ceremony, eaten as food, or provide shelter. These species may be difficult to substitute with others in the territory.

Drainage basin: Area of land, surrounded by elevation, within which all the streams drain into the same water body.

---

1   James D. Mauseth, "Introduction to Plants and Botany," *Botany: An Introduction to Plant Biology* (Burlington, MA: Jones and Bartlett Learning, 2017), 766.

Ecological niche: The sum of abiotic environmental conditions (light, moisture, etc.) and biotic interactions (competition, predation, etc.) that limit where a species can live.[2]

Ecosystem: All the living beings (plant, animal, and fungi) in a given area along with their physical habitat (soil, lake, rock, etc.).[3] For example, a marsh ecosystem can be made up of ducks, fish, rice worms, Manomin, cattail, water, organic soil, water, rock, and much more.

Elder: An Anishinaabe person who carries and embodies cultural teachings. An Elder is not determined solely by age, but by experience.

Foodweb: The set of living beings within an ecosystem who are connected through relationships of predation, herbivory, or decomposition. Energy is transferred from plants to herbivores, who in turn transfer their energy to predators. Since some beings consume the same food as others, energy is transferred through ecosystems in a web-like pattern.[4] For example, energy is gathered by plants, who may then be eaten by insects, who may then be eaten by many different bird species, who may in turn fall prey to an eagle.

Photosynthesis: Process through which plants take carbon dioxide from the air, energy from the sun, and water from their environment in order to create the sugars they need to grow and function. Oxygen is released as a by-product of photosynthesis.

Plant sentience: A term that encompasses a plant's ability to communicate, establish social networks, and respond to environmental challenges.

Pollination: The process through which pollen is deposited into the ovary of a flower by wind, water, insects, or mammals—leading to fertilization and subsequent development into a seed.

Seven Generations Principle: A decision-making framework that prompts individuals to consider the long-term consequences of their choices. Individuals who adopt a Seven Generations framework are encouraged to consider whether their actions honour ancestral teachings and ensure future well-being.

Time immemorial: A term used by Anishinaabeg to refer to the time before European impact. This term also honours centuries of Indigenous territorial occupation and care that extend beyond the reaches of human memory.

---

2   Stanton Braude and Bobbi S. Low, "An Introduction to Methods and Models in Ecology, Evolution, and Conservation Biology" (Princeton: Princeton University Press, 2010), 257.

3   Mauseth, "Introduction to Plants and Botany," 767.

4   Mauseth, "Introduction to Plants and Botany," 770.

SELECTED BIBLIOGRAPHY

Aagaard, Kevin, Josh Eash, Walt Ford, Patricia J. Heglund, Michelle McDowell, and Wayne E. Thogmartin. "Modelling the Relationship Between Water Level, Wild Rice Abundance, and Waterfowl Abundance at a Central North American Wetland." *Wetlands* 39, no. 1 (2019): 149–60. http://doi.org/10.1007/s13157-018-1025-6.

Adelson, Naomi. "The Embodiment of Inequality: Health Disparities in Aboriginal Canada," *Canadian Journal of Public Health* 96 (2005): S45–S61. https://doi.org/10.1007/BF03403702.

Adler, Shawn, and James Whetung. "Foraging for Wild Rice with Chef Shawn Adler." *CBC Life*. 10 December 2019. Video, 6:30. https://www.youtube.com/watch?v=NRdVnJwgW1s.

Aherin, Robert, and Christine Todd. "Developmental Stages of Children and Accident Risk Potential." *Agricultural Safety and Health, University of Illinois Extension.* Accessed 3 July 2020. https://web.extension.illinois.edu/agsafety/fact-sheets/devstage.cfm [https://perma.cc/TKW5-55HT].

Aiken, S.G., P.F. Lee, D. Punter, and J.M. Stewart. *Wild Rice in Canada.* Toronto: NC Press Limited and Agriculture Canada, 1988.

Anderson, Kim. *Life Stages and Native Women: Memory, Teachings, and Story Medicine.* Winnipeg: University of Manitoba Press, 2011.

Archibold, O.W. "Wild Rice." In *Encyclopedia of Food Science and Nutrition*, edited by Benjamin Caballero, Luiz Trugo, and Paul M. Finglas, 6183–6189. 2nd ed. Cambridge, MA: Academic Press, 2003.

Arthington, Angela. *Environmental Flows: Saving Rivers in the Third Millennium*. Berkeley: University of California Press, 2012.

Arzigian, Constance. "Middle Woodland and Oneota Contexts for Wild Rice Exploitation in Southwestern Wisconsin." *Midcontinental Journal of Archaeology* 25, no. 2 (2000): 245–68.

Bansal, Sheel, Shane C. Lishawa, Sue Newman, Brian A. Tangen, Douglas Wilcox, Dennis Albert, Michael J. Anteau et al. "*Typha* (Cattail) Invasion in North American Wetlands: Biology, Regional Problems, Impacts, Ecosystem Services, and Management." *Wetlands* 39, no. 4 (2019): 645–84. https://doi.org/10.1007/s13157-019-01174-7.

Benton-Banai, Edward. *The Mishomis Book: The Voice of the Ojibway*. Minneapolis: University of Minnesota Press with Indian Country Communications, 1988.

Big-Canoe, Katie, and Chantelle A.M. Richmond. "Anishinaabe Youth Perceptions About Community Health: Toward Environmental Repossession." *Health and Place* 26 (2014): 127–35. https://doi.org/10.1016/j.healthplace.2013.12.013.

Boyd, M., C. Surette, J. Surette, I. Therriault, and S. Hamilton. "Holocene Paleoecology of a Wild Rice (*Zizania* sp.) Lake in Northwestern Ontario, Canada." *Journal of Paleolimnology* 50 (2013): 365–77.

Boyd, Matthew, Clarence Surette, Andrew Lints, and Scott Hamilton. "Wild Rice (*Zizania* spp.), the Three Sisters, and the Woodland Tradition in Western and Central Canada." *Midwest Archaeological Conference Inc. Occasional Papers* 1 (2014): 7–32.

Branstner, Christine. "Archaeological Investigations at the Cloudman Site (20CH6): A Multicomponent Native American Occupation on Drummond Island, Michigan 1992 and 1994 Excavations." Report submitted to the Consortium for Archaeological Research, Michigan State University. East Lansing: Michigan State University, 1995.

Brose, David S. *The Dunn's Farm Site; 20LU22: A Late Middle Woodland Event in Northwest Michigan*. Kalamazoo, MI: Imprints from the Past, 2016.

Cidro, Jaime, Bamidele Adekunle, Evelyn Peters, and Tabitha Martens. "Beyond Food Security: Understanding Access to Cultural Food for Urban Indigenous People in Winnipeg as Indigenous Food Sovereignty." *Canadian Journal of Urban Research* 24, no. 1 (2015): 24–43.

Corntassel, Jeff. "Re-Envisioning Resurgence: Indigenous Pathways to Decolonization and Sustainable Self-Determination." *Decolonization: Indigeneity, Education and Society* 1, no. 1 (2012): 86–101.

SELECTED BIBLIOGRAPHY

Crawford, Gary W., and David G. Smith. "Paleoethnobotany in the Northeast." In *People and Plants in Ancient Eastern North America*, edited by Paul E. Minnis, 172–257. Washington, DC: Smithsonian Books, 2003.

Cunningham, Myrna. "Chapter V: Health." In *United Nations, Permanent Forum on Indigenous Issues, State of the World's Indigenous Peoples*, edited by Broddi Sigurdarson, 156–87. New York: United Nations, 2009.

Dawson, K.C.A. "The MacGillivray Site: A Laurel Tradition Site in Northwestern Ontario." *Ontario Archaeology* 34 (1980): 45–68.

———. "The Martin-Bird Site." *Ontario Archaeology* 47 (1987): 33–57.

———. "The Mound Island Site: A Multi-Component Woodland Period Habitation Site in Northwestern Ontario." *Ontario Archaeology* 30 (1978): 47–66.

Densmore, Frances. "Uses of Plants by the Chippewan Indians." Extract from *Forty-Fourth Annual Report of the Bureau of American Ethnology*. Washington, DC: Government Printing Office, 1928.

Dore, William G. *Wild-rice*. Ottawa: The Queen's Printer for Canada, 1969.

Dysievick, Kristi E., Peter F. Lee, and John Kabatay. *Recovery of Wild Rice Stand Following Mechanical Removal of Narrowleaf Cattail*. Windsor, ON: International Joint Commission, 2016.

Earle, Lynda. "Traditional Aboriginal Diets and Health." *National Collaborating Centre for Aboriginal Health*. Prince George, BC: National Collaborating Centre for Aboriginal Health, 2011.

Echo-Hawk, Roger C. "Ancient History in the New World: Integrating Oral Traditions and the Archaeological Record in Deep Time." *American Antiquity* 65, no. 2 (2000): 267–90.

Elliott, Bethany, Deepthi Jayatilaka, Contessa Brown, Leslie Varley, and Kitty K. Corbett. "'We are not being heard': Aboriginal Perspectives on Traditional Foods Access and Food Security." *Journal of Environmental and Public Health* 1 (2012): 1–9. https://doi.org/10.1155/2012/130945.

Fannucchi, William A., Genevieve T. Fannucchi, and Lyle E. Nauman. "Effects of Harvesting Wild Rice, *Zizania aquatica*, on Soras, Porzana Carolina." *Canadian Field-Naturalist* 100, no. 4 (1986): 533–36.

Federal Interagency Stream Restoration Working Group (FISRWG). *Stream Corridor Restoration: Principles, Processes, and Practices*. Washington, DC: FISRWG, 1998.

Fernald, Merrit Lyndon, Alfred Charles Kinsey, and Steve William Chadde. *The New Edible Wild Plants of Eastern North America*. Sullivan, IN: Orchard Innovations, 2019.

First Nations Information Governance Centre (FNIGC). *First Nations Regional Health Survey (RHS) 2008/10: National Report on Adults, Youth and Children Living in First Nations Communities*. Ottawa: FNIGC, 2012.

Food and Agriculture Organization of the United Nations. *The State of Food and Agriculture: Climate Change, Agriculture and Food Security*. Rome, Italy: Food and Agriculture Organization, 2016.

Ford, Richard I. "Ethnobotany in North America: An Historical Phytogeographic Perspective." *Canadian Journal of Botany* 59 (1981): 2178–88.

Frideres, James. *Indigenous People in the Twenty-First Century*. 3rd ed. Don Mills, ON: Oxford University Press, 2020.

Griffin, Kersten O. "Paleoecological Aspects of the Red Lake Peatland, Northern Minnesota." *Canadian Journal of Botany* 55 (1977): 172–92.

Grover, Linda LeGarde. *Onigamiising: Seasons of an Ojibwe Year*. Minneapolis: University of Minnesota Press, 2017.

Hatala, Andrew R., Darrien Morton, Chinyere Njeze, Kelley Bird-Naytowhow, and Tamara Pearl. "Re-Imagining Miyo-Wicehtowin: Human-Nature Relations, Land-Making, and Wellness among Indigenous Youth in a Canadian Urban Context." *Social Science and Medicine* 230 (2019): 122–30. https://doi.org/10.1016/j. socscimed.2019.04.012.

Huber, James Kenneth. "Palynological Investigations Related to Archaeological Sites and the Expansion of Wild Rice (*Zizania aquatica* L.) in Northeast Minnesota." PhD diss., University of Minnesota, 2001.

Intergovernmental Panel on Climate Change (IPCC), Rajendra K. Pachauri, and Leo Meyer, eds. *Climate Change 2014: Synthesis Report*. Geneva, Switzerland: IPCC, 2015.

Johns, Timothy, and Bhuwon R. Sthapit. "Biocultural Diversity in the Sustainability of Developing Country Food Systems." *Food and Nutrition Bulletin* 25, no. 2 (2004): 143–55.

Johnson, Elden. "Archaeological Evidence for Utilization of Wild Rice." *Science* 163, no. 3864 (1969): 276-277.

Joseph, Bob. *21 Things You May Not Know About the Indian Act: Helping Canadians Make Reconciliation with Indigenous Peoples a Reality*. Port Coquitlam, BC: Indigenous Relations Press, 2018.

Kimmerer, Robin Wall. "Returning the Gift." *Minding Nature* 7, no. 2 (2014): 18–24.

Kinew, Kathi Avery. "Manito Gitigaan—Governing in the Great Spirit's Garden: Wild Rice in Treaty #3." PhD diss., University of Manitoba, 1995.

SELECTED BIBLIOGRAPHY

Kuhnlein, Harriet, and Oliver Receveur. "Dietary Change and Traditional Food Systems of Indigenous Peoples." *Annual Review of Nutrition* 16, no. 1 (1996): 417–42. https://doi.org/10.1146/annurev.nu.16.070196.002221.

Landry, Véronique, Hugo Asselin, and Carole Lévesque. "Link to the Land and *Mino-Pimatisiwin* (Comprehensive Health) of Indigenous People Living in Urban Areas in Eastern Canada." *International Journal of Environmental Research and Public Health* 16 (2019): 1–10. https://doi.org/10.3390/ijerph16234782.

Lee, P.F. "Ecological Relationships of Wild Rice, *Zizania aquatica*. 5. Enhancement of Wild Rice Production by *Potamogeton robbinsii*." *Canadian Journal of Botany* 65, no. 7 (1987): 1433–38. https://doi.org/10.1139/b87-198.

Lemke, Stefanie, and Treena Delormier. "Indigenous Peoples' Food Systems, Nutrition and Gender: Conceptual and Methodological Considerations." *Maternal and Child Nutrition* 13, no. 3 (2017): 1–12. https://doi.org/10.1111/mcn.12499.

Lennstrom, Heidi A., and Christine A. Hastorf. "Interpretation in Context: Sampling and Analysis in Paleoethnobotany." *American Antiquity* 60, no. 4 (1995): 701–21.

Mallik, A.U. "Small-Scale Succession Towards Fen on Floating Mat of a *Typha* Marsh in Atlantic Canada." *Canadian Journal of Botany* 67, no. 5 (1989): 1309–16. https://doi.org/10.1139/b89-174.

Mancuso, Stefano, and Alessandra Viola. *Brilliant Green: The Surprising History and Science of Plant Intelligence.* Washington, DC: Island Press, 2015.

Mauseth, James D. *Botany: An Introduction to Plant Biology.* 6th ed. Burlington, MA: Jones and Bartlett Learning, 2017.

McAndrews, John H. "Paleobotany of a Wild Rice Lake in Minnesota." *Canadian Journal of Botany* 47 (1969): 1671–79.

McNally, Mary, and Debbie Martin. "First Nations, Inuit and Métis Health: Considerations for Canadian Health Leaders in the Wake of the Truth and Reconciliation Commission of Canada Report." *Healthcare Management Forum* 30, no. 2 (2017): 117–22. https://doi.org/10.1177/0840470416680445.

Meeker, James E. "The Ecology of 'Wild' Wild-Rice (*Zizania palustris* var. *palustris*) in the Kakagon Sloughs, a Riverine Wetland on Lake Superior." In *Proceedings of the Wild Rice Research and Management Conference*, edited by Lisa S. Williamson, Lisa A. Dlutkowski, and Amy P. McCammon-Soltis, 68–83. Carlton, MN: Great Lakes Indian Fish and Wildlife Commission, 1999.

Minnesota Department of Natural Resources (MNDNR). "Natural Wild Rice in Minnesota: A Wild Rice Study." Report submitted to the Minnesota Legislature by the Minnesota Department of Natural Resources. St. Paul: MNDNR, 2008.

Moffat, Charles R., and Constance M. Arzigian. "New Data on the Late Woodland Use of Wild Rice in Northern Wisconsin." *Midcontinental Journal of Archaeology* 25, no.1 (2000): 49–81.

Molles, Manuel C., and James F. Cahill. *Ecology: Concepts and Applications*. 2nd ed. Whitby, ON: McGraw-Hill Ryerson, 2011.

Monckton, Stephen G. "Plants and the Archaeology of the Invisible." In *Before Ontario: The Archaeology of a Province*, edited by Marit K. Munson and Susan M. Jamieson, 124–33. Montreal: McGill-Queen's University Press, 2013.

Moyle, John B. "Wild Rice in Minnesota." *Journal of Wildlife Management* 8, no. 3 (1944): 177–84.

Myrbo, A., E.B. Swain, D.R. Engstrom, J. Coleman Wasik, J. Brenner, M. Dykhuizen Shore, E. B. Peters, and G. Blaha. "Sulfide Generated by Sulfate Reduction is a Primary Controller of the Occurrence of Wild Rice (*Zizania palustris*) in Shallow Aquatic Ecosystems." *Journal of Geophysical Research: Biogeosciences* 122, no. 11 (2017): 2736–53. https://doi.org/10.1002/2017JG003787.

Neufeld, Hannah T., Chantelle A.M. Richmond, and Southwest Ontario Aboriginal Health Access Centre. "Impacts of Place and Social Spaces on Traditional Food Systems in Southwestern Ontario." *International Journal of Indigenous Health* 12, no. 1 (2017): 93–115. https://doi.org/10.18357/ijih112201716903.

———. "Exploring First Nation Elder Women's Relationships with Food from Social, Ecological, and Historical Perspectives." *Current Developments in Nutrition* 4, no. 3 (2020): 1–11.

Oelke, E.A., J. Grava, D. Noetzel, D. Barron, J. Percich, C. Schertz, J. Strait, and R. Stucker. *Wild Rice Production in Minnesota*. Minneapolis: University of Minnesota, 1982.

Ontario Federation of Indigenous Friendship Centres (OFIFC). *Ganohonyohk—Giving Thanks: Understanding Prosperity from the Perspectives of Urban Indigenous Friendship Centre Communities in Ontario.* Toronto: OFIFC, 2020. https://ofifc.org/?research=ganohonyohk-giving-thanks-indigenous-prosperity.

Panci, Hannah, Melonee Montano, Aaron Shultz, Travis Bartnick, and Kim Stone. *Climate Change Vulnerability Assessment: Integrating Scientific and Traditional Ecological Knowledge.* Odanah, WI: Great Lakes Indian Fish and Wildlife Commission, 2018.

Pickett, Keri, dir. *First Daughter and the Black Snake*. 2017; Pickett Pictures, 2017. 1h 44m. DVD.

SELECTED BIBLIOGRAPHY

Pillsbury, Robert W., and Melissa A. McGuire. "Factors Affecting the Distribution of Wild Rice (*Zizania palustris*) and the Associated Macrophyte Community." *Wetlands* 29, no. 2 (2009): 724–34. https://doi.org/10.1672/08-41.1.

Poff, N. LeRoy, J. David Allan, Mark B. Bain, James R. Karr, Karen L. Prestegaard, Brian D. Richter, Richard E. Sparks, and Julie C. Stromberg. "The Natural Flow Regime." *BioScience* 47, no. 11 (1997): 769–84. https://doi.org/10.2307/1313099.

Raster, Amanda, and Christina Gish Hill. "The Dispute Over Wild Rice: An Investigation of Treaty Agreements and Ojibwe Food Sovereignty." *Agriculture and Human Values* 34, no. 2 (2017): 267–81. https://doi.org/10.1007/s10460-016-9703-6.

Reading, Charlotte. "Structural Determinants of Aboriginal Peoples' Health." In *Determinants of Indigenous Peoples' Health in Canada: Beyond the Social*, edited by Margo Greenwood, Sarah de Leeuw, Nicole Marie Lindsay, and Charlotte Reading, 3–17. Toronto: Canadian Scholars' Press, 2018.

Reo, Nicholas J., and Laura A. Ogden. "Anishnaabe Aki: An Indigenous Perspective on the Global Threat of Invasive Species." *Sustainability Science* 13, no. 5 (2018): 1443–52. https://doi.org/10.1007/s11625-018-0571-4.

Richmond, Chantelle A.M., and Catherine Cook. "Creating Conditions for Aboriginal Health Equity: The Promise of Healthy Public Policy." *Public Health Reviews* 37 (2016): 1–16. https://doi.org/10.1186/s40985-016-0016-5.

Richmond, Chantelle, Marylynn Steckley, Hannah Neufeld, Rachel Bezner Kerr, Kathi Wilson, and Brian Dokis. "First Nations Food Environments: Exploring the Role of Place, Income, and Social Connection." *Current Developments in Nutrition* 4, no. 8 (2020): 1–8. https://doi.org/10.1093/cdn/nzaa108.

Simpson, G.M. "A Study of Germination in the Seed of Wild Rice (*Zizania aquatica*)." *Canadian Journal of Botany* 44, no. 1 (1966): 1–9.

Skinner, Kelly, Rhona M. Hanning, Ellen Desjardins, and Leonard J.S. Tsuji. "Giving Voice to Food Insecurity in a Remote Indigenous Community in Subarctic Ontario, Canada: Traditional Ways, Ways to Cope, Ways Forward." *BMC Public Health* 13, no. 1 (2013): 1–13. https://doi.org/10.1186/1471-2458-13-427.

Skinner, Kelly, Erin Pratley, and Kristin Burnett. "Eating in the City: A Review of the Literature on Food Insecurity and Indigenous People Living in Urban Spaces." *Societies* 6, no. 2 (2016): 1–17. https://doi.org/10.3390/soc6020007.

Statistics Canada. *Aboriginal Peoples in Canada: Key Results From the 2016 Census.* Last modified 25 October 2017. https://www150.statcan.gc.ca/n1/daily-quotidien/171025/dq171025a-eng.htm?indid=14430-1&indgeo=0.

Steeves, Taylor A. "Wild Rice: Indian Food and a Modern Delicacy." *Economic Botany* 6, no. 2 (1952): 107–42. https://doi.org/10.1007/BF02984871.

St. George, Scott. "Streamflow in the Winnipeg River Basin, Canada: Trends, Extremes and Climate Linkages." *Journal of Hydrology* 332, no. 3–4 (2007): 396–411. https://doi.org/10.1016/j.jhydrol.2006.07.014.

Stults, M., S. Petersen, J. Bell, W. Baule, E. Nasser, E. Gibbons, and M. Fougerat. *Climate Change Vulnerability Assessment and Adaptation Plan: 1854 Ceded Territory Including the Bois Forte, Fond du Lac, and Grand Portage Reservations.* Duluth, MN: 1854 Ceded Territory, 2016.

Tarasuk, Valerie, Andy Mitchell, and Naomi Dachner. *Household Food Insecurity in Canada, 2014.* Toronto: Research to Identify Policy Options to Reduce Food Insecurity, 2014.

Thomas, A.G., and J.M. Stewart. "The Effect of Different Water Depths on the Growth of Wild Rice." *Canadian Journal of Botany* 47 (1969): 1525–31.

Tobias, Joshua K., and Chantelle A.M. Richmond. "'That land means everything to us Anishinaabe . . .': Environmental Dispossession and Resilience on the North Shore of Lake Superior." *Health and Place* 29 (2014): 26–33. https://doi.org/10.1016/j.healthplace.2014.05.008.

Truth and Reconciliation Commission of Canada. *Truth and Reconciliation Commission of Canada: Calls to Action.* Winnipeg, MB: Truth and Reconciliation Commission of Canada, 2015.

VanDerwarker, Amber M., Dana N. Bardolph, Kristin M. Hoppa, Heather B. Thakar, Lana S. Martin, Allison L. Jaqua, Matthew E. Biwer, and Kristina M. Gill. "New World Paleoethnobotany in the New Millennium (2000–2013)." *Journal of Archaeological Research* 24, no. 2 (2016): 125–77.

Vennum Jr., Thomas. *Wild Rice and the Ojibway People.* St. Paul: Minnesota Historical Society Press, 1988.

Walker, Brian, C.S. Holling, Stephen R. Carpenter, and Ann P. Kinzig. "Resilience, Adaptability and Transformability in Social-Ecological Systems." *Ecology and Society* 9, no. 2 (2004): 1–9.

Walker, Sandra. *The Path to Wild Food: Edible Plants and Recipes for Canada.* Edmonton, AB: Lone Pine Publishing, 2018.

Weir, Cynthia E., and Hugh M. Dale. "A Developmental Study of Wild Rice, *Zizania aquatica* L." *Canadian Journal of Botany* 38 (1960): 719–39.

Whipple, Dorothy Dora. *Chi-mewinzha: Ojibwe Stories from Leech Lake.* Minneapolis: University of Minnesota Press, 2015.

SELECTED BIBLIOGRAPHY

Willows, Noreen, Paul Veugelers, Kim Raine, and Stefan Kuhle. "Associations between Household Food Insecurity and Health Outcomes in the Aboriginal Population (Excluding Reserves)." *Health Reports* 22, no. 2 (2011): 15–20.

Wisconsin Department of Natural Resources (WDNR). *Wild Rice: Ecology, Harvest, Management.* Madison, WI, n.d.

Wright, Patti J. "Methodological Issues in Paleoethnobotany: A Consideration of Issues, Methods, and Cases." In *Integrating Zooarchaeology and Paleoethnobotany: A Consideration of Issues, Methods, and Cases,* edited by Amber M. Derwarker and Tanya M. Peres, 37–64. New York: Springer, 2010.

Yost, C.L., M.S. Blinnikov, and M.L. Julius. "Detecting Ancient Wild Rice (*Zizania* spp. L.) Using Phytoliths: A Taphonomic Study of Modern Wild Rice in Minnesota (USA) Lake Sediments." *Journal of Paleolimnology* 49 (2013): 221–36.

Younging, Gregory. *Elements of Indigenous Style: A Guide for Writing By and About Indigenous Peoples.* Edmonton, AB: Brush Education, 2018.

Yu, Zicheng, J.H. McAndrews, and D. Siddiqi. "Influences of Holocene Climate and Water Levels on Vegetation Dynamics of a Lakeside Wetland." *Canadian Journal of Botany* 74 (1996): 1602–15.

Zhang, Xuebin, K.D. Harvey, W.D. Hogg, and Ted R. Yuzyk. "Trends in Canadian Streamflow." *Water Resources Research* 37, no. 4 (2001): 987–98.

Zilberstein, Anya. "Inured to Empire: Wild Rice and Climate Change." *William and Mary Quarterly* 72, no. 1 (2015): 127–58.

CONTRIBUTORS

COMMUNITY ADVISORS

Allan Luby, Niisaachewan Anishinaabe Nation, is a band member, federally licensed captain, and expert navigator. He has been President of Lake Navigation Ltd., which operates a 200-passenger capacity vessel, since 1987. Luby agreed to share his water expertise with the Manomin Project by maintaining boating equipment and acting as a river guide for the 2018 and 2019 field seasons. Luby also transports band members along the river to participate in land-based activities co-hosted by the University of Guelph and Niisaachewan Anishinaabe Nation.

Elder Archie Wagamese, Niisaachewan Anishinaabe Nation, began harvesting Manomin on the Winnipeg River in the 1950s. Over thirty years of guiding experience deepened Wagamese's understanding of the river as he observed water levels and water quality to provide tourists with a safe adventure. During his lifetime, Wagamese expressed an interest in sharing his knowledge on the influence of dam development on the ecosystem, highlighting relationships between animal (e.g., beaver, muskrats, and ducks) and plant life (e.g., Manomin). He was also interested in sharing his knowledge of transit routes and related harvesting areas that were and continue to be influenced by changing water levels. Before his death in December 2021, Wagamese actively guided the Manomin Project.

Barry Henry, Niisaachewan Anishinaabe Nation, is the Economic Development Officer (EDO) for his community. As EDO, Henry helps to develop plans for the use of traditional lands. The Manomin Project is one such initiative as field restoration could allow band members to reclaim Manomin harvesting, processing, and sales in their territory. More than that, field restoration would allow band members to restore reciprocal relationships with Manomin. As a member of the Manomin Project, Henry has played a key role welcoming students to Niisaachewan Anishinaabe Nation and coordinating Elder interviews in the band office and on the land.

Elder Clarence Henry Jr., Niisaachewan Anishinaabe Nation, began visiting Manomin fields on Lake of the Woods in the 1950s. At this young age, Henry learned how to process Manomin by watching his family at work. He is interested in changing markets for Manomin and economic factors that influence people's decision to pick Manomin. Henry is a future- and solution-oriented Elder who has expressed an interest in environmental modification to restore Manomin on the Winnipeg River. He is aware of past restoration attempts (e.g., damming and seeding) on reserve and is willing to comment on their perceived effectiveness.

Elder Danny Strong, Niisaachewan Anishinaabe Nation, began harvesting Manomin in the late 1960s. Strong continued picking by canoe, as conditions allowed, until his death in January 2023. He was interested in how the harvest is carried out and can be supported by families into the future. Strong identified picking techniques that may facilitate crop regeneration. He also shared techniques for replanting Manomin fields after the harvest. He was interested in supporting crop revitalization by encouraging individuals to build relationships with Manomin.

MANOMIN

Elder Guy Henry, Niisaachewan Anishinaabe Nation, began caring for Manomin in the 1970s as a young boy while watching his grandparents harvest by canoe on the Winnipeg River. Currently, Guy works alongside his community on several projects to restore sturgeon and bat populations, Manomin fields, and to maintain sources of renewable energy. Along with his knowledge of Manomin care, he has shared places where the ancestors would process the harvest by dancing on Manomin placed in holes formed from the bedrock. He also recommended an additional Manomin field for ongoing research, noting its high yields in years past. Having learned about Manomin from his family, Guy remains committed to passing on his extensive knowledge of the natural world to the next generation. Guy enjoys being out on the water, learning new things, and contributing to his community through the many projects he is involved with.

Elder John Henry, Niisaachewan Anishinaabe Nation, began picking Manomin on the Winnipeg River in the 1960s. He continues to harvest Manomin, as conditions allow, today. Henry is interested in developing water-level recommendations to restore Manomin. He is also interested in the spin-off effects Manomin restoration may have along the Winnipeg River, noting that declines in field productivity have caused declines in duck and goose hunting. He associates crop restoration work with the economic potential of the region. Henry has also worked on the Grievance Committee since the 1990s, fostering an interest in research as a foundation for reconciliation.

Kii'zhii'bob'binse, Adik dodem. Niisaachewan/Waabaaseemong is my home community. Reno Cameron is my English name. I am a proud father of four beautiful daughters and one handsome son. I have walked with my wife for fourteen years. My father was Larry Henry. He worked with the Ontario Provincial Police (OPP) for fourteen years and was chief for one term. He moved into mental health for some time and took on the role of working with the Indian Residential School. Our Father was called home in

2022. My Mother is Shelia Cameron-Copenace. She has worked in schools for some years and has been involved in childcare services all her life. She continues to work in that field.

Elder Larry Kabestra Sr., Niisaachewan Anishinaabe Nation, began harvesting Manomin at a young age. Larry participated in other traditional activities as well. He was known by community members as an expert fisherman, hunter, and guide. During his lifetime, Larry committed to sharing his cultural teachings and language with Youth. He inspired others to learn both on the land and through college or university (should they so choose). In his forties, Larry completed his Economic and Community Development degree with the University of Manitoba—an accomplishment that blazed a trail for others. Before his death in 2023, Larry participated in land-based activities to help pass his Manomin teachings down to the next generation. He did so with patience and with humour.

Chief Lorraine Cobiness, Niisaachewan Anishinaabe Nation, has over a decade of experience as Chief of Niisaachewan First Nation. She oversees the Manomin Project. From her position, Cobiness sets research priorities, reviews progress reports, and establishes objectives for research dissemination and use. She has experience collaborating with industry and government to manage the Kenora Forest. She is keen to apply these relationship-building and negotiation skills to water management in the Upper Winnipeg River drainage basin.

Elder Nancy McLeod, Niisaachewan Anishinaabe Nation, was taught to honour all Creation by her Elders. Through her participation in the Manomin Project, Nancy hopes to show others how to maintain respectful relationships with their plant and animal relatives. Nancy teaches that we must treat our lands, waters, and each other with care.

Elder Sherman Kabestra, Niisaachewan Anishinaabe Nation, has been harvesting Manomin for over sixty years. He thinks it is important for people to understand how introduced plant species (like "bog" or hybrid cattails) affect Manomin growth and the health of ancestral fields. Sherman has located and towed members of the Manomin Project back to shore, sharing teachings while keeping the team safe in the territory. A special editorial shout-out to Elder Kabestra for the rescue!

Elder Terry Greene, Niisaachewan Anishinaabe Nation, is a traditional Elder who opened the Manomin Project in 2018. He began harvesting Manomin as a youth. In the 1970s, he participated in seeding initiatives in the Lake of the Woods District. Greene is willing to reflect on the pros and cons of this experience to inform crop restoration at Niisaachewan. He asserts that Manomin harvesting is a Treaty Right. As such, Greene is also committed to passing on information that could be used to empower Anishinaabe youth to learn and to practice skills associated with treaty living.

Elder Theresa Jourdain (née Kabestra), Niisaachewan Anishinaabe Nation, began harvesting Manomin with her family in the mid-1950s. Jourdain has expressed an interest in observing hybrid cattail, referred to as "bog," and managing its spread throughout traditional harvesting areas. She has also experimented with removal techniques (e.g., axing vegetation). Jourdain would like to develop and share her understanding of "bog" and other species that complicate Manomin growth. She is also interested in discussing species that appear to improve plant health. For example, Jourdain perceives lily pads as a potential fertilizer.

The editors would also like to acknowledge and thank **Josephine Kylne** and **Karen Bluebird** for sharing during community events and showing the support needed to continue the project.

AUTHORS

Andrea Bradford @manominproject, obtained her PhD from Queen's University, focusing her dissertation on the ecohydrology of the Minesing Wetlands in Ontario. She has been a faculty member in Water Resources Engineering at the University of Guelph since 2002 and has provided expert testimony on the impacts of development on streams and wetlands. She is passionate about advancing management and design approaches to meet the needs of aquatic systems and protect the well-being of the people who depend upon them. The Manomin Project has stimulated collaboration and learning that Andrea, who is a settler, has applied to both research and enhancing undergraduate engineering education. She was awarded the University of Guelph Faculty Association Distinguished Professor Award for Innovation in Teaching in 2020.

Brittany Luby @manominproject, is the author of four children's books, including *When the Stars Came Home, Mnoomin Maan'gowing/The Gift of Mnoomin, Mii mandaa ezhi-gkendmaanh/This Is How I Know*, and *Encounter*. Luby is also the author of *Dammed: The Politics of Loss and Survival in Anishinaabe Territory*, a piece of historical non-fiction for adult readers. Luby has won numerous awards for both her fiction and non-fiction writing, including the Ruth & Sylvia Schwartz Children's Picture Book Award (2022), Best Book in Canadian Environmental History (2022), and the Governor-General's History Award for Excellence in Scholarly Research (2021). She has been and continues to be trained by the Grievance Committee and the Elders at Niisaachewan Anishinaabe Nation to raise awareness of Crown-Anishinaabe relations in what is colonially known as Canada. Writing is Luby's way of fulfilling this responsibility to her ancestral community, Niisaachewan Anishinaabe Nation.

Edward Benton-Banai, a spiritual teacher of the Lac Court Orielles Band of the Ojibway Tribe, was a co-founder of the American Indian Movement, as well as the founder and executive director of the Red School House in what is currently St. Paul, Minnesota. He was called home in 2020.

Giizhiigokwe Sandra Indian, born and raised at Onigaming, Lake of the Woods, has been an accredited teacher for three decades, teaching many subjects at schools at Whitefish Bay and Onigaming in Northwestern Ontario. She has also taught in Minnesota. She was one of the first walkers around Lake Superior and is a well-regarded Knowledge Keeper. She pursues her wish for more Anishinaabeg to speak Anishinaabemowin by sharing her language and stories online.

Hannah Neufeld is an Associate Professor and holds the Canada Research Chair in Indigenous Health, Wellbeing and Food Environments. Her research approach for twenty-five years has been community-based, working with Indigenous families and communities on the revitalization of food systems and supporting maternal child feeding practices within Canada and internationally. She has contributed to infant nutrition policy, knowledge translation platforms with the World Health Organization and led two co-edited volumes, *Indigenous Experiences of Pregnancy and Birth* along with *Recipes and Reciprocity: Building Relationships in Research*.

Jana-Rae Yerxa is Anishinaabe from Couchiching First Nation in Treaty #3 territory. She has a Master of Social Work degree from Lakehead University, and a Master of Arts in Indigenous Governance from the University of Victoria. She is faculty and curriculum developer in Anishinaabe Gikendaasowin at the Seven Generations Education Institute.

Jane Mariotti @manominproject is a settler ecologist with a passion for community-centred research and land-based food systems. She is currently pursuing a master's degree in Environmental Science at the University of Guelph, where her research focuses on boreal soil fertility and sustainable agriculture in the Northwest Territories. Her field experience within Canada includes environmental monitoring in Ontario and the Northwest

Territories. She has also worked abroad in Costa Rica. Her involvement with the Manomin Project began in 2021 as an undergraduate research assistant, and since then has included fieldwork on the Upper Winnipeg River as well as various research and administrative tasks.

Jill McConkey is Senior Editor at UMP. She has an MA in Canadian History and has worked in scholarly publishing for nearly twenty-five years.

Joseph Pitawanakwat is Ojibway from Wikwemikong Unceded Indian Territory on Manitoulin Island, Ontario. He is an educator who specializes in plant-based medicine. He is the founder and director of Creators Garden, a year-round, Indigenous outdoor education-based business. Pitawanakwat focuses on plant identification, sustainable harvesting, and teaching everyone of the linguistic, historical, cultural, edible, ecological, and medicinal significance of plants through experience. He is currently pursuing a master's in Environmental Studies at York University and has learned from hundreds of traditional knowledge holders. Pitawanakwat has uniquely blended these teachings with Western knowledge and is a community-recognized plant-based knowledge holder.

Kathi Avery Kinew has worked with First Nations and Treaty Chiefs organizations for more than fifty years. She has also taught Indigenous Studies courses at the University of Manitoba for more than twenty-five years. Kathi is the author of "Manito Gitigaan: Governing the Great Spirit's Garden" (1995), her PhD dissertation at the University of Manitoba. She is honoured to call Onigaming her home.

Kezhii'aanakwat Ron Kelly is an honoured Elder, who was brought up on both sides of Lake of the Woods—Northwest Angle #33 First Nation on the west and Ojibways of Onigaming on the east. He continues his traditional way of life. Kezhii'aanakwat is an accredited teacher of many subjects at the Mikinaak Onigaming School where he has taught for forty-five years. He is currently doing cultural and land-based language teaching for the school.

He is a teacher of language teachers, having taught Anishinaabemowin at the Lakehead University Summer Institute for about a decade. He has shared his knowledge at many language and education conferences, in fluent Anishinaabemowin. Kezhii'aanakwat has also shared his proficiency in writing Anishinaabemowin in syllabics and with the double vowel system, encouraging others to do so.

Kristi Leora Gansworth is a citizen of Kitigan Zibi Anishinaabeg, and a scholar focusing on Anishinaabe responsibilities. Her poetry and writing are an ongoing engagement with her existence as Anishinaabekwe and she is currently at work on a full-length collection of poems.

Margaret Lehman @manominproject is a settler researcher who joined the Manomin Project in May 2019. Lehman is currently working on the land and caring for her plant relations in lands protected by the Dish with One Spoon Covenant.

Michelle Johnson-Jennings, PhD, EdM, a Choctaw Nation–enrolled tribal member, is director of the division of environmentally based health and land-based healing at the University of Washington's Indigenous Wellness Research Institute. She holds the Canadian Research Chair in Indigenous Community Engaged Research. Dr. Johnson-Jennings founded and directed the Research for Indigenous Community Health Center at the University of Minnesota and was awarded a U.S. Fulbright scholarship to conduct research in New Zealand. She has been invited to present her research at numerous professional conferences held in the Czech Republic, New Zealand, Mexico, Canada, and the United States. She is on the editorial board of the *Indigenous Policy Journal*.

Patees Dorothy Copenace was born and raised at Ojibways of Onigaming, Lake of the Woods. She is a fluent Anishinaabemowin speaker and an honoured Elder in Onigaming and throughout Treaty #3 and Anishinaabe territory.

Pikanagegaabo William Yerxa was born on the Little Eagle Reserve in Northwestern Ontario. He learned to harvest Manoomin from his parents, Bert and Francis Yerxa, and has continued this vital Anishinaabe practice for seventy years. Alongside his wife, Florence Yerxa, he has continued to teach his children, grandchildren, and great-grandchildren how to traditionally harvest and prepare the sacred grain.

Samantha Mehltretter @manominproject, PhD, is a settler researcher working on the Manomin Project, a community-driven collaborative research project with Niisaachewan Anishinaabe Nation and the University of Guelph. She completed her bachelor's in Water Resources Engineering at the University of Guelph in 2015, and subsequently worked in Coastal Engineering for two years before pursuing graduate research. Her interest in the social and environmental impacts of engineering led to her involvement in the Manomin Project. Mehltretter was awarded the prestigious National Science and Engineering Research Council Alexander Graham Bell Canada Graduate Scholarship to complete her doctoral research, which investigated Manomin growth on the Upper Winnipeg River. She is an Assistant Professor of teaching at the University at Buffalo in the department of Civil, Structural, and Environmental Engineering.

Sean Sherman (The Sioux Chef), Oglala Lakota, born in Pine Ridge, South Dakota, has been cooking across the United States and the world for the last thirty years. His main culinary focus has been on the revitalization and awareness of Indigenous foods systems in a modern culinary context. Sherman has been the recipient of a 2015 First Peoples Fund Fellowship, 2018 Bush Foundation Fellowship, National Center's 2018 First American Entrepreneurship Award, 2018 James Beard Award for Best American Cookbook, and a 2019 James Beard Leadership Award.

Shane Chartrand, of the Enoch Cree Nation, is at the forefront of the re-emergence of Indigenous cuisine in North America. Raised in central Alberta, where he learned to respect food through raising livestock, hunting, and fishing on his family's acreage, Chartrand relocated to Edmonton as a young man to pursue culinary training. In 2015, Chartrand was invited to participate in the prestigious international chef contingent of Cook It Raw and has since competed on Food Network Canada's *Iron Chef Canada* and *Chopped Canada*. Currently, Chartrand is the executive chef at the acclaimed SC Restaurant at the River Cree Resort and Casino in Enoch, Alberta, where he transforms his diverse influences and experiences into culinary art.

Victoria Jackson, PhD, is a settler scholar whose research focuses on seventeenth-century Wendat childhood. She completed her doctoral work in 2020 at York University in Toronto, Ontario, Canada. Today, Jackson works in the Indigenous postsecondary education sector in Ontario.

ILLUSTRATIONS

Dani Kastelein is an artist, illustrator, designer, and intern architect at Brook McIlroy. They are of mixed heritage, including Dutch, French, and Métis. Dani holds kinship ties that extend from the Red River to the surrounding regions of Georgian Bay as a Drummond Island descendant. As such, their responsibilities extend to the Anishinaabeg Nations within the boundaries of their historic community. Their research and art often explore the complexities of historic and contemporary Indigenous experiences related to water access and the preservation of harvesting traditions. Dani earned a Master of Architecture degree from the University of Waterloo School of Architecture and was part of the charter class of the Bachelor of Architectural Studies program at the McEwen School of Architecture.

INDEX

bold page numbers indicate illustrations

A

Ackley, Fred Junior, 61

Aherin, Robert, 54

ah-sub-bi' (net), 24

alders (*Alnus*), 27

Amafo Hashi (Grandfather Sun in Choctaw), 84

ancestor, 6–7, **8**, 9–10, 14, 43, 49, 59, 61–62, 75, 78, 82–87, 138–40, 143, 150–51, 154, 155–57, 197

andawenjigewin (hunting and trapping), 16

Anderson, Kim, 55

Anishinaabe-Aki: anaerobic processes, 72; biodiversity of, **12**, 58–59, 72, 76–77, 79, 91, 93, **94–95**, 96, 101, **107**, **111**; cultivating resilience, 102–4, 105–6; drainage basin and, 98, 100; ecosystem disruptions, 91–92, 96–98, 100, 101–2, 104–5; effects of temperature on, 100–1; knowledge transfers within, 13; sense of belonging in, 50, 57, 59, 61, 119, 127–28; Upper Winnipeg River, 3, 51, 58, 89–90, **94–95**, 97, 104, 106; Whitefish Lake, 27–28, **30**, 33, 35

Anishinaabeg: barriers to knowledge transfer, 3–4, 122–23, 163; effects of Residential Schools, 3–4, 119, 122, 124, 137–38, 144–46, 170n5; environmental stewardship of, 14, 16, 77, 80–82, 96–97; ethical Manomin research projects and, 41–42; foodways of, 16, 76, 115; forms of reconciliation, 138–39; gender roles in the Manomin harvest, 52, **53**, **63**, **65**, **66**; knowledge transfers from, 41, 51–52, 74, 93, 126–27, 138; on other-than-humans, xi, xii, 58, 78–79; reciprocal relationship with Manomin, 7–8, 10, 11, 14, 57–59, 90, 139, 141–42, 146–47, 160; relational philosophy of, 6–7, 9, 91, 105, 142–43, 147–50, 182n2; rights of, 4–5, 18–19, 116, 125, 129, 142–43, 163–64, 166–68; role of children in the Manomin harvest, 3–4, 13, 51–52, 54–55, **56**, 57, 85, **136**; role of Elders in the Manomin harvest, 14, 16, **20**, 52–53; Seven Fires Prophecy and, 9, 21–25, 49, 52, 143–44; Seven Generations Principle, 6–7, **8**, 50, 59–62, 155–58; traditional harvest practices of, 16, 60, **63–69**, **114**; traditional hunting practices of, 16, 61, 76, 78–79; treaty making practices of, 139–40, 141–42. *See also* Anishinaabemowin; First Nations peoples; Indigenous communities; Manomin; settler-colonist activities

Anishinaabemowin (Anishinaabe language), 19; activity words, 16–17; animal words, 22; etymology of Apakweaashk, 76–77; etymology of Gziibinashk, 74–75; etymology of Kandamo, 78–79; etymology of Mak'akiimdaas, 80; etymology of Manomin, xii, 90, 141; etymology of

Minominkeshiihn, 77–78; etymology
of Zagaswe, 140; hunting and fishing
words, 16, 24; philosophical words, xii–
xiii, 21, 91, 139–40; plant words, 16;
seasonal words, 14, 16–17, 52

apakweaashk (cattail), 76–77, 101

archaeology: collection methods, 32,
36–38, difficulty collecting evidence,
35–40; ricing jigs, 28, 34, 39; types of
evidence, 31–32, 41

Aristotle, xi

Arzigian, Constance, 34

asemaa (tobacco), 14, 58

B

bagida'waawin (fishing with gill nets in
open waters), 16

Ba-wahn' (Dakota people), 24

Baw-wa-ting', 24

beaver, **12**, 36, 93, **95**, 140–41, 208

Benton-Banai, Edward, 9

berry broth, 47

biboon (winter), 16

Bill C-31, 120

Bimaadiziwin (the Good Life), 139–40

biota, 72, 92, 96, 101, 104

Blair Garden, 126

Bowron, Joseph, 60

Boyd, Matthew, 35

Branstner, Christine, 37

broadleaf arrowheads (*Sagittaria
latfolia*), 27

Brose, David, 31

C

Canada, Government of, xiii–xiv, 3–4, 5,
17–18, 117–18, 163, 166–67. *See also*
settler-colonist activities

canoes, 14, 16, 17, 20–21, 23–24, 33–34,
39–40, 50, 52–55, 57, 60, **69, 70**, 77,
83–84, **109**, 146, 160

cedar, 17

ceremony, 14, 17, 19, 22, 24, 61,
139–41, 145–46

chenopods (*Chenopodiineae*), 27, 39

children: cultural teaching of, 6, 50–51,
59, 61–62; Indigenous demographics,
117, 120, 123; roles in Manomin
harvest, 3–4, 13, 51–52, 54–55, 57,
85; stages of development, 54. *See also*
Residential Schools

Choctaw people, 83–84

colonialism, xiii–xiv, 4–6, 9, 18–19, 115,
124–25, 138–39, 166–68. *See also*
settler-colonist activities

copyright, 163–64, 167–68

Crawford, Gary, 37

Creator, the (Gitchie Manito, Gitchi
Manidoo), 7, 9, 14, 17, 22, 49, 57, 90,
142, 146, **154**, 175n5

cultural keystone species. *See* Manomin

Curve Lake First Nation, 41

D

dabasendiziwin (humility), 91

dagwaagin (early fall), 16

Dakota people (Ba-wahn'), 24

damselfly, **111**

Densmore, Frances, 50, 55, **63, 65**

Detroit River, 23

INDEX

Dore, William, 79, 93

dumplings, 43–47

Dunn's Farm (archaeological site), 31

E

Elders: knowledge transfers from, 13, 41, 51–52, 74, 93, 122–23; on environmental change, 90–91, 97–98, 101, 105; role in the Manomin harvest, 14, 16, **20**, 52–53, **154**. *See also* individual Elders

Enoch Cree Nation, 131

F

firs (*Abies*), 27

First Nations Food, Nutrition and Environmental Study (FNFNES), 115

First Nations peoples: barriers to knowledge transfer, 3–4, 122–24, 163; fostering community, 125–27. *See also* Anishinaabeg Indigenous communities

flotation method, 37

food insecurity, 115–16, 118, 119, 122, 125

food sovereignty, 116, 121, 125, 128

Friendship Centre Movement, 118–19

G

Gansworth, Kristi Leora, 59

generations: future, 6, 10, 61–62, 77–78; next, 8, 19, **154**

genocide, 18, 155. *See also* Canada, Government of; settler-colonist activities

Gete-Anishinaabeg (Anishinaabe ancestors), 14

gift, 7, 9, 14, 16–17, 24, 55, 57–58, 62, 72, 75, 79–80, 82–83, 90, 97, **114**, 119, 141–42, 143, 146–47, **154**, 155, 158, 160, 168, 174n4

Gitchie Manito (the Creator), 22, 175n5

Gi-ti-gay'-wi-nini-wug' (planters or keepers of the Creator's garden), 21

gitigewin (planting gardens), 16

Giizhiigokwe (Sandra Indian), 8

gratitude, xii, 10, 17, 58

Great Lakes region, 1, **2**, 3, 9, 28–29, 34, 36, 40. *See also* Anishinaabe-Aki

Great Web of Being, 9–10, 58, 62, 77, 78, 96. *See also* plant beings; Seven Generations Principle

Greene, Terry (Elder), 51, 53, 89, 92

Grover, Linda LeGarde, 52

Gziibinashk (Scouring Rush/*Equisetum hyemale*), 72, **73**, 74–75

H

Hastorf, Christine A., 37–38

Hawk (relative), 58–59

helper species, 12, 58–59, 61, 77–79, 92, 159–60

Henry, Barry, 51

Henry, Clarence (Elder), 3–6, 51–52, 55, 97, 161

Henry, Guy (Elder), **20**, **48**, **154**

Henry, John (Elder), **12**, 51, 54, 57, 92

Hill, Christina Gish, 51

Holden, Bill, 79

hooks, bell, 149

hunting and trapping (andawenjigewin), 16, 141

I

Indian Act, the, 3, 4, 6, 120

Indigenous communities: barriers to knowledge transfer, 3–4, 122–24; barriers to women, 124–25; ethical Manomin research projects and, 40–41; food insecurity and, 115–16, 118, 119, 122, 125; food sovereignty of, 116, 125, 128, 129; health determinants in, 115–16, 117–18; transferring traditional knowledge, 120–24, 137–39; urban food environment and, 10, 120–22, 125–26. *See also* Anishinaabeg; First Nations peoples; settler-colonist activities; individual nations

Indigenous Language Rights, 166–68

iskaagamizigewin (spring), 14

J

Jennings, Derek, 83

Jourdain, Theresa (Elder), 51, 55, 89

K

Kabestra, Larry (Elder), 51, **113**

Kandamo (Lily Pad), **x**, 27, 78–79, 80

kashkatin (freeze-up), 16

Kavanaugh, Francis (Grand Chief of Treaty #3), 7

Kelly, Alice (Elder), 61–62

Kezhii'aanakwat (Elder Ron Kelly), 8, 9, 17

Kimmerer, Robin Wall, xii–xiii, 58

Kinew, Kathi Avery, 8, 58–59

knockers, **64**, 83, **136**

Kylne, Josephine (Elder), 51

L

Lake of the Woods, 13, 49, 97

Lennstrom, Heidi A., 37–38

Linde, C.C., 173n8

Linnaeus, Carl, 5

Luby, Allan, 60

M

MacGillivray (archaeological site), 27–28, **30**

macrobotanical evidence, 31

Madeline Island (Mo-ning-wun'-a-kawn-ing), 25

maize (corn), 33–34, 35, 39, 177n33

Mak'akiimdaas (Pitcher Plant/*Sarracenia purpurea*), 80, **81**, 82, 184n19, 184n21–22

Mamakwa, Sol, 166–67

Manito Gitigaan (the Great Spirit's Garden), 8, 14, 141

Manitoulin Island, 24

Manomin: anatomy of, **48**, **70**, **110**; Anishinaabe stewardship of, 8, 17, 34–35, 50, **65**, **69**, 105–6, **154**; archaeological evidence of, 30, 31–34, 40; as a relative, 142–43; climate change and, 33, 100–1; cultivation of, 4, 14, **65**, **69**, 182n46; distribution of, 1, **2**, 29, **88**; effects of human development on, 101–2, 104–5; effects of water levels on, 98, 100; gender roles in the harvest of, 52–53, **63**, **65**, **66**; harvest ceremonies and, 14, 58, 63; harvest processes, 33–34, 50–51, 53–55, **63**, **65–68**, 83–85; helper species to, 58–59, 61, 92, 159–60; in the larger ecosystem, 35, 76–77, 93, **94–95**, 96, 101–2, 103, **111–12**; in traditional diets, 39, 115, 146–47, 149; letter to, 151–52; life cycle of, 16, **26**, 76–77, 92–93, **99**, **107–10**, **113**, 159; political aspect of, 138–39, 149–50; reciprocal relationships with humans, 7–8, 10–11, 57–59, 139, 141–42, 147–49, **154**, 160; reseeding efforts, 41, 60–61, **64–65**, **69**, 90–91, 103–4; role of children in the harvest of, 3–4, 13, 51–52, 54–55, **56**, 57, 85, **136**; role of Elders in the harvest of, 14, 16, **20**, 52–53, **154**; settler-colonist activities and, 90, 97; Seven Fires Prophecy and, 9, 49, 143–44; taxonomy of, 1, 3. *See also* Anishinaabe-Aki; Anishinaabeg; wetlands

Manomin Advisory Committee, 161

Manomin and Bergamot (recipe), 43–47

Manomin Project, 51, **112**, 164–65, 184n1

Manomin with Mushrooms (recipe), 131–35

Manoominikewi-giizis (Harvest Moon), 16, 52, 137

Martin-Bird (archaeological site), 27–28, **30**

mashkikiikewin (making medicines), 16

McGuire, Melissa A., 96

McLeod, Nancy (Elder), 51

McLester, Ron Deganadus, 59–60

Menominee, Ginnifer, **114**

Metekamiganang (Elder Doug Skead), 14

microbotanical evidence, 31–32

Middle Woodland period, 28, 31, 37

Midewiwin Society, 22–25, 174n4, 175n6

miinan (blueberries), 16, 44

Minnesota, 31–32, 35, 40, 101

Minominkeshiihn (Yellow Rail), 77–78

miskominag (raspberries), 16, 44

Mi-ti-goo-ka-maig' (whitefish), 24

Mo-ning-wun'-a-kawn-ing (Madeline Island), 25

Moose (relative), 58, 78–79, 93, 183n18

Morris, Alexander, 140–41

Mound Island (archaeological site), 28

Moyle, John B., 50

Mskomini giizis (Raspberry Moon), 52

mushrooms, 131–35

muskrat, 14, 93, **94**

N

Nanabush, 58

Ngũgĩ wa Thiong'o, 141

Niagara Falls, 22

niibin (summer), 16, 29, 54, 100, 104

Niisaachewan Anishinaabe Nation (NAN): conditions of publication, 161; ethical Manomin research projects and, 184n1; on environmental disruption, 101; on Manomin harvest, 51–52, 55, 58; on settler-colonist activities, 97; teachings of, xi, 89–90

Northwest Angle Treaty (Treaty #3), 13, 17–19, 140

Nymphaea odorata (water lilies), **x**, 27

O

ode'iminan (strawberries), 16

Ode'miin giizis (Strawberry Moon), 52

offering, 14, 31, 37, 58, 84, 97, 140

Ogden, Laura, 96–97, 105

Ojibways of Onigaming, 13, 21, 24–25, 141, 146, 174n9

Ontario Federation of Indigenous
Friendship Centres (OFIFC), 118–19

Onush Lakchi, 83. *See also* Manomin

Onush Lakchi/Manomin, Berries, and Love
(recipe), 83–87

osasawiminan (chokecherries), 16

oshkitagwaagin (early fall), 16

other-than-humans. *See* helper species

P

paashkiminisigan'an (sauces or jams), 16

paddy rice (*Oryza* spp.), 1, 3

pagita'an (ice break up), 14

paleoethnobotany, 29, 31, 34,
35–36, 37–39

Patees (Dorothy Copenace), 8

pawa'iminaanan (pin cherries), 16

Paypom, Allan (Elder), 173n8

Peacock, Thomas (Elder), 7–8

Peters, G.R., 34

photosynthesis, 71, 76, 101

phytoliths, 31–32, 33, 38, 39

Pikanagegaabo (Elder William [Willie]
Yerxa), 137–38, 141–44, 145–49, **153**

Pillsbury, Robert W., 96

Pine Portage, 90, 97, 105, 106

plant beings, **x**, xi–xii, 10, 71–76, 78–82.
See also Great Web of Being; Manomin

pollen, **26**, 31, 32, 33, 38–39, 92

pondweed (*Potamogeton
gramineus*), 27, 96

prayer, 14, 61, 87, 141

R

ragweed (*Ambrosia*), 27, 33

Raster, Amanda, 51

recipes: Manomin and Bergamot, 43–47;
Manomin with Mushrooms, 131–35;
Onush Lakchi/Manomin, Berries, and
Love, 83–87

Reo, Nicholas, 96–97, 105

Residential Schools, 3–4, 18, 119, 122–23,
144–48, 170n5

rice worm, 78, 92–93, **112**, 159, 198

ricing jigs, 28, 34, 36, 39

Robbins's pondweed (*Potamogeton
robbinsii*), 27, 96

Royal Commission on Aboriginal
Peoples, 161

S

sagakinige (winter activities), 17

seasons: growing season, 96, 100, 104, **112**;
harvesting season, 3, 5, 139, 142; mating
season, 78; six seasons of care, 14, 172n1

sedges (*Cyperaceae*), 27, 33

sediment core studies, 32–33, 38

settler-colonist activities: environmental
dispossession, xiii–xiv, 4–5, 90, 120,
123–24; land encroachment, 10, 18,
116; Residential Schools, 3–4, 119,
122, 124, 137–38, 144–46, 170n5;
treaty negotiations, xiii, 17–18, 140–41;
Western (European) botanical standards,
xi–xii. *See also* Canada, Government of

Seven Fires Prophecy, 9, 21–25, 49,
52, 143–44

Seven Generations Principle, 6–7, **8**, 50,
59–61, 155–58

Seven Grandfather Teachings, 91, 140

INDEX

shaabozigaweba'igewin (pushing the gill nets under the ice), 16

Simpson, Leanne, 139–40

Smith, David, 37

Southwest Ontario Aboriginal Health Access Centre (SOAHAC), 118, 192n41

Spirit Island, 24

Spokni Chunkash (Grandmother Spider in Choctaw), 84

spruce, 17

St. George, Scott, 100

St. Lawrence River, 1, 22

star duckweed (*Lemna trisulca*), 96

Stark, Heidi Kiiwetinepinesiik, 139–40

Steckle Heritage Farm, 126

Steeves, Taylor A., 5, 103

Stevens, Stephanie, **136**

Strong, Danny (Elder), 51, 53, 55, 57, 60, 100

Surette, Clarence, 37

T

Tea Garden, 126

Todd, Christine, 54

Toronto Council Fire Native Cultural Centre, 119

Treaty #3 (Northwest Angle Treaty), 13, 17, 18–19, 140

Truth and Reconciliation Commission of Canada, 18, 117, 162, 167

Turtle Island, xiii, 1, 29, 34, **114**. *See also* Anishinaabe-Aki

Typha spp., 101–2

U

United Nations Declaration on the Rights of Indigenous Peoples (UNDRIP), 18, 163–64, 166

United States, Government of, 18. *See also* settler-colonist activities

University of Manitoba Press (UMP), 164–66

University of Waterloo's Environmental Reserve, 126

Upper Winnipeg River, 3, 51, 58, 89–90, **94–95**, 97, 104, 106

urban environment, 117–18, 119–22, 124, 128–29

urban gardens, 125–29

V

Vennum, Thomas, 51

Veracini, Lorenzo, xiv

W

Wagamese, Archie (Elder), 51, 97–98

Walker, Sandra, 73

Walpole Island, 23

water lilies (*Nymphaea odorata*), **x**, 27, 78–79

Waterdrum, 23–25, 175n6

Wauzhusk Onigum First Nation, 14

wetlands, **x**, 5, **88**; anaerobic processes, 72; biodiversity of, **12**, 58–59, 72, 76–79, 91, 93, **94–95**, 96, **107**, **111**; change over time, 36–37; cultivating resilience, 102–6; drainage basin and, 98, 100; ecosystem complexity, 91–92; ecosystem disruptions, 96–98, 100–2, 104–5; effects of temperature on, 100–1. *See also* Anishinaabe-Aki

Whetung, James, 41

Whipple, Dorothy Dora (Elder), 58

White Owl Native Ancestry Association (WONAA), 125–26

Whitefish Lake, 27–28, **30**, 32–33, 35

wiigwaas (birchbark), 16–17

wild rice. *See* Manomin

willow tree (*Salix*), 27, 33

winter season (biboon), 16–17, 21, 55, 59, 79, 100, **107**, 142

Wisahkotewinowak Collective, 126–27, 129

Wisconsin, 101

Y
Yerxa, Jana-Rae, xiii, 143–49, **153**

Yost, Chad L., 38

Z
Zaagaswe'idiwag ("offering smoke to each other" / pipe ceremony), 140–41

ziigwaan (spring), 14, 16, 20, 98, 103–4, **107**, **108**

Zizania spp. *See* Manomin